Uneasy Warriors

Uneasy Warriors

*Gender, Memory, and Popular Culture
in the Japanese Army*

Sabine Frühstück

UNIVERSITY OF CALIFORNIA PRESS
Berkeley • *Los Angeles* • *London*

University of California Press, one of the most distinguished university presses in the United States, enriches lives around the world by advancing scholarship in the humanities, social sciences, and natural sciences. Its activities are supported by the UC Press Foundation and by philanthropic contributions from individuals and institutions. For more information, visit www.ucpress.edu.

University of California Press
Berkeley and Los Angeles, California

University of California Press, Ltd.
London, England

Every effort has been made to identify and locate the rightful copyright holders of all material not specifically commissioned for use in this publication and to secure permission, where applicable, for reuse of all such material. Credit, if and as available, has been provided for all borrowed material either on-page, on the copyright page, or in an acknowledgment section of the book. Errors, omissions, or failure to obtain authorization with respect to material copyrighted by other sources has been either unavoidable or unintentional. The author and publisher welcome any information that would allow them to correct future reprints.

Library of Congress Cataloging-in-Publication Data

Frühstück, Sabine.
  Uneasy warriors : gender, memory, and popular culture in the Japanese Army / Sabine Frühstück.
    p. cm.
  Includes bibliographical references and index.
  ISBN 978-0-520-24794-9 (cloth : alk. paper)—
  ISBN 978-0-520-24795-6 (paper : alk. paper)
  1. Japan—Armed Forces. 2. Sociology, Military—Japan. 3. Popular culture—Japan. 4. Japan—Armed Forces—Women. I. Title.
  UA845.F68 2007
  306.2'70952—dc22
                                    2007011432

Manufactured in the United States of America

16 15 14 13 12 11 10 09 08 07
10 9 8 7 6 5 4 3 2 1

This book is printed on New Leaf EcoBook 60, a 100% recycled fiber of which 60% is de-inked post-consumer waste, processed chlorine-free. EcoBook 60 is acid-free and meets the minimum requirements of ANSI/ASTM D5634-01 (Permanence of Paper).

Contents

Illustrations

Acknowledgments

Over the past nine years the research for this book has taken me from the Japanese defense attaché's offices in Vienna to similar places in Tokyo, and from there, to military bases across Japan. I am indebted particularly to all those members of the Self-Defense Forces who put up with me long term, despite the fact that to many the outcome of my research must have remained unclear and possibly suspect. If I succeeded over the years at building a network of Self-Defense Forces members and affiliates, it is mostly thanks to a handful of lieutenant colonels and colonels who have been supportive and creative in their methods of helping me connect with their peers across Japan. Most of them seemed impressed, amused, and occasionally exhausted. They were most probably quietly unnerved that I showed up year after year insisting that I needed yet more information, wanted to carry out more interviews, and that the book would take an unclear number of additional years to complete.

Thomas Ludwig has continued to ask me the most probing questions, has cautioned and encouraged, and has joined me in laughing and sighing about the details of research and writing. Tak Fujitani, Laura Miller, Glenda Roberts, and Jennifer Robertson have read the entire manuscript for the press to come up with many important suggestions, most of which I hope I was able to incorporate. I also wish to express my gratitude for invaluable exchanges and critical comments on different incarnations of parts of the book by friends and colleagues including Tarak Barkawi, Jim Bartholomew, Aaron Belkin, Eyal Ben-Ari, Elise Edwards,

Cynthia Enloe, Gerald Figal, Joshua Fogel, Ute Frevert, Harry Ha-
rootunian, Dick Hebdige, André Hertrich, David Holloway, Glenn
Hook, Haruko Iwasaki, Kawano Hiroshi, David Leheny, Sepp Linhart,
Angus Lockyer, Stewart Lone, Stephan Miescher, Laurie Monahan,
Norman Naimark, John Nathan, Dick Samuels, Jim Sheehan, Aaron
Skabelund, Brigitte Steger, Suzuki Akira, Tanaka Hiromi, Tanaka
Masakazu, Tan'o Yasunori, Tsutsui Kiyoteru, Ueno Chizuko, and Bert
Winther-Tamaki, as well as my graduate students Teresa A. Algoso and
Susan McArver. At the University of Vienna, Nakamura Yōko, Rumi
Onodera, and Tomoyama Kaori transcribed some of the hundreds of
hours of interviews. At the University of California at Santa Barbara, Ya-
mamoto Natsuki, Boden Davidson, and Diana Mao contributed in im-
portant ways to the preparation of visual and quantitative data that I
draw from in this book.

The response to some of the main ideas, which I was invited to present
at the following institutions, also helped me tremendously to sharpen my
focus and critical depth: the universities of Vienna and Tokyo (1999); the
University of Michigan, the University of California at Berkeley, Stanford University, and Yale University (2001); Kyoto University (2003); the
University of California at Irvine (2004); and Harvard University (2005).
I am also grateful for the discussions that followed conference presentations at the annual meetings of the Association for Asian Studies (2004
and 2006); the symposium on *Transformation of Experience: Interpreting the 'Opening' of Japan* at Berkeley (2004); the conference on *Gender and Nation: Japanese Perspectives,* held at the Tokyo Women's Plaza
(2004); and the annual meeting of the Vereinigung für sozialwissenschaftliche Japanforschung in Berlin (2004).

Four months of collaborative research with Eyal Ben-Ari in 1998 and
1999 preceded the work for this book and resulted in two articles, one
in the *Journal of Japanese Studies* (2002) and another in the *American
Ethnologist* (2003). Similarly, I have discussed some of the findings from
field trips to army bases together with Tanaka Masakazu, Miyanishi
Kaoru, Fukuura Atsuko, and Nishio Fumi in an article in *Jinbun Gakuhō*
(2005). In Kyoto, Tanaka Masakazu has created the first network of anthropologists, historians, and political scientists who have begun to critically examine military establishments across Asia. I feel privileged to
have been one of their first non-Japanese members. My home base for
the last few years, the Department of East Asian Languages and Cultural
Studies at the University of California at Santa Barbara, and particularly
Allan Grapard and Ron Egan, continue to be an important source of in-

tellectual inspiration and emotional support, and has once again graciously allowed me a one-year leave to finish this book. In Santa Barbara, the members of the Military, Society and Citizenship Research Focus Group, under the leadership of Aaron Belkin, have been particularly helpful in my gaining a broader transnational and interdisciplinary perspective.

The following grants and fellowships have facilitated the research and writing of this book: a research grant from the Humanities and Social Sciences Division at the University of Vienna (1999); Faculty Research Grants (2002, 2003, 2004), a Regents' Humanities Faculty Fellowship (2003), and a Faculty Award from the Interdisciplinary Humanities Center (2005), all at the University of California at Santa Barbara; a Japan Studies Grant from the North East Asia Council of the Association for Asian Studies (2002); and the Stanford Humanities Center External Faculty Fellowship (2005/2006). In Japan, I was the co-recipient of a collaborative research grant provided by the Japanese Ministry of Education during the time I spent as a visiting research professor at the Institute of Research in Humanities, Kyoto University (2003). My fellow fellows at the Stanford Humanities Center have been particularly helpful in framing some of the larger theoretical questions this book addresses.

Patricia Marby Harrison continues to be an extraordinarily careful and reliable reader. I am grateful to Reed Malcolm, Kalicia Pivirotto, Sue Heinemann, Sandy Drooker, and Janet Villanueva at the University of California Press, who have expertly ushered this book to completion.

Note on Asterisked Names and Abbreviations

Throughout this book, to protect people's identities, I have used pseudonyms for both my fieldwork sites and the people I interviewed. These pseudonyms are indicated by an asterisk the first time they appear. Occasionally, however, I do use real names, and in these cases I have permission to do so. As a courtesy to my interviewees, I have not included any comments in this book that I was told off the record.

The following abbreviations are used in my discussion:

ASDF	Air Self-Defense Force
GSDF	Ground Self-Defense Force
IJA	Imperial Japanese Army
IJN	Imperial Japanese Navy
JDA	Japan Defense Agency
MSDF	Maritime Self-Defense Force
NDA	National Defense Academy
NMDA	National Medical Defense Academy

Introduction

The moment I stepped onto the base exercise ground in the exceptionally hot summer of 2001, I realized that this part of my research would be different from anything I had done before. Clad in a Ground Self-Defense Force (GSDF) uniform, I wondered what a week of basic training in the army would bring. What new insights could I expect from wearing fatigues, moving on command, saluting service members, accompanying new recruits to various field trainings, eating in the mess hall, and sleeping in an army bunk bed? How would this kind of research experience affect my perspective on the Self-Defense Forces and possibly the armed forces more generally?

A week of participant observation at the Kibita* GSDF base on Honshū constituted only a small part of my overall research effort, but it seemed particularly significant: No scholar before me—Japanese or foreign—had ever had that opportunity. After Mishima Yukio's spectacular suicide in 1970, the military administration had become wary of a political backlash should events get out of hand and was not keen on letting outsiders take a close look at their troops' everyday lives. Mishima had enlisted in April 1967 under his real name, Hiraoka Kimitake, and eventually trained a group of young men at the GSDF Fuji Officers' Candidate School (Fuji Gakkō), which I had visited twice by the time of my own "basic training." At that time, the Self-Defense Forces' administration thought that having a famous writer among its troops was a brilliant public relations stunt (Nathan 2000 [1974]:220–223, 227; Sugihara and Sugihara 1997). That fantasy collapsed on November 25, 1970, when

Mishima and his followers from the Shield Society (Tatenokai), which he had founded, took over the GSDF base in Ichigaya, Tokyo. They held a general hostage and appealed to the Self-Defense Forces to overthrow the democratically elected government before Mishima ended his own life by ritual suicide. He did so in the building of the former Army Academy (Rikugun Shikan Gakkō), the principal school of the Imperial Japanese Army, which serves as a memorial hall within the Japan Defense Agency (JDA) today (Nathan 2000:270–281; see also Naito 2001). As I show in this book, the Self-Defense Forces have come a long way since then.

It took me three years, many different strategies and networking efforts, and a good deal of persistence to get inside Kibita GSDF base. It all began with a conversation in the offices of a Japanese military official in Vienna in the spring of 1998. Colonel Fujiwara Toshio*, a soft-spoken GSDF officer with excellent German language skills, provided me with a handful of contacts to other officers in Japan. On my first visit to the Japan Defense Agency (then still located in Roppongi, Tokyo) I had two letters in my pocket: one from the Austrian minister of defense, the other from the Austrian ambassador to Japan. Both were addressed to the director of the JDA and requested support of my research. Numerous phone calls to and from the JDA led nowhere for a long time, so I pursued other avenues of research. But I never received permission, either in writing or by phone, to enter a base for the purpose of participant observation. Doors finally began to open, however, and eventually Fujiwara, with whom I had met at least once a year since his return to Japan, let me know that one of his former seniors at the NDA had agreed to let me onto the base he commanded.

By the time I arrived at Kibita GSDF base, I had been engaged in research on the Self-Defense Forces for three years. The purpose of my stint on base was to gain additional insight into service members' everyday lives in order to better understand the place of the military in present-day Japan. I had first become interested in the military while writing a book on the emergence of sex as an object of scientific research (2003). Although people off-handedly refer to taboos in the context of sex and sexuality in Japan, I found the notion of taboo applied much more aptly to military matters. From the 1880s through the early 1940s, whether at times of war or peace, the military in Japan had been everywhere, permeating every element of modern culture from the sciences to the arts, from the state to the individual. Postwar Japan, by contrast, seemed to resemble Roland Barthes's vision of Tokyo: a city that possesses a center that is empty and remains invisible (1982 [1970]:31–32). Here was a nation-state with a powerful military that remained largely invisible, rarely speaking out, let alone being spoken about. In 1998, when I began my research, only a few scholars were studying the Self-Defense Forces; indeed, many scholars of Japan seemed uninterested in or even apprehensive about studying the Self-Defense Forces. In the United States, the lack of interest in studying the military as an institution might be explained by the Vietnam debacle, which left the military morally tainted and thus seemingly not worthy of anthropological research (Ben-Ari 2004:340). In Japan, the reasons more likely range from the Self-Defense Forces' unconstitutionality to their lackluster status because of the constraints on combat. Since its first issue in 1965, the *Journal of Military History (Gunji Shigaku)* has been mainly occupied with the intricacies of specific battles the Imperial Army and Navy fought and has published only a handful of articles on the Self-Defense Forces. Finally, in 2004, they put out a special issue on the Self-Defense Forces for their fiftieth anniversary. Japanese feminists have not taken up the issue of militarism or shown interest in the Self-Defense Forces' attempts at the integration and equal treatment of women, partly because of their pacifist convictions. Only recently have they begun to question the customary contradiction between feminism and militarism in postwar Japan and to appeal to women generally and female service members in particular to "change the Self-Defense Forces from within" (Ueno 1998; Shimada Y. 2002; Satō 2004). One Japanese sociologist explained the lack of sociological interest in the Self-Defense Forces to me by suggesting that it did not matter what kinds of lives service members lived because they were politically irrelevant. A Japanese anthropologist was convinced that the Self-Defense Forces were not a worthwhile subject of research because they were not a "real" military and thus were "weak." Other dismissive responses seemed to arise from concern that my research might legitimize the Self-Defense Forces.

This prohibition of scholarship is highly problematic because, after all, the military is at the intersection of a number of crucial debates that have contributed to redrawing the line between the military and civil society. These debates and their outcomes have repercussions for the Self-Defense Forces. But even beyond the specificities of Japan, and my own motivations and interests, we live in a particularly salient time for an investigation of military establishments.

Since the end of World War II, societies the world over, especially the

United States, have undergone a steady militarization, from the increase in military budgets to the intrusion of the military into civilians' lives, from the normalization of military ideals to the amalgamation of the military and civilian spheres into an inseparable entity. The end of the cold war should have triggered a massive disarmament. Instead, after an eleven-year period of worldwide decreases, military budgets—an important indicator of militarization—have been rising again. World military expenditure in 2005 represented a real-terms increase of 3.4 percent since 2004, and of 34 percent over the ten-year period from 1996 to 2005. This dramatic reversal was related primarily to enormous increases in the U.S. military budget, which now accounts for almost half of the world total, but Japan's real military expenditure has also contributed. In 1999 it was 20 percent higher than a decade earlier, even though Japan's GNP percentage share had remained at roughly 1 percent.[1]

According to data from the Stockholm International Peace Research Institute, Japan ranked as the fourth-largest military spender with a defense budget of $42.1 billion, or 4 percent of the world share. The other top five spenders are the United States ($478.2), the United Kingdom ($48.3), France ($46.2), and China ($41.0). In purchasing power parity terms, however, Japan ranks only eighth behind the United States, China, India, Russia, France, the United Kingdom, and Saudi Arabia (SIPRI 2005).

As the feminist political scientist Cynthia Enloe (1990, 1993) has shown, signs of militarization are not always as blatant as in military budgets; they may also be seen in the "step-by-step process by which a person or a thing gradually comes to be controlled by the military or comes to depend for its well-being on militaristic ideas" (Enloe 2000:3). Andrew J. Bacevich (2005:2), a graduate of the U.S. Military Academy and a Vietnam veteran and historian, put it somewhat differently. He wrote that Americans have fallen prey to a militarism that manifests itself in a romanticized view of soldiers, a tendency to see military power as the truest measure of national greatness, and outsized expectations regarding the efficacy of force. To a degree without precedent in U.S. history, Bacevich claimed, Americans have come to define the nation's strength and well-being in terms of military preparedness, military action, and the fostering of (or nostalgia for) military ideals. Indeed, the militarization of U.S. society has advanced so far, agrees the anthropologist Catherine Lutz (2001:8), that the distinction between civilian and military has become an artificially maintained illusion. The sociologist Michael Manneven observed that the notion of civilian control of the military has become meaningless, since civilians have become the leading militarists (see Bacevich 2005:63).

Observers of Japan claim that while most of Japan's postwar history has been characterized by a pronounced anti-militarism that starkly contrasts to developments in the United States, a quiet, hidden militarization has recently become more visible. Postwar Japan started out from a specific military-societal configuration that constituted a decisive gesture of departure from its imperialist and wartime past. From 1872 to 1945 the Imperial Japanese Army (IJA) had held enormous social and political power, but the Self-Defense Forces radically broke with this tradition and were placed under civilian control. In the process, the Self-Defense Forces were politically and socially marginalized and rendered almost invisible in the wider society. The IJA had fought its enemies in the name of establishing and expanding the Greater Japanese Empire, which ceased to exist in 1945. The Self-Defense Forces differ in engaging exclusively in noncombat operations. They have rescued victims of earthquakes, mud slides, forest fires, and plane crashes; they have rebuilt destroyed infrastructure and participated in U.N. peace-keeping missions (kokusai heiwa kyōryoku katsudō); and on a more mundane level, they have built sports grounds and secured large-scale event sites. Most significantly, they have not once engaged in warfare.[2]

The year 2004, however, marked the first deployment to a war zone since the Asia-Pacific War.[3] On January 9, 2004, the first GSDF and Air Self-Defense Force (ASDF) units were dispatched to Samawa, Iraq, sanctioned by the Law for the Humanitarian Aid and Special Measures in Iraq (Iraku jindō fukkō shien tokusoho), which had been formulated on December 3, 2003. According to the law, the Self-Defense Forces were to "help reconstitute the security of the Iraqi people's lives and establish the political entities on which democratic measures depend" (Zaidan Hōjin Bōei Kōsaikai/Securitarian 2004a:10–11).[4] The highly contested deployment had enormous symbolic significance for Japan's present-day military. It initiated a series of major changes in Japan's security makeup and expedited the transition of the Self-Defense Forces from a position of almost complete oblivion at the margins of public interest to one at the center of political discourse and popular attention (Yoshida T. 2003). Japanese debates about potential military threats had mostly taken place behind the closed doors of military experts and security policy strategists. Now these issues were being discussed in public. National television stations and newspapers that had largely been apprehensive about reporting on the Self-Defense Forces, except for token annual events and scandals (such as a drug scandal in the Maritime Self-Defense Force [MSDF]; *Asahi Shinbun* September 29, 2005), began featuring stories about the Self-Defense Forces. International events, including North Korea's announcement in early 2003 that it possessed nuclear weapons, which was reaffirmed in early 2005, as well as its nuclear test on October 9, 2006, have intensified debate about the condition, preparedness, and suitability of the Self-Defense Forces (Pilling 2004b). In 2004, when the National Defense Plan for the first time explicitly defined China and North Korea as potential threats to Japan's security, the military's public profile increased and national as well as international media created the impression that Japan had radically shifted course from an antimilitary to a nationalist and possibly militarist regime—a view that I hope to put into perspective in this book.

The military is also the elephant in the room in the debate about modern Japan's conflicted relationship to its wartime history. A series of events has suggested a commitment to eliminate history from public consciousness, including the establishment of the Japanese Society for History Textbook Reform and the Association for the Advancement of a Liberalist View of History, the ministerial approval of history textbooks that whitewash Japan's wartime past, and then Prime Minister Koizumi Junichirō's visits to a shrine dedicated to fallen soldiers, including war criminals. One consequence, according to critics across almost the entire political spectrum, is that the history of the modern period is slipping from living memory in Japan whereas it is being kept alive vividly in Japan's former colonies, creating a gap that has continued to wreck regional relations (Philling 2006). A high school teacher in Okinawa, where teachers teach their students Okinawa's history only up to the Battle of Okinawa, neglecting all subsequent military developments, is ready to take his share of the blame. "This is our responsibility," he says; "we keep pushing for peace, peace while we do not study war and know nothing about the military" (Ishikawa M. 1995:109).

This notion of Japan's commitment to peace is recorded in the constitution, which has been more frequently evoked in recent years. The 2005 defense white paper prominently featured the Iraq mission and noted that as a member of the United Nations, Japan contributed and "collaborated within the limits of the Japanese constitution"—a constitution, it is important to remember, that prohibits Japan from maintaining a standing army. Thus, the current debate on constitutional revision touches the very heart of Japan's postwar national posture, with the legitimacy of the armed forces being the most prominent concern.[5]

Currently, Article 9 reads: "Aspiring sincerely to an international peace based on justice and order, the Japanese people forever renounce war as a sovereign right of the nation and the threat of use of force as a means of settling international disputes. In order to accomplish the aim of the preceding paragraph, land, sea, and air forces, as well as other war potential, will never be maintained. The right of belligerency of the state will not be recognized" (Inoue K. 1991:275). In April 2005, the Lower House Panel on the Constitution (Shūgiin kenpō chōsa-kai), set up originally as a result of the Persian Gulf War in 1991, produced a 723-page report *(Shūgiin kenpō chōsa-kai hōkokusho)*. The report lays out how a revision would affect the military and suggests Article 9 be revised in order to clarify the legality of the Self-Defense Forces and to state unambiguously the nation's right to self-defense (*Asahi Shinbun* April 16, 2005). With pundits on both the right and the left favoring a revision (Hook and McCormack 2001), it is more likely than ever to happen. In the interim, however, it is important to ask what it means for service members to work and risk their lives in the name of a state that has declared their very organization illegal. My research into service members' everyday experiences, motivations, career choices, and attitudes toward issues that highlight the armed forces speaks to this central paradox of military-societal relations in Japan: the contradiction between Article 9 and the existence of Japan's armed forces. Beyond that are the paradoxes in maintaining a military force in any democracy: the contradiction between prohibitions of violence in civilian life and the military's training and potential demand for violent acts, and the contradiction within a profession that teaches people how to use violence so that they will avoid it, that prepares them for something so that it will not happen, and that ultimately proves their ability by remaining unnecessary.

The Self-Defense Forces have been hesitant and cautious pioneers among military establishments. By carefully constraining and recasting their potential for violent acts in the name of the Japanese state, they have foreshadowed transformations by which military establishments worldwide have only recently begun to be affected, so much so that military sociologists have appropriated the term "postmodern" for this new type of military (Moskos, Williams, and Segal 2000). From their very beginnings, the Self-Defense Forces have been entrusted with the kinds of missions most military establishments—most notably the U.S. military— have only recently added to their list of operations, including community works, disaster relief, and peacekeeping. Anthony Zinni, a retired general of the U.S. Marine Corps and former commander in chief of United

States Central Command, is confident that the kind of "real soldiering" that characterized the wars of the twentieth century is coming to an end. Zinni spelled out his vision of the future of the U.S. military and ostensibly the armed forces of other postindustrial democratic countries, such as Japan:

> ... we ignore the real war-fighting requirements of today. ... We want to find a real adversarial demon—a composite Hitler, Tojo, and Mussolini—so we can drive on to his capital city and crush him there. Unconditional surrender. Then we'll put in place a Marshall Plan, embrace the long-suffering vanquished, and help them regain entry into the community of nations. ... But it ain't gonna happen ... we're going to be doing things like humanitarian operations, consequence management, peacekeeping and peace enforcement. Somewhere along the line, we'll have to respond to some kind of environmental disaster. ... The truth is that military conflict has changed and we have been reluctant to recognize it. ... Odd missions to defeat transnational threats or rebuild nations are the order of the day, but we haven't as yet adapted. (Urquhart 2004:32)[6]

On the following pages, I examine how the Self-Defense Forces have made sense of those "odd missions" Zinni envisions as the future of the military. The Self-Defense Forces' steps toward a new kind of military establishment have not, however, provided a smooth transition to different modes of militarized gender, a cozy relationship to civilian society, or even an uncomplicated relationship to their past. In fact, even though more military establishments are adopting characteristics and missions similar to those of the Self-Defense Forces, members of the Self-Defense Forces often see themselves as falling short of what they imagine a real, normal military to be.

A brief history of the Self-Defense Forces is needed before an in-depth analysis of their current condition. Japan's postwar armed forces were founded on July 8, 1950, as the National Police Reserve (Keisatsu Yobitai) in the wake of America's involvement in the Korean War and were later renamed and inaugurated as the Self-Defense Forces (Jieitai) on July 1, 1954.[7] Japan's Self-Defense Forces consist of three services (ground, sea, and air), which are equipped with the latest military technology (tanks, ships, planes, and a variety of state-of-the-art weaponry, although no nuclear weaponry) and have all of the organizational facets common to armed forces (territorial divisions, brigades, and training methods) (Bōeichō 1999:437, graphs 46 and 47). This book focuses on the largest service branch, the army or Ground Self-Defense Force (GSDF), which has about 148,000 troops. The Air Self-Defense Force

(ASDF) has 46,000 and the Maritime Self-Defense Force (MSDF) has 44,000 service members. With 37.8 percent of the national budget, the GSDF receives the largest share.[8]

Since the 1950s, military-societal relations in Japan have undergone gradual but important shifts, typically in the aftermath of various engagements of the Self-Defense Forces. In 1960, the Self-Defense Forces were on the brink of being mobilized to suppress domestic unrest: in the largest mass demonstration in Japan's history, hundreds of thousands of ordinary citizens protested the renewal of the Treaty of Mutual Cooperation between Japan and the United States of America (Nichibei Anzen Hosho Jōyaku), which was to tie Japan permanently to U.S. security interests in the region. Before the political unrest erupted, Sugita Ichiji, GSDF chief of staff, had sent a confidential Plan to Mobilize for the Maintenance of Order to a number of high-ranking officers under his command (Sase 1980:94). Many of these officers, he later recalled, did not want to even think about mobilizing the Self-Defense Forces against the Japanese population and were hoping that the police would take care of suppressing a demonstration.[9] In such an inflammatory atmosphere, the strength of the public's anti-war and anti-military sentiment helped deter the JDA from using force against the protesters (Yamamoto 2004:229). The mass protest dissipated when Prime Minister Kishi Nobusuke—who had served as minister of commerce and industry in Tojo Hideki's government from 1941 to 1945 and was then jailed as a class A war criminal until 1948—resigned because of public furor over the treaty and Ikeda Hayato took office to announce his income-doubling plan. The movement against the security treaty with the United States eventually splintered into local anti-base movements, and today it is barely spoken of in the public arena, with the exception of Okinawa, where protests are directed primarily against the U.S. bases there (Angst 2003; Asato 2003; Ishikawa 1995a; Takazato 1996, 2003).

The next watershed for military-societal relations in Japan came in the aftermath of the Persian Gulf War during the early 1990s, which had an impact on both the self-perception of service members and public opinion of the Self-Defense Forces (Ishikawa 1995b; Hook 1996). Japan contributed $12 billion to the Gulf War and in April 1991 sent mine sweepers to the Persian Gulf in the Self-Defense Forces' first international deployment ever. The United States fiercely criticized Japan for not putting its soldiers at risk (Uwe Schmitt, *Frankfurter Allgemeine Zeitung*, January 9, 1995). This criticism prompted the JDA to engage in a more concerted effort at professional image-building (Bessatsu Takarajima

1991; Inoguchi 1991; Ito 1991; Yamaguchi 1992) and triggered a debate about Japan's responsibilities in the international arena and its contributions to international security *(kokusai kōken)*. Despite the doubts about the Self-Defense Forces' roles beyond Japan's borders, Japan's participation in international peacekeeping missions has been given *post facto* legitimacy, a strategy that has boosted approval of the Self-Defense Forces as well (Hook 1996:125–126).[10] The first such mission was to Cambodia in 1992, soon after the law that regulates Japan's participation in peacekeeping missions (Kokusai heiwa kyōryokuhō) passed. The Japanese contingent was accompanied by an impressive press corps set on documenting their every move (Katzenstein 1996a; Dobson 2003). Although the majority of the Japanese population continues to oppose militarism at home and in wars abroad, in the aftermath of the first peacekeeping missions the public has increasingly accepted a constrained international role for the Self-Defense Forces.

The international criticism Japan faced for its purely monetary contribution to the Gulf War coincided with increasing domestic support for Japan to play a larger political and possibly military role in the international arena. According to Glenn Hook (1996), the end of the cold war and the Gulf War have also cast doubt on the simple equation of overseas dispatches and the participation in an aggressive war.

A large-scale natural disaster marked another milestone on the Self-Defense Forces' march to public approval and a moment of intense media exposure. Initially, after the Self-Defense Forces mobilized to rescue survivors of the Kōbe-Awaji earthquake on January 17, 1995, the Self-Defense Forces came under intense scrutiny and were criticized by national and international media for the lack of a prompt and organized response. In the long run, however, the earthquake and its aftermath forced the military to modernize its disaster relief operation equipment and training, and later high-ranking commanders and soldiers alike viewed their involvement in the rescue operation as highly rewarding and thus successful. Various morale-boosting stories of saving someone's life circulated among the ranks for a long time. Subsequently, entire cohorts of newly recruited service members and cadets at the National Defense Academy (NDA) joined the Self-Defense Forces, hoping primarily to be dispatched to a disaster relief site, to rescue people who would be grateful to them, and to possibly be acknowledged in TV news reports for their efforts.[11] Rescuing people from the aftermath of a natural disaster had an enormous identity-building significance for practically all service members.

Similarly, at the end of 1998, the press celebrated the eighty-man unit from a GSDF base near Nagoya that had recently returned from Japan's first international disaster relief mission to Honduras in November and December. The Honduras mission and ongoing peacekeeping operations boosted service members' self-esteem and were highlighted by the military administration for two reasons: they communicated to politicians and to the national and international public that the military could perform well in an international arena, contributing to the international community, and they allowed the military to gain favorable exposure in an ambiguously civilian/military context.

In early 1999, however, the North Korean "missile incident" raised new concerns about an impending military threat and contributed to debates about Japan's military capability and the functionality of the U.S.–Japan security alliance. The media addressed the failure of the Self-Defense Forces and the U.S. forces in Japan to prevent the incident and, more generally, the capability of the Self-Defense Forces in worst-case scenarios. The liberal press again questioned the constitutional legitimacy of the Self-Defense Forces; the right exploited the opportunity to criticize the restrictions preventing the Self-Defense Forces from acting like a "normal," "conventional," or "modern" military organization (Katahara 2001). These conflicts have persisted with Japan's more recent involvement in Iraq, and negotiations at the interface between military and society continue to make an impression on service members' self-perception.

This book is organized into five chapters that address the various issues involving the Self-Defense Forces from different angles. The first chapter provides my view and microanalysis of the rhythms of everyday life on a GSDF base, which reveals the issues service members struggle with—issues that I examine from different perspectives in later chapters. Just as anthropologists claim that they gain enhanced understanding of the human subjects of their research through participant observation, Self-Defense Forces public relations officers believed that I would best understand the Self-Defense Forces if I experienced their lifestyle firsthand. I don't share this belief but do think that the immediacy and physicality of my stint on base contributed to my attempts to temporarily see military matters through the eyes of a recruit.

In chapter 2, I analyze the construction of masculinities in the military. Historically, war has enforced an extreme version of male behavior as the ideal model for all such behavior, by emphasizing the physical prowess of military men enhanced by machines, and by distilling national identity into the abrupt contrast between winning and losing. The more technologically advanced war has become, however, the less plausible battlefield action has been as a source of traditional military honor and masculine identity (Braudy 2003:xvi, 251). The question then emerges of what might constitute heroism and how constructions of militarized masculinity work in a military that has not been involved in combat since its very foundation. For many male service members, joining the Self-Defense Forces is marked by a sense of defeat in some area of their lives: a failed entrance exam at a regular university leaves some with no choice but to enter the NDA; a low-income background closes doors to costly formal technical training, which some hope to receive in the Self-Defense Forces; or a vague feeling of disappointment in their job situation or the lack of job alternatives in their community leads them to the Self-Defense Forces. In an effort to overcome this sense of defeat, the Self-Defense Forces use gender politics to establish service members as "true men" and heroes of a new kind. Rather than privileging the combat soldier, however, I argue that negotiations around militarized masculinities draw on a number of existing modes of masculinity.

The situation for female service members, involving the construction of a militarized femininity, is quite different yet closely intertwined with that for males, as chapter 3 describes. The personnel and public relations apparatuses of the Self-Defense Forces skillfully represent female service members in a way that addresses the anxieties about the maleness of the military and attempts to connect the military to wider society and mass culture. I argue that many women emerge from the ranks of the Self-Defense Forces as "feminist militarists," aware of both their tremendous importance to the Self Defense Forces' public image and their marginal position within the ranks.

In chapter 4, I examine the strategies that the Self-Defense Forces employ in crafting their internal and public stature. I argue that they take advantage of the techniques of advertising and popular culture to camouflage, normalize, and trivialize the armed forces in the eyes of the public. These efforts range from the use of comic series and mascots to narrate their roles to a young audience; to recruitment posters that feature pretty women in casual clothes; to mass festivals that attract entire families—all attempts to familiarize the Japanese population, in historically and culturally specific ways, with a military that otherwise presents itself as isolated, marginalized, and misunderstood.

In chapter 5, I ask how the military valorizes a past that is marked by defeat. Looking at base museums against the backdrop of more prominent war and military museums, I trace numerous instances of the historization and dehistorization within and around the Self-Defense Forces and analyze what kinds of institutional ersatz histories the Self-Defense Forces create. I argue that the Self-Defense Forces try to forge a communal memory that will increase service members' morale and enable them to reposition themselves in Japanese society and the international security landscape. Base museums as the main sites of these efforts employ three strategies of representation—locality, historicity, and symbolism—that help humanize Imperial Army members and reconcile the relationship between the IJA and the Self-Defense Forces.

The epilogue addresses some of the larger questions behind my sociocultural and historical analysis—questions about new forms of militarization, the shape of the military of the future, and the notion of the normal state. The Self-Defense Forces promote themselves as a military establishment one moment and play down their military stature the next. Japanese troops at home and—since 1992—abroad have labored under a legally ambiguous status, a distinct lack of appreciation, and potentially hostile public opinion.[12] How and why does the military in Japan affect the tensions between a reputation for impotence and weakness and a reputation for potency and militarism? In what ways do service members negotiate their doubts about the political relevance of a military establishment that has one of the largest budgets in the world? How do they handle their uncertain status as successors to Japan's imperial armed forces, which so memorably shocked the United States and the world with their attack on Pearl Harbor on December 7, 1941, and their concerns about potency despite having the most sophisticated and modern military technology at their disposal? By the same token, what do conventional notions of a military's irrelevance, weakness, and impotence mean in today's world, in which military establishments are increasingly driven by ever-more-sophisticated technologies rather than by manpower, populated by military bureaucrats rather than by combatants, and whose role in combat more often resembles the role of superheroes in computer games than real life experience (Wright 2004)?

By shedding light on the condition of the Japanese military, this book aspires to examine an uneasiness intrinsic to the Japanese military and which other military establishments increasingly encounter: an uneasiness regarding their roles in their own society and abroad, the respectability of different kinds of missions, the variety of masculinities that military organizations produce, and the professional identities of troops more generally.

CHAPTER I

On Base

We must remember the true nature of our role as members
of the Self-Defense Forces, and refrain from taking part in
political activities, reflect deeply on the distinguished mission
bestowed on us as members of the Self-Defense Forces, and
take great pride in our work. By the same token, we must
devote ourselves unstintingly to training and self-discipline
and, in the face of events, be prepared to discharge our duties
at risk to ourselves.

> From "The Ethos of Self-Defense Forces Personnel,"
> adopted on June 28, 1961 (cited in Bōeichō
> 2005:546–547)

With the help of private first class Tama Keiko*, it had taken me about half
an hour to get into thick cotton fatigues and boots whose leather had been
hardened by the sweat of dozens of soldiers who had worn them before
me. The pants needed to be stuck into the boots. Superfluous cloth had to
be tightly folded back. The boots had to be evenly laced up, and the laces
tucked into the boot shafts. The shirt had to be tucked into the pants so
that the creases on the front and back of the shirt formed extensions of the
creases on the front and back of the pants. The belt was supposed to hold
everything in place, without hindering movement. All buttons had to be
properly closed. The cap had to be placed on my head and pulled down to
right above my eyebrows so that my eyes were protected against the bright
summer sun but still could be seen by others when I looked straight ahead.[1]

I had left my pleasantly air-conditioned office at the University of
Tokyo and taken the bullet train for several hours and a local train for
another two, arriving in the small town of Kibita at mid-morning on July
16, 2001, to spend a week of "basic training" at a GSDF base. Two uniformed men had jumped out of a Jeep to greet me at the station and drive
me to the base. Entering the base through the guarded gate, the two men
showed their identification cards and exchanged salutes with the service

members on guard duty. The younger of the two men was a private who did not introduce himself. The older one was Major Ono Shun*, the man in charge of the public relations office on the base. Ono had carefully prepared my visit and was in charge of arranging interviews with new recruits and their drill sergeants. In this chapter, I take a close look at the internal mechanisms of a GSDF base through the lens of a week of basic training. Narrating this experience allows me to identify and introduce some of the key sites, people, and issues that make up a base and characterize the everyday lives of Japanese service members.[2]

THE RULES OF ENGAGEMENT

This book draws from the methods of anthropology and cultural studies, including intensive interviews and participant observation, as well as the analysis of historical and present-day documents, texts, and visual materials. Between the summer of 1998 and the spring of 2004, I spent about nineteen months conducting fieldwork in Japan. I believe that these stints—the longest was for a period of eight months in 1998–99—considerably added to the credibility I had as someone interested in "understanding" (with all its ambiguities) the Self-Defense Forces. Altogether I interviewed about 195 people: officers, officer candidates, noncommissioned officers, and privates serving in the infantry, artillery, transport, communications, airborne, medical, and public relations; and international cooperation units and departments. The service members I spoke to related their motivations, experiences, and visions of their own futures and that of the Self-Defense Forces.

I encountered service members at all stages of their careers, from lieutenants to three-star generals and admirals, first- to fourth-year cadets at the NDA, and new recruits just three months into basic training. In general, these men and women were between the ages of eighteen and fifty, but my subjects also included veterans in their sixties, seventies, and eighties. Service members talked to me in the field in between training sessions, in meeting rooms of base headquarters, in their offices, in coffee shops and restaurants, and in their homes. In geographical terms, their experience ranged widely, including bases in Kyushu, Shikoku, Kansai, Tokyo, and Hokkaido in Japan, as well as foreign postings. In some cases, tours of duty had been extended for up to six months for missions to Mozambique, Cambodia, the Golan Heights, and Honduras. Japanese defense attachés could be posted abroad for as long as several years. About 90 percent of my interviewees were men. They can roughly be categorized into members of the GSDF chief of staff *(Rikujō bakuryōchō)*, officers *(shōkō kurasu no kanbu)*, noncommissioned officers *(kashikan)*, and enlisted service members *(rikushi)*. I will refer to all of these people as "service members" throughout the book unless a more precise definition is necessary. In addition to service members, I interviewed other people with close ties to the Self-Defense Forces. Among these were academics at both the NDA and the NMDA.[3] I also consulted with researchers at a number of research institutes, which are in some way affiliated with the Self-Defense Forces, the JDA, and the Ministry of Foreign Affairs and deal with military research. I interviewed a retired commander of the U.S. Northern Army who was at the time the CEO of a military technology corporation; a former member of the Japanese Imperial Army; a representative of the Self-Defense Forces' veteran association, and a retired general (who was then a security consultant to Tokyo governor Ishihara Shintarō); and foreign defense attachés to Japan from South Korea, Italy, Germany, and the United States. Lastly, I spoke with journalists who report primarily on military matters in newspapers and magazines, ranging from the *Yomiuri Shinbun* and *Mainichi Shinbun* to *Securitarian* and *Jane's Defense Weekly*.

Several service members and veterans allowed me to take a closer look at their personal lives by inviting me to their houses, where I talked with my (usually male) interviewee for many hours over lunch, dinner, or coffee and cake. In most cases I met their wives, who participated in the conversation, provided their views of their lives as service members' wives, and commented on their husbands' statements. In a few cases I also met their children, some of whom had never talked to a foreigner before.

By visiting many different military sites, I was able to trace typical service members' careers, which take them all over Japan. As a formal visitor of base commanders, I was allowed to spend full days at various bases, including Iruma ASDF base, Nerima GSDF base, and Matsudo GSDF base. Although arrangements at each base differed, generally an aide to the base commander picked me up at the nearest station or at the entrance to the base, took me to the commander's office, and after a polite exchange of greetings and a brief introduction of myself and my project, a guide was appointed to show me around. The guides provided me with general information about the base and introduced me to several people engaged in their respective activities. On one base I interviewed Self-Defense Forces personnel individually but in the presence of my guide. At other bases I had the chance to both interview people individually at work or during lunch, and away from my guide in more casual, less controlled settings.

I spent time on several bases on open house days and attended military festivals. At the annual open house of the NDA, which allows, like any Japanese festival, for a great deal of playfulness despite the otherwise rigid character of the institution, some cadets showed up in Imperial Army uniforms, a few appeared in former German SS *(Schutzstaffel)* uniforms, and others had nude photographs of themselves pinned onto a board next to a brief self-introduction in the hopes of finding girlfriends among the visitors. I explored the NDA campus, ate lunch in the cafeteria, visited classrooms, and spoke to people in meeting rooms and study rooms. All of this gave me insight into what the daily life of cadets is like on the hills above Yokosuka Bay, a few minutes away from the American base, and on the very spot where, during the first half of the twentieth century, Imperial Army officers had also been trained. In addition, I visited the campuses of the NMDA and the General Staff College in Ebisu. I attended the annual parade of the GSDF base in Asaka, where then-prime minister Obuchi Keizō spoke on the need for the tough training of the Self-Defense Forces in the aftermath of the 1999 North Korean "missile incident" (a threat to Japanese territory). During a second trip to the Iruma ASDF base, along with thousands of visitors, I watched different kinds of airplanes flying overhead. There, I also closely followed a Miss ASDF Contest. A female officer introduced the participants; representatives of various companies congratulated them; and uniformed Self-Defense Forces veterans presented them with gifts. I spent an incredibly hot day in early August 1999 at the Matsushima ASDF festival watching a performance by the Blue Impulse Team, who after a round of applause, were joined by a female model for visitor photographs. Several days on two different occasions at the muddy training ground at Mt. Fuji and the Fuji Officers' Candidate School (Fuji Gakkō) in Gotemba provided me with insights on senior cadets' last maneuver before graduation (figure 1). They chatted with me, dug defense holes, and prepared for and went on a 30-kilometer night march, greeting me in the morning upon their arrival. I returned to the Fuji school a few years later, in 2003, for the school's forty-ninth anniversary festival.

Some of my interviewees were wary, and some were delighted to talk with me.[4] They often took on the role of social elder and/or military expert as they related the lessons of their lives and their hopes for the future. Against the backdrop of the Self-Defense Forces' rather unfavorable reputation, and—in many cases—their individual socioeconomically

FIGURE 1. A National Defense Academy cadet takes a break during the last maneuver of his senior year at the Self-Defense Forces training ground at the foot of Mt. Fuji, July 22–23, 1998. (Photograph by the author)

disadvantaged backgrounds, many service members seemed eager to talk to me about their careers. Service members of all ranks were surprised and pleased that someone from the outside was interested in their every-day lives, their relationships, and their opinions of their work and the world in general. For some, I must have provided the first opportunity to be singled out to speak about their lives. The relative openness of many interviewees—especially of those at the end of their careers—might also be attributed to the sense that the Self-Defense Forces are not duly recognized and appreciated. For the first time, here was their chance to tell all to somebody who was willing to listen.

Officers transfer every two or three years, and thus contacts I made were often temporary. On the one hand, it has been difficult to keep in touch and follow up on conversations I had over the years. On the other hand, these circumstances have led to new opportunities. I was able to repeatedly interview a number of officers who had transitioned from desk posts in the JDA to base commander positions in rural Japan or from international posts back to desk posts in the JDA, undergoing at least one major promotion in the process. I also had the opportunity to interview successors to various positions, thus being able to observe the considerable range of differences in personality, ambition, and vision that each individual brings to a post.

Other important contacts developed through several encounters— some formal, others almost coincidental. In one case, an official visit to the JDA was unsuccessful until I ran into the officer I was looking for at a live-firing demonstration at the foot of Mt. Fuji. He was excited about having just achieved a major promotion. He told me right then and there that he would be able to arrange a base visit for me, during which I would be able to interview ten service members who had just returned from a prestigious international mission.

Another important contact developed out of a farewell party for a foreign defense attaché in Tokyo. There, an ASDF general told me I reminded him of his son, a sociologist (who did not intend to follow in his father's footsteps). Two days later, he sent me an email and invited me to the base. Later he arranged for me to attend the annual live-fire demonstration at the Mt. Fuji Training Ground (Kita Fuji Enshūjo) and introduced me to a GSDF base commander he had been friends with since his days at the NDA. In another case, a young female GSDF veteran, who had self-published comics about her experiences in the Self-Defense Forces, not only told me about her career as a service member, but also introduced me to an officer couple and accompanied me to their house, where I was able to speak with them for an entire afternoon. I found that the more often I returned to the field, the less dependent I became on higher-ranking officers; each time I met people who knew somebody in the Self-Defense Forces or knew somebody with a connection to the Self-Defense Forces. A friend's sister-in-law, for example, turned out to be a nurse in a Self-Defense Forces' hospital, and a scholar friend's advisee was a graduate of one of the Self-Defense Forces' high schools.

Many of them were outspoken about their appreciation for and their criticism of the Self-Defense Forces.

More than most other institutions, military establishments are held together by clear-cut hierarchies of rank, specialization, and branch of service. The hierarchical structure is instilled in service members from the day they join, and it is represented on everything they see and wear: uniform chest pockets, sleeves, shoulders, caps, and unit banners in the form of colors, cherry blossoms, stripes, and a variety of other symbols. Given these fairly conservative norms in the Japanese military (and the conservative nature of the larger Japanese society), I was not sure what kind of response I could expect from service members. Furthermore, as suggested by the walls and fences around bases, the presence of guards at the entrance to bases, and the procedures required to enter bases—the need to show identification cards, and in the case of visitors, fill out visitor forms—the armed forces are, to a considerable degree, closed to outsiders.[5] Setting aside the relative unease that many Japanese men and women feel when dealing with a foreigner, the Self-Defense Forces administration might well have suspected that I would at least inconvenience, if not unduly burden, the base authorities. I often had to be accompanied, driven, and picked up again, and thus I took up a lot of somebody's time in that regard. The number one rule of the Self-Defense Forces—safety—applied to me as well, and occasionally I had to be kept out of the way of combat and other field exercises where (fake) ammunition was used. My health and fitness also were not taken for granted. I did not carry heavy equipment when I accompanied units to their various field trainings, but dealing for hours at a time with the summer heat, high grass, and unwieldy ground meant that I had to frequently assure the drill sergeants that I was all right. And if I was the only woman present, the lack of bathrooms became an additional potential problem.

As with any institution (Douglas 1986), the military depends on a high degree of secrecy in order to monitor and control its image. This was true of the Self-Defense Forces, as well, and all the information that they produce and disseminate about themselves. Scholars who have analyzed organizations as varied as theater troops, sports teams, and confectionary factories have suggested that Japan's organizations and institutions are particularly rigid in how they close themselves off (Edwards 2003; Kondo 1990; Robertson 1998). But some concerns about secrecy are specific to the military. Commanders I spoke to felt that a base and its units are the core of their organization, and they worried that both the service members who talked to me and I myself were to some degree beyond their control. They worried about what I would hear and see, and how I would interpret that.

My role was defined by many factors beyond my control as well. Stories that might have been told to a military professional or a man were perhaps deemed inappropriate in conversation with me, a scholar, a foreigner, and a woman. In one instance, had I been someone else, a captain might not have apologized before ranting against the integration of women because "they cannot urinate in the field and they take menstruation leaves of absence." Perhaps those service members who had participated in combined exercises with the United States Forces, Japan (USFJ) would not have criticized their American opponents so straightforwardly if I had been an American citizen. Perhaps female service members who told me about sexual harassment cases that had brought their female subordinates to tears would not have gone into as much detail if I had been a male scholar. Perhaps the positive acceptance of homosexuals, and the almost universal conviction among individuals that they had never encountered a gay man or woman within the Self-Defense Forces, may have seemed more appropriate in interactions with a foreign woman like myself rather than with a man, who may have been uncomfortable discussing non-normative masculinity. The assumption that I must be a sympathetic outsider was established as much by my general interest in service members' lives (rather than a specifically problematic aspect of the military) as by the general unfavorable perceptions of the military that led to constant self-monitoring and self-legitimization. Once it was established, however, that I had no interest in publishing my research findings in the Japanese tabloids, the need for caution and secrecy diminished. I came to be seen primarily as an academic, a profession that enjoys a relatively high prestige in Japan; most service members I spoke to expressed their admiration when they learned that I was affiliated with the University of Tokyo and Kyoto University, two of Japan's elite schools.

The influence that base authorities had on the personnel selected for interviews should not be underestimated, but I did interview a variety of people with diverse views about their personal careers and the Self-Defense Forces as an organization. Some of the people I interviewed were chosen by the administration, some were spontaneously chosen by a field commander during exercises, and others were introduced through a third person outside the military. Occasionally service members were concerned that their individual experience would not be representative, and I had to convince them that it was indeed their own personal views on life in the Self-Defense Forces that interested me. Many were highly articulate and engaging. A lieutenant colonel I interviewed while his superior was working at a desk in the same office, for example, did not hesitate to dismiss his superior's excitement about the success of a mission he had directed. Several officers of the same rank violently disagreed with one another over the benefits of sending a deployment to Iraq in order to improve the Self-Defense Forces' reputation. Just back from a peacekeeping operation, one captain detailed for me the paradox of assuming that service members refrain from having sex during the six months they were posted abroad while also supplying condoms for them on base and information about "safe brothels" in the area of deployment. Similarly, the foreign defense attaché who seemed determined to provide me with the official line on his country's view of the Self-Defense Forces and the "excellent cooperation" between them and his country's armed forces became quite agitated when we touched on Japanese officers' scandalous lack of historical knowledge. And, in the presence of his fellow Japanese officers, a Korean officer visiting the General Staff College in Tokyo did not hesitate to claim that Japanese soldiers did not measure up to their Korean counterparts. In fact, he suggested, they weren't real soldiers at all.

In sum, the discernible boundaries between the mostly male service members and me, the outsider, which put many aspects of my visit beyond my control, may have impeded my research, but my outsider status in various ways also facilitated intimate, informal, and critical statements by the service members I interviewed.

HEADQUARTERS

My first stop after changing into the uniform was the commander's office in the headquarters building. In contrast to the headquarters of the Self-Defense Forces in Ichigaya, Tokyo, which combines the charm of a postmodern, glass and concrete government facility with the look of a medieval Japanese castle, the local headquarters here were housed in a bare, square building. The entrance hall held a glass display case filled with trophies from sports competitions as well as a certificate of participation in a United Nations Disengagement Observer Force (UNDOF) operation. Several men from this base had participated in the Self-Defense Forces' first peacekeeping mission to Cambodia, from July 1992 through September 1993. International missions are a mark of prestige for both the individual service members and the regiment. Major Ono

explained to me that the Self-Defense Forces' ambiguous image has improved primarily because of successful peacekeeping missions and the
group's role in rescue and relief missions after the Kōbe-Awaji earthquake in 1995 (despite the initial criticism that the Self-Defense Forces
were slow to mobilize and otherwise inefficient).

Ono had not been involved in the disaster relief activities in the Kōbe
area, but he knew from his experiences on a similar, if smaller, mission
what it must have been like for those service members who were. In
1974, right after he had completed his basic training, his unit was mobilized to bring a forest fire under control. It was horrific, he said, and
he had thought he might be killed. "I feared for my life then," he remembered with a shudder, "but luckily none of our troops were killed."
Major Ono Shun, a man of about fifty who took his job very seriously
and did not easily smile, had joined the Self-Defense Forces in 1973. He
had planned to retire after a few years in order to take over his father's
construction business, but he enjoyed it so much that he stayed on. His
father, who was fifteen when the Asia-Pacific War (1931–45) ended, vig-
orously opposed his son's decision to join the new military because he
equated the Self-Defense Forces with the Imperial Army. Ono's grand-
father, by contrast, who had not been drafted during the war, encouraged him to join the Self-Defense Forces. It is the rhythm of life on and
around a base, the outdoor field training, and the company of (mostly)
men that many service members like Ono cherish about their profession.
Asked about his current job as the head of the public relations office on
the base, a position that he had held for over a year, Ono said that he
would much rather be a platoon leader in the field again. However, as
he was by his own estimation too old to keep up with the young men
(and possibly women) in the field, Ono did not expect to be returning to
a field assignment.

When we entered the commander's office, Colonel Katō Seigo*, a tall
man in his early forties, awaited us behind a heavy wooden desk. The
large office also housed a sofa and a meeting area, a glass case with memorabilia, and a red carpet that ran from the door to the desk. Colonel
Katō welcomed me to the base, encouraged me to turn to Ono as I would
to a father throughout my weeklong visit, and expressed his hope that I
would get something out of my stint on base. I had been introduced to
him through one of his former juniors at the NDA, someone I had been
in touch with for the past three years and who constituted a major piece
of my contact network within the armed forces. Occasionally, base commanders who allowed me on base to carry out interviews or service

members I interviewed off-base explained to me that they had felt obliged to agree to my requests because they owed my contact person a favor. In some cases, however, the support I received from service members must have been motivated by curiosity and perhaps flattery. In others, it was an act of mutual obligation among officers who had been classmates at the NDA, in the same officers' course at some point in their early career, or simply friends. One base commander barely disguised his unwillingness to comply with my contact person but felt obliged to do so for reasons that remained a mystery to me. Commander Katō, however, did not let on whether he was returning a favor or whether I was putting my contact person in his debt.

After the brief encounter with the commander, Ono accompanied me to the public relations office on the ground floor of the headquarters building. Four service members, including private first class Tama Keiko, worked there under Ono. All of them sat at desks, busy with clerical work when we entered. I had a few minutes to take a look at the newsstand where several base newspapers and magazines were available, ranging from basic facts on the three services, recruitment and public relations material, and Self-Defense Forces periodicals such as *Securitarian, Asagumo,* and *Sōyū.* There I also noticed videos of maneuvers, special forces' training, the annual live-fire demonstration, and other public events, which are available at base stores and large bookstores. The videos are made by Self-Defense Forces photographers and are generally shown to external sympathizers, including representatives of companies that support particular events or that send their newly recruited personnel to one-week experience and training programs on a base; representatives of schools who invite recruitment officers to instruct their middle or high school students on the Self-Defense Forces; and organizations that neighbor bases, with whom the Self-Defense Forces tries to develop and maintain good relations.

Public relations officers serve not only officers and enlisted personnel, but also the journalists and photographers who work for magazines and newspapers published by the JDA, as well as the newsletters that are produced and published by individual Self-Defense Forces bases. This division's main responsibilities are to create, manage, and control information reaching the wider public, which includes efforts to almost completely suppress information about incidents that may harm the Self-Defense Forces' image—accidents, suicides, and criminal offenses committed by service members. The public relations office on each base organizes several types of annual events, which may include the celebration of the foundation day of the base; a cherry blossom festival; an Obon festival; and a sports festival open to the public in an effort to project an image of the Self-Defense Forces as an open, accessible *(hirakareta Jieitai)* organization.

In addition to these festivities on base, Ono and his staff spent a considerable portion of their time organizing the participation and cooperation of service members in local community events. This local regiment, he told me, was called upon frequently for what the Self-Defense Forces refer to as "activities for the collective good" that function as community outreach and are intended to contribute to the "deepening of the understanding of the Self-Defense Forces in the local population." During the previous year alone, service members from the Kibita regiment helped out at eleven large local events that ranged from festivals to sports competitions. For the festivals, service members wore traditional costumes and participated in processions; other service members, clad in their fatigues, prepared a playing field for a sports event. The public relations apparatus in the JDA enthusiastically embraces these opportunities to show the troops at their best—that is, as an organized, friendly, and strong group of men and women. Individual service members on this and many other bases I had visited were less enthusiastic. Even though they get compensated with time off for the time they spend engaging in these community activities, Ono said, they generally dislike these tasks because they involve a commitment outside of their regular work hours, often on Saturdays and Sundays (Terada 2001; Ishikawa 1995b).

IN THE BARRACKS

The Kibita GSDF base barracks for male service members are one- to three-story buildings. One sergeant is in charge of each floor. The "head of the room" *(heya-chō)*—usually the man who has been on the base the longest—is in charge of sorting out problems among roommates. The rooms are shared by four men of the same rank. On some bases, there are bunk beds and the number of troops per room differs. On the Kibita GSDF base, the transition to four-men rooms is quite recent and was undertaken in order to make life in the Self-Defense Forces more attractive, especially for those men who are perhaps far away from a comfortable family home. The reduction of troop numbers per room is only one small way in which the Self-Defense Forces try to attract and retain more service members. The NDA, for example, had tried different kinds of models with ever-smaller numbers of cadets per room until the number reached just two cadets per room. In addition to the quest for privacy, it was hoped that smaller numbers in each room would also undercut the instances of freshmen hazing by senior cadets. In the late 1990s, however, the NDA had to return to four cadets per room since a smaller number had led to "disciplinary problems." Each service member at Kibita GSDF base has one iron bed and a small locker for personal belongings, some of which are piled up under the bed, on a small desk, or over a chair. "They are not supposed to have anything of value in their rooms," the floor sergeant explained to me, but stereos and television sets are tolerated to "establish a sense of privacy and individuality." When he joined in the 1970s, this sergeant recalled, at least ten men shared one room and no personal equipment was allowed. Instead of doors, the rooms had curtains that did not allow for any privacy at all. Outside the Kibita barracks rooms, in the hallways, uniform caps hang on wooden knobs. The walls are bare except for posters that summarize the "virtues of service members." The linoleum floors shine. A full-length mirror covers the wall on each floor where the staircase turns.

The women's barracks differ in important ways. On other bases, female service members have complained about being housed in the oldest, shabbiest, and most inconveniently located buildings, but here at Kibita the barracks for female service members were recently renovated in order to accommodate female troops (Fukukawa K. 1995). While gray and green are the prevailing colors in the much older barracks for male service members, bright yellow, orange, and pale pink dominate the women's bathrooms. The floor of the common room is partly covered with straw mats and only partly with linoleum. Special common areas are designated for doing laundry and hanging up clothes to dry. A small air-conditioned room is reserved for smoking. There I had my first chat with Shōkai Rumi* and Tama, who turned out to be a crucial source of information on the intricacies of everyday life on base, particularly for women. Men used a part of the building, but the door to the women's barracks was locked, and a sign at the entrance warned off trespassers: "The entry of men is prohibited." Any man found in the women's quarters would be fired, Tama noted.

Over the next hour or so our conversation touched on the two women's motivations for joining the armed forces, their current frustrations, and their plans for the future. Both in their early twenties, they enjoyed the physical work and the opportunity to keep fit in contrast to "sitting in front of a computer all day," which was what they imagined would have awaited them elsewhere. The question of whether they should quit the Self-Defense Forces, they told me, was always on their minds. Private Shōkai, in only her second year of soldiering, did not plan to stay in the Self-Defense Forces forever; nor did she have other plans for her future. Tama had been in the Self-Defense Forces for four years and seemed more desperate to make a decision soon. On the one hand, Tama contemplated, she would find it difficult to quit now because she had just been promoted. On the other, she believed that only if she quit soon would she be able to train for some other career. Having joined the Self-Defense Forces right after graduation from high school, Tama regretted that she had never had the chance to experience university life. As for many service members, the Self-Defense Forces was not her primary career choice. She wanted to become a policewoman but did not pass the exam, which is more competitive than the one for the Self-Defense Forces. When she joined the Self-Defense Forces she wanted to train as a nurse or as a communication expert in order to acquire skills that would be useful later outside the military, but her preference was ignored by her superiors. She was posted to an infantry unit, a branch of service with a particularly low number of women. Tama's husband served in the same regiment. She appreciated this arrangement, which allowed them to live together, but was still frustrated by the posting. In contrast to other branches of the armed forces, Tama explained, "work in the infantry does not provide opportunities to acquire skills one could use off-base and outside the military."

Throughout a career in the Self-Defense Forces, service members frequently submit lists with several possible postings ordered by preference. The final decision, however, is made by the military administration and generally remains unclear to the person in question. Of course, postings, transfers, and promotions are based on the assessment of a service member's skills, but there are also other considerations such as age, as well as the internal logic of the armed forces. In Tama's case, for example, her posting to an infantry unit might have been affected purely by the oversupply of women in nursing units and the need to spread women more evenly throughout the armed forces.

Both female privates occasionally felt that they were wasting their time and taxpayers' money. They were sure that the public perceived them as a burden to the national budget and the ailing economy. Sometimes, Tama said, the feeling of uselessness was overbearing. It bothered her that the police were always shown on television and in films as the heroic protectors and saviors of the community, but service members who "train much harder do not ever appear on television and are not considered heroes at all. We are not even appreciated," Tama claimed. We're "viewed as tax thieves," added Shōkai. When Shōkai suggested that their bad reputation might be related to the fact that the Self-Defense Forces had never been involved in a war, Tama asked her whether she ever wanted a war. "No, of course not," Shōkai replied. "That would be right-wing thinking," she added. Both service members saw the Self-Defense Forces as being in a political dilemma, which Tama understood as follows: The right wants to restore the emperor to his prewar and wartime position in order to invade other countries. The left is anti–Self-Defense Forces and anti-war. In between these two extremes, it is difficult for the Self-Defense Forces to gain any solid ground. Even though the generation of service members with war experience as members of the Imperial Army have long since retired, and none of the current service members have been involved in combat, Tama notes, talk about war is common in the mountains during strenuous field exercises. "When we sat around utterly exhausted from several days of training in the forest without returning to the base once, sooner or later the conversation would turn to war. If a war broke out," Tama claimed, "most of us, men or women, would quit." The main reason in her view was that many young privates joined the Self-Defense Forces for the relative job security it offered in the current economic recession. While job security has always been a motivational factor for privates and sergeants, it has become ever more important for higher-ranking troops since the beginning of the recession in the early 1990s.

Tama hinted at another problem intrinsic to female service members' experiences in the armed forces. "From the outside it looks as if there were no discrimination of women because theoretically everything is organized by rank, but in reality there is a lot of discrimination." Already in their short military careers, the glamour of the Self-Defense Forces promised in the shiny, multicolored brochures had worn off. "I do not want to be treated like a woman," Tama said, emphasizing that her primary motivation for joining and remaining in the Self-Defense Forces was the desire to compete with and win against men. She sounded sad when she said that perhaps that should not have been the only reason to stay on. She knew that women were not allowed on the front lines "because of the possibility of rape by the enemy." Considering that "there is no war anyway," she found this a rather "ridiculous excuse to slow down women's promotions and careers." Gender discrimination, however, pervades even the smallest of everyday acts. When Tama was dating the man to whom she is now married, she had to keep it a secret, even though she suspected that everybody knew about their relationship. They did not talk to each other on base in order to avoid rumors that would have negatively affected both of them, as intimate relations among service members are discouraged and even prohibited among cadets at the NDA. Once she married, Tama said she never sat down next to men in the cafeteria, for example, and avoided talking to any of them privately, which could not have been easy as she was one of only a dozen women in a regiment of several hundred troops. If she did, she claimed, some of these men would start talking about her and spread the rumor that she must be having an affair. "As a woman, one sticks out so much and is under permanent observation," she explained.

THE MESS HALL

I got a glimpse of the constant surveillance Tama was so conscious of when I had lunch with her in the huge mess hall. Upon entering I concentrated on taking off my cap and holding it under my left arm while picking up a tray and putting some of the food onto dishes on my tray: soup, rice, meat, vegetables in a thick sauce, peaches for dessert. The food—oily and salty—told its own story of military life. The view that soldiers do hard physical work and thus must eat food with a high caloric value was obviously taken to heart here. The high level of salt was meant to make up for all the sweating during the daily exercises. This kind of food, which does not cater to any particular regional cuisine or taste, is fairly cheap, so it can be prepared in large quantities and kept warm for several hours.

Tama barely looked up when she searched for an empty table. Her manner was controlled and disinterested. Gone was the young, animated woman from our earlier conversation who had seemed worried that at her young age she might already have made an irreversible mistake by joining the Self-Defense Forces. In contrast to the chat in the female barracks, when she was reflective and articulate about her experience, in the mess hall she remained decisively silent. I quickly realized that this was not a place for conversation. She was still the same short and petite young woman, but in professional mode she seemed both invisible and ready to take on anyone and anything that might cross her path. I tried to eat as fast as she did. The game show that was on at full volume on the television added to the deafening noise of moving chairs, boots, and the kitchen staff at work. Some men sat in pairs and groups; others sat and ate by themselves. Besides the two of us, I did not see a single other woman. Some men looked up when we entered. Very few of them talked to each other. All gulped down the food in big chunks, jumped up, and left one after the other. Clearly this was not a place to linger. When we were finished, we lined up to shove the remaining food on our plates down a drain, briefly rinsed the dishes, and put them into a water basin where they soaked before being washed by the kitchen staff. Leaving the mess hall I put my cap back on and stepped out into the bright sunlight.

IN THE FIELD

The morning highlight for the rest of the week was my participation in basic training *(kyōren* and *kihon kunren)*. Clad in the green fatigues that were buttoned up to my neck, I stood at attention or at ease, marched, turned 45 degrees, 90 degrees, 180 degrees, turned around, saluted with cap or helmet, saluted with bare head, bowed toward the flag, and stood still during the noon roll call in 104-degree summer heat. The orders were yelled in a staccato that made it almost impossible for me to identify simple words such as "Ki o tsuke!" (Attention!) or "Yasume!" (At ease!). The sergeant constantly corrected every move I made. I stood with my feet too far apart. I marched too stiffly or not stiffly enough. I turned too late. I pushed my chin forward too much. I turned like a dancer instead of like a soldier in a formation of soldiers. I felt silly with the helmet on my head. While hearing him yell orders and struggling to put the correct foot forward, a number of thoughts crossed my mind. Why was participant observation considered a key to understanding? Why had I left the cool of the university offices and libraries to stomp around at attention, sweat running down my spine? Worst of all, when I turned in the wrong direction for the fourth time, I cracked an embarrassed smile. The sergeant cut into my thoughts. "Promise me one thing. Do not smile as long as you are on the training ground! Never!" His warning was superfluous; my concentration distracted me from the embarrassment, but it took days before I began to do things right more often than not and escape the angry rebukes.

I spent the afternoons mostly accompanying units to different kinds of field exercises *(butai kengaku)*, ranging from rifle shooting or aiming and firing mortars (figure 2) to combat training that involved firing machine guns at the troops designated as enemy units, in the woods a few miles from the base *(sentō kunren)*.

Several regiments throughout the country are designated to train the bulk of new recruits. Only in March and April, when their numbers get

FIGURE 2. Service members of the GSDF during mortar training on Kibita GSDF base in the summer of 2001. (Photograph
by the author)

too high to be completely absorbed by these regiments, is the overflow
trained on bases near the recruits' hometowns. Basic training consists of
two phases, three months each. During the second phase, new recruits
are split up according to the specialties in which they receive special
training. When the six months are over, privates resume their service in
respective units on bases all over Japan, and NDA graduates move on to
the GSDF officer training facility in Kurume, Kyushu.

My comrades for a week were high school and university graduates as well as people who had held other jobs before joining the Self-Defense Forces. All of them were new recruits *(shin taiin)* three months into basic training. Female recruits are trained in all-female units at the GSDF Asaka camp about half an hour from Ikebukuro station, Tokyo, during the first three months, but they join the men during the second phase of their basic training (Bōei Kenkyūkai 1996:66–67).

According to Self-Defense Forces regulations, the goal of the first phase of basic training is to "awaken an awareness for a service member's mission, the cultivation of the basic skills, including discipline, ethics and a strong sense of responsibility, proficiency in group life, and the training of physical strength" (Bōei Kenkyūkai 1996:46, 65–66). Subjects covered the first three months include spiritual training *(seishin kyōiku)* or mental preparation *(kokorogamae)*, public service, basic knowledge across different specialties, combat and combat technique training, and sports (Bōei Kenkyūkai 1996:66).[6] In addition to these components, service members also are encouraged to develop their "love for people" *(hito o ai shi)* and their patriotism *(kuni o ai shi,* also referred to as *aikokushin* and *sokokuai)*. Patriotism, according to the regulations, brings together the "love for one's region" *(kyōdō ai)* and the "love for one's race/ethnic nation" *(minzoku ai)* (Bōei Kenkyūkai 1996:57–60).

At the time I encountered them, during my "training," recruits still spoke a language quite different from their recruiters' slogans, which I discuss in chapter 4. Every day, they said, was completely regimented, from the roll call at 6 A.M., when they assembled for an early morning run, to 10 P.M., when the lights were turned off.[7] Basic training was "really tough" for some and "not as tough as expected" for others, but then there was the struggle of taking care of one's uniform, being permanently away from one's family (a first for many), the thousands of rules that needed to be followed, and never a minute of privacy. They learned the unwritten rules of NDA cadet hierarchy, where "seniors are emperors, juniors are humans, sophomores are slaves, and freshmen are garbage" (Sekizaki 1995:178). They endured the bullying of older cadets or recruits, and some looked forward to the days when they would be in the position to pass on some of the hardships to the next class. During the first few months, new recruits on bases all over Japan and cadets at the NDA cry on the phone when talking to their mothers. Some of them do not return to base or the campus from their first weekend off after three weeks of continuous training. Most of those who enter the second phase of basic training, however, will stay on for at least one two-year contract.

A major part of my time on the Kibata GSDF base was taken up with interviewing two dozen privates, cadets, and sergeants during their breaks from field exercises—a setting that made for hurried but also more spontaneous and straightforward interviews (figure 3). While I imposed the artificiality of the interview onto the situation and had them sit down in the grass with me (out of earshot of their units), the training ground was clearly their space. The conversation—especially with sergeants and older service members—flowed so freely that I could hardly keep up with my note taking. Service members who seemed confident and content with their careers and career prospects in the Self-Defense Forces and service members who were high-ranking and older were all more comfortable about being interviewed. Service members who enjoyed their jobs cracked jokes about it more often but were more likely to speak critically of their personal experiences and of the Self-Defense Forces as an organization. Some of the privates whose fathers were veterans of the forces had never considered a different career and seemed eager to embrace the challenges of field training. Sergeants who had spent their lives in the field, training numerous cohorts of troops, did not seem to trouble themselves with the concerns of those officers who were in charge of the public relations apparatus and of managing the *esprit de corps*, troop morale, self-image, and to some degree the public representations of the armed forces. Sweat dripped from their foreheads while I asked them a range of questions about their career paths, impressions of new recruits, and how they had met their wives. Huge ants crawled up my sleeves. Sunstroke always seemed imminent.

Sergeant Sakurai Susumu* exuded the kind of confidence that came from being sure of his expertise, his role, and his place within the Self-Defense Forces. He saw his task as one of getting new recruits into shape, physically and mentally. He had trained new recruits for more than fifteen years and was sure that he had seen it all: the sweat, the tears, the quitters.[8] "Recruits," he was convinced, "have always been more or less the same." But when prompted, he did seem to shake his head about the young generation. "Some have never even done their own laundry. Most are only children and are not used to functioning in a unit. Some even fight back tears," he laughed, "just because I yell at them." Other drill sergeants told similar stories. "Young people today have to be trained for one week just to make sure that they get rid of their long or dyed hair, that they understand that they cannot have spots on their uniforms, or leave the buttons of their pants open when they eat" (Oka 1998:212). But all too soon the interview was over. Back in the grass that reached up to my waist, and in the bushes, where a kind of hide-and-seek com-

FIGURE 3. A GSDF service member during an interview with the author.

bat training was in process, machine guns went off in rapid succession, and I lost sight of sergeant Sakurai and the unit under his command.

Mortar training on the base training ground was a very different affair. Four men lined up behind each mortar, which looked like a little cannon. At the command, they ran to the mortar, moved it into firing position opposite a target, adjusted the viewfinder, and a few seconds later yelled something that indicated to the sergeants clocking them that they were done. Timing and speed were everything. The men were out of breath from their efforts, and their uniforms were drenched in sweat. It took a while before the drill sergeant let them take a break so that one group could show me how the mortar worked. Trying to catch their breath, they explained mostly by gesturing and said very little. Soldiering is a fairly wordless job.

On one of the following days, I got to watch a rifle exercise. In the field, rifle training consisted of holding the rifle in different positions, and eventually lying down on one's stomach, spreading one's legs wide for balance, lifting the rifle up on one's elbows, aiming, and then shooting at a target. I could not see whether anybody actually hit the target. The privates got up, returned to their starting points, and started all over again. They repeated this for several hours. The repetitions were meant to automate a series of movements that seem impossible to perform

when your heart is pounding and your hands are trembling from ex-
haustion or nerves, and all the while your body is splayed on the ground
in a position for maximum balance.

THE RECRUITMENT OFFICE

The recruitment office in Kibita is one of about fifty throughout Japan
where all told about a thousand service members work. It is small and
barely identifiable from the outside; inside it is crammed with brochures
and recruitment records. I have visited more than a dozen of these offices,
which typically are located in hard-to-find corners of faceless buildings,
close to the main railway station of a town or a major subway stop in a
city. The two main tasks of these offices are recruiting new personnel and
introducing retiring service members to businesses in the region.

There are four main tracks. Students of Self-Defense Forces high
schools are all male and typically enlist because of a dire socioeconomic
situation at home. Most of them later join the armed forces as privates,
partly because very few achieve a scholastic level that allows them to pass
the entrance examination at the NDA or other universities. Cadets at the
NDA and the NMDA are trained to become the elite officers of the Self-
Defense Forces.[9] Graduates of other universities also enter the officers'
track after completing basic training. Enlisted soldiers enter into two-
year contracts, although many stay in the Self-Defense Forces for more
than ten years.

The recruitment office in Kibita is located directly next to the railway
station and is directed by Major Terasaki Makoto*, a graduate of the
NDA who is in his late forties and is a local resident. There are eleven
high schools, one university, and one two-year college in the region.
Terasaki suggested that the low number of secondary schools might be
responsible for the lack of young men and women from the area who
make it into the NDA.

In the early 1970s, one recruitment officer began to use direct mail
and posted hundreds of recruitment posters. He won a prize for that in-
novative recruitment strategy, which subsequently was adopted nationwide (Sase 1980:212). Today, by contrast, Terasaki and officers like him,
equipped with piles of glossy, multicolored brochures, flyers, and Self-
Defense Forces gadgets, visit schools in order to talk to students about
joining the Self-Defense Forces. Many schools, however, do not allow
them onto the school grounds in the first place. Even when he does find
a sympathetic school headmaster, Major Terasaki pointed out, recruit-

ment officers have to appear in civilian clothes rather than in their uniforms in order to "remain as low key as possible and not draw attention to themselves." In rural areas and small towns, recruitment officers will send out recruitment material directly to families whom they know have a son who will soon be graduating from high school (Shimoyachi 2003). Despite these recruitment efforts, recruitment officers fail to fill the ranks, and the recruitment of high school graduates who are targeted for sergeant careers has become particularly problematic because of the low birth rate and the decreasing number of people who do not go on to a college or university (Bōeichō 2001b:250, Oka 1998:127–129).

The recruitment offices also handle the local distribution of recruitment posters and other public relations material and the initial screening of applicants, which consists of a conversation about the person's motivations to join, family background and schooling, and visions of his or her future in the Self-Defense Forces. This conversation is the first opportunity for recruitment officers to talk about opportunities the Self-Defense Forces offers for acquiring, at no extra cost, special skills, such as large vehicle licenses or technical expertise, that are useful outside the armed forces. After this interview, applicants take a formal written exam that covers several high school subjects, including Japanese language, mathematics, and an essay on a subject of the applicant's choice. Candidates who pass the exam undergo another more substantial interview at which recruitment officers try to learn more about the candidate's motivation and personality. A physical exam, for which the basic criteria are good health, a height of at least 155 centimeters for men and 150 centimeters for women, and a weight within 20 kilograms of the norm, completes the evaluation process.

Recruitment strategies have changed considerably over the decades and recruitment has become somewhat easier during the past fifteen years because of the recession and also possibly because of some improvement in the Self-Defense Forces' image. Recruiting for the Self-Defense Forces, however, has remained one of the less desirable jobs and most certainly a dead end for an officer who already has a stalled career. Terasaki recalled with some measure of horror the stories older service members have told of their recruitment efforts. In the 1950s and 1960s, being a recruitment officer was the most problematic. "One's career was measured according to how many heads one was able to recruit, and at that time that seemed impossibly difficult. It was a no-win situation" (see also Sase 1980:205). The Self-Defense Forces had the greatest recruitment problems before the oil crisis in 1973. Recruitment officers were

practically ordered to recruit whomever they could find, without any regard for ability. Recruitment officers in the 1970s were so desperate to
increase their figures that they resorted to approaching young men on the
street (Sase 1980:206–210). One veteran recalled his own recruitment at
that time. Born in a little town in Kyushu, he had gone to Tokyo in order
to enter a professional school. He was studying for the entrance exam
and had a job to support himself. One day as he sat on a bench in Ueno
Park and watched the passers-by, a man called out to him, "Brother, you
have a good body. Are you a university student?" He replied that he was
just a night school student. He thought the remark a bit strange, but the
man seemed sincere. The man said, "In fact there is a good job for you.
Shall we go to a coffee shop and talk it over?" As it turned out, the man
was from the same town in Kyushu, the student trusted him, and they
went to a coffee shop. There the man identified himself as a recruiter for
the Self-Defense Forces. The young man was attracted by the possibility
of attending college while working in the Self-Defense Forces. He applied
that same day, passed the exam, and joined on June 1, 1970 (Nezu
1995:8–9).

Recruitment in Okinawa has probably always been considerably
tougher than elsewhere in Japan. One recruiter in Okinawa, for example, found the recession to be a blessing for the Self-Defense Forces.
Sergeant Izumi Kenichi was prepared for a tough job when he was transferred to Okinawa, where one-fourth of the fifty-three city and town
governments refused to support the recruitment efforts of the Self-
Defense Forces despite laws that ostensibly forced local governments to
do so. Considering Okinawa's history, Izumi understood the lack of sympathy for the Self-Defense Forces. But after the economic bubble of the
1980s burst, the number of applicants rapidly increased, and by 1996,
he and other recruiters were dealing with three times as many applicants
as in 1991. Once they had accepted one in two applicants, he reported,
but now they accepted only one in 3.5 applicants. This constituted quite
a shift from the 1970s when demonstrators in Okinawa shouted slogans
like "Self-Defense Forces go home!" or "Do not come to Okinawa a second time, Japanese military!" (Ishikawa M. 1995:236–238).

Such recruitment successes, however, obscure a demographic situation that has begun to affect all of Japan and promises to be particularly
dramatic in Okinawa. The recruitment pool has begun to shrink dramatically (Oka 1998:127–129). In the 1990s, there were roughly two
million eighteen-year-old men and women. More than half (1.2 million)
of those young people went into professional secondary schools or col-

leges and thus were no longer candidates for a career as a private in the Self-Defense Forces.

In contrast to the often aggressive rejection in earlier decades, the most common response from students today, according to Terasaki, is their lack of interest, which in his mind is rooted in a "lack of a sense of purpose" *(mokuteki ishiki ga nai)*. His assessment of local youth was mild, however. He had not forgotten that he too had found himself at the NDA and later in the Self-Defense Forces because of a number of random circumstances, including a failed entrance exam elsewhere. At the time he, too, had not had a clear goal or an understanding of or interest in national defense. His trajectory was typical for a large number of officers now in their forties and fifties. Very few had thought of the NDA as their first-choice university. Most had failed an entrance exam at a more prestigious school. What drew or pushed them to the NDA and into the Self-Defense Forces were service member fathers; an impoverished socioeconomic background; the need or desire to become independent from parental support; the hope that the NDA would straighten out their lives; and, of course, the possibility of a university education, for which they did not have to pay, with the option of resuming a civilian life after graduation. The NDA promised all of those benefits. Just like their seniors in the Self-Defense Forces, freshmen at the NDA gave all of these explanations for opting for the NDA.

Given the dire recruitment situation in his district, Terasaki knew he could not be picky about the reasons why men and women wanted to join the Self-Defense Forces, but he appreciated enthusiasm more than educational background and intelligence. He found that the opportunity to use their "real (physical) strength" *(jitsuryoku-shugi)* as service members was the strongest motivator among young men who joined in the region and hinted that these men were less likely to be disappointed with what they found in the Self-Defense Forces. Here, almost all applicants were men, and he spoke of female applicants only when I pressed him. "Of the women who are admitted into the Self-Defense Forces," he said, "80 to 90 percent in this region quit when they have children." This attitude of benevolent patronization, shared by many men of his generation, and one that is found across organizations, keeps many women from pursuing a career. Terasaki saw this trajectory of women's lives as a natural outcome, though, and not as an organizational or economic problem for the Self-Defense Forces.

THE HALL OF HISTORICAL MATERIALS

Service members were hesitant to speak about the legacy of the Imperial Army during my interviews. Kibita and numerous other bases, however, have made an enormous effort to capture and exhibit the local regiment's past in base museums. The Kibita base museum opened in the 1960s. The role of the Hall of Documents, or Hall of Historical Materials, as it is also called, is to collect and preserve artifacts in such a way that they represent the history of the Self-Defense Forces and their predecessors in a simple, factual manner.[10] The exhibits came together with a lot of help from local support groups—including branches of the Young People's Association (Seinenkai), the Parents' Association (Fukeikai), the OB or Veterans Association (Taiyūkai), the General Defense Association (Ippan Bōei Kyōkai)—and the Association of Bereaved Families under the guidance of the Self-Defense Forces' local public relations office. All of these organizations have their own ties to bases throughout Japan and together form a support network that connects service members to the wider population. For the Kibita base museum, local support groups sent out letters to their members and veterans of the Imperial Army in the region and received most of the exhibits from them. Thus, in depending on local families to supply artifacts, the museum represents history from a distinct local view; references to and representations of the Imperial Army beyond the local regiment are conspicuously rare.

Staff Sergeant Shimoda Hiromasa*, in charge of museum tours and one of Ono's subordinates, who was close to retirement, was delighted to give me a tour of what he seemed to think of as his museum. Occasionally the soft-spoken man guided veterans, and on rare occasions schoolchildren from the region, through the two rooms of the Hall of Historical Materials. The main audience, however, was the new recruits who were undergoing basic training on the base and had not, Shimoda was sure, "learned anything about the Imperial Army in their schools." The regiment's history did not just begin in 1951 when the National Police Reserve was renamed the Self-Defense Forces; indeed, it went back much further, as the trajectory of the building that housed the museum attested and as Shimoda was proud to point out. The building had undergone a remarkable metamorphosis, one echoed in numerous museums on other bases across the country. Originally, it had housed the headquarters of an Imperial Army infantry regiment. When the Imperial Army was formed in the 1870s, Shimoda explained, the local population was very poor and many wanted to join the military because they imagined a better life there than on their impoverished farms (as in other parts of Japan, oldest sons typically were exempt from recruitment). The basic criteria for enlisting were good overall health and—just as in the Self-Defense Forces today—a height of at least 155 centimeters. In 1898, the new local infantry regiment was established and its headquarters moved into the building. It remained there until the end of the Asia-Pacific War in 1945. According to Shimoda, soldiers from the local regiment "were mobilized during the Russo-Japanese War [1904–5], the Manchurian Incident [1931], the China Incident [1937], and to the Philippines throughout the Asia-Pacific War. Almost 20,000 soldiers from this base died during these wars."

After the end of the Asia-Pacific War, the building continued to be used as a headquarters but this time by the local section of the Allied occupation forces. After the Imperial Army had been dismantled and the Self-Defense Forces adapted the base, the building was "returned" to the Self-Defense Forces in the early 1950s. Thus, Shimoda proudly emphasized, his Self-Defense Forces regiment has a history of more than fifty years whereas many other bases were founded almost twenty years later. The one-story brick building had been restored several times since it was first erected. Walking up a few steps, I saw that a narrow hallway split the building into two rooms of equal size. The door to the right led into the room for the "History of the Former Army" (Kyūgun-shi). The door to the left led to a room designated for artifacts that ostensibly document the history of the Self-Defense Forces. At the entrance to this room, the three-foot-high Hotei-sama, one of the seven deities of fortune, symbolized the virtue that lies in being "content with what one has and making an effort to do better"—a modest civilian message that is decisively removed from the conventional notions of heroism, patriotism, and militarism I had expected to find.

A few undated woodblock prints depicted a decisive battle in the prefecture more than four hundred years ago, an event that marked the start of Japan's military history in the region. The old flag, Shimoda explained to me, had eight rays that represented the chrysanthemum, the symbol for the imperial household. Originally the flag was used for all kinds of occasions; now it is used only by the MSDF except for local festivals, when the Kibita GSDF regiment uses it as a regimental banner (rentaiki). Shimoda confided that he included the emperor in his thoughts and prayers about protecting the country. He imagined the emperor as an institution "that has been there for a long time and will still be there when [he is] dead." The thought of the imperial household's continuity, however comforting to him, necessitated here and elsewhere the suppression of the emperor's war responsibility. In his opinion, "the symbol of Japan formally had been the commander in chief of the Imperial Army but in reality had no power at all." A colored photograph of the Meiji emperor and empress was hung next to the declaration of the Sino-Japanese War. A colored photograph of the Shōwa emperor decorated a copy of the Imperial Rescript for Soldiers and Sailors. Exhibits in narrow glass cases included medals and stripes for military ranks, draft notices, letters from soldiers to their wives and families, uniforms, and boots. The items were undated, and the responsibility of explaining what they were and what they signified was left to Shimoda.

Shimoda had no illusions about the attitude of new recruits toward the museum and his lecture. He was certain that new recruits "do not care at all about the Hall of Historical Materials or anything [I have] to say about it," but he considered it his duty as a history buff to teach them about the "necessity to protect one's family, one's friends, the local community, and one's country *(kuni)*." These ties were obvious to him, but he said they "seem lofty to most of the young men and women who join the Self-Defense Forces these days." Shimoda's attempt to bridge the gap between the attitudes of new recruits and the ideology of their profession as proclaimed protectors of Japan echoed the first official statement about the postwar military's purpose, allegedly given in March 1951 by Hayashi Keizō, then the first commander-in-chief of the GSDF. Hayashi envisioned the new military as driven by "the love of parents and siblings of our own blood, our wives and children, for the Japanese people and land" (Bōei Kenkyūkai 1996:49).[11]

Shimoda framed his explanations with another officially sanctioned notion, namely that "the Self-Defense Forces is not a military force." I had heard this proclamation countless times, repeated like a mantra across ranks, age groups, and gender. For some service members it was a source of pride. For others it constituted the main obstacle to true professionalism. Regardless, Shimoda emphasized that there is a telling difference between the Self-Defense Forces of today and the Imperial Army. In the Imperial Army, he said, soldiers were treated so badly that during battles they shot their commanders in the back. In the GSDF, by contrast, and especially in the infantry (he used both the Imperial Army term *hohei* and the Self-Defense Forces term *futsūka*), good interpersonal relations were considered the most important ingredient of a functional unit. His explanation hinted at the already numerous attempts to acknowledge the problematic or horrific sides of the IJA in order to set the Self-Defense Forces apart from it.

Moving into the room for the history of the Self-Defense Forces, I saw a machine gun, several recent uniform styles, and public relations material on a blackboard—all displayed without a discernible order or explanations, indicating to me that no one had a clear idea of how the history of the Self-Defense Forces should be documented. In separate glass cases, portrait photographs of middle-aged and older women (with their names) were exhibited under the title "Honorary Mothers" (Mazā no katagata). During the Asia-Pacific War, these women were members of the local branch of the Patriotic Women's Association (Aikoku Fujinkai),[12] so why were their photographs here rather than in the room reserved for the Imperial Army? Indeed, exhibits related to prewar and wartime women filled about a third of the exhibition space in the Self-Defense Forces' room. I assumed these wartime representations of women had been placed in this room because of the lack of space in the first room, but it deepened my impression of the uncertainty people felt regarding how and what to tell about the Self-Defense Forces. There were no photographs of commanders, service members, or missions, and thus the story of the Self-Defense Forces remained faceless and hard to follow.

The legacy of the Imperial Army and the difficulty of creating a history of the Self-Defense Forces were problems that existed beyond the museum's walls. On the last afternoon of my stay on the base, Tama and Sergeant First Class Ueda Tarō* took me on a sightseeing tour that turned into a trip into Japan's military past. A small Shintō shrine was our first stop. When the priest finished with a tour group, he walked with us. "The new recruits on the local navy base come to visit the shrine every year," the priest explained on the way around the shrine, but "the army recruits do not." Later, Tama explained that whether new recruits visit the shrine depends on the "commander's personality," rather than on different views the navy and the army have about Shintoism, the state religion under Japan's wartime regime (when all other religions were carefully repressed). The legacy of the Imperial Army as an oppressor of ordinary (Japanese) people, a perpetrator of war crimes, and—most of all—a defeated force has always affected the GSDF, which generally shies away (more so than do the MSDF and the ASDF) from public connections to the wartime regime, be it the Imperial Army or representations of state religion. Aside from individual commanders' preferences, the MSDF's command decision to visit the shrine can also be seen as an expression of the marked difference in these other branches' wartime roles. Tama addressed that possibility and told me that, according to her brother, who was a service member in the MSDF, "the MSDF keep their traditions alive. The GSDF does not." He viewed the army's image as "dark" *(kurai)*. "Dark" is a word that has often been used to describe the Japanese war experience, with reference not only to the darkening of rooms during air raids but also, more importantly, to a negative time darkened by meaningless hardships, as in the phrase "dark war clouds" (Buchholz 2003:298). Tama suggested that it was because of these occasional rivalries that the GSDF hardly ever trained with the MSDF, even though the GSDF frequently carried out joint maneuvers with the ASDF.

Leaving the shrine behind us, we crossed a concrete bridge built in a fake Edo style—just one of the many heavy-handed efforts to turn the town into a place with some traditional flair and a sense of community *(machi-* and *furusato-tsukuri)*. Outside a tiny bicycle rental shop we sat down on a bench and had sodas. Ignoring both Tama and me, an old man at the bicycle rental shop approached Ueda and asked him whether he was a service member. Then he told him that he had been stationed in Okinawa during the Asia-Pacific War, where everybody from his unit was killed except for him. He cheered Ueda on by repeatedly calling out that "there is only one nation" *(Kokutai wa hitotsu shika nai)*. Ueda vaguely nodded but did not respond. Tama grinned at him and made a face at me, dismissing the old man's words. Ueda raised his eyebrows to her as if to say, "What!?" Tama just kept grinning at him. Then, Ueda finished his cigarette, and with the uncomfortable encounter over, we returned to the base, where we passed by the museum one more time.

HONORABLE DISCHARGE

The evening before my departure a farewell barbeque was organized for me. It took place in a corner of the base where picnic tables and wooden benches had been arranged in a semicircle. Sukiyaki stoves were on the tables, and service members served beer. The appearance of Commander Katō had been carefully coordinated so that he arrived last. I sat next to the commander at a table of six. About eighteen service members were there, including the commander, the aide-de-camp, several officers, and some of the sergeants I had observed and interviewed in the field during the week. There were also four representatives, including one woman, from the local Young People's Association, whom I had interviewed earlier that day about the association's relationship and collaboration with the bases and the Self-Defense Forces more generally. Both a Shintō priest and a veteran, now the owner of a local small business, were introduced to me as "local supporters of the Self-Defense Forces." Ono served as the master of ceremonies. First, toasts. Individual introductions followed. Each service member introduced himself with his rank and name, place of birth, the name of the base where he had served previously, his specialty within the military, hobbies, family status, and the number of children he had. All of this information was listed very quickly and orderly and thus appeared to be a rather common exercise at occasions such as these. After the first few introductions, only the commander and I continued to listen and applaud; everybody else was already having fun talking to one another and preparing food on the stoves. Only when Commander Katō finally stood to speak did the group fall silent again, with everyone's attention focused on him. Clearly a socially adept man, he started on a folksy note designed to both impress and bond with his troops and to overcome differences of rank in the presence of civilian outsiders, including myself. Yet he was able to also demonstrate his ability to perform his duties as commander and his skills as a man of the world.

Born in Tokyo, Commander Katō lived apart from his family, who had stayed in the city. Katō's daughter was already in college, and his wife liked to be close to her in Tokyo. And, he added smiling, she had no interest in moving out to the country where she did not know anybody and would not get to see him much anyway. Commander Katō was a career officer, and it turned out that over the six-year span of my fieldwork, he was reassigned three times—from an office post in the old JDA in Roppongi, then to his current command, and later back to the JDA again, which in the meantime had been relocated to Ichigaya. He tried to see his family every third weekend. Even though that was not always possible, he was luckier than many men in the Self-Defense Forces. Many officers and service members live separated from their wives and families because of the sheer difficulty of moving a family every two or three years on transfers. As long as the children are little, moving is easy, but most parents shy away from repeatedly taking their children out of school once they begin middle school, afraid that the moves will affect their performance and chances to get into a good high school and university. Those who leave their families behind in remote rural areas of Shikoku, Kyushu, or Hokkaido often see their families only three or four times a year, for just a few days at a time.

Katō introduced me by mentioning a conversation we had had when

I first met him at the beginning of the week. He had asked me whether I preferred speaking English or Japanese. I replied that I would prefer speaking Japanese, given that English was not native to either of us. He pointed out how impressed he had been by my saying that. The other men muttered appreciation. I used the opportunity to express my gratitude. A Taikō performance by five service members followed.[13] Within two hours the party was virtually over. Suddenly, the president of the Young People's Association stood in the middle of the barbeque site, and everybody stood up and turned to him. He threw his arms up and shouted "Banzai!" three times, followed by three collective shouts by everybody else. The party quickly dissolved. On the way out, one of the drill sergeants gave me his card and asked me to send him my publications on the Self-Defense Forces because he was sure that "the men told [him] different things than they had told [you]."

The commander and a few other men, including Majors Ono and Terasaki, then took me along to a second dinner off-base, the almost obligatory second gathering or *nijikai*. For the second dinner, the commander changed into a dark suit and necktie. The other men wore more casual pants and short-sleeved shirts. Service members are hardly seen in their uniforms in public places off-base, so this change of clothes was not surprising; for them it was only one of the many routines intended to help them blend in with civilian society. Service members with whom I had dinners or drinks off-base had always been in civilian clothes.

A rented bus took us up into the hills nearby where we had dinner in a Japanese-style room of a hotel with a splendid view of the valley. The hotel owner was introduced to me as yet another "supporter of the Self-Defense Forces." Considering that we were the only guests on a Friday night, I wondered whether the gesture of support was not mutual. The hotel owner led us all up a steep staircase. Sitting on cushions on a floor covered with straw mats, we had a rather extensive dinner—first sushi, then a series of other dishes, together with beer and rice wine. I sat across from the commander at a long, narrow table. The commander used this occasion to massage the egos of his sergeants, "as the men who really make a base work [while] commanders come and go and are totally dependent on their support." To my left, Major Terasaki got quite drunk and increasingly persistent with romantic propositions, to which I responded as graciously as possible. Everybody else just ignored him, although I did sense disapproval of his behavior from Ono, who sat at the other end of the table.

Eventually, the conversation turned to security matters and Japan's position in the international arena. Like many officers with international experience, Commander Katō's thoughts on military matters in Japan and abroad were closely tied to American security policy: "The American focus on security policies has shifted from Europe and Russia to Asia, particularly China and North Korea. Both of these countries are potential future threats to Japan." China, said Katō, trained officers and privates but did not train sergeants, a shortcoming that rendered the Chinese military dysfunctional at that point. He was unsure, however, how this practice might change within the next ten years. He suggested that the improvement of diplomatic relations with China was preferable to rearmament, but later he criticized the Japanese government for providing so much economic aid to China.[14] Whereas North Korea featured as an unknown element because of the unpredictability of its leader Kim Jong Il, Katō found that South Koreans were much more patriotic than the Japanese and attributed that difference to the conscription system there. The other men remained mostly silent or uttered their agreement, and I realized that the commander's speech was at least as much directed at them as it was a response to my questions. Thus it came as no surprise that, when asked about the ongoing discussion on constitutional reform, Katō favored the revision (kaizō) of Article 9. In recent years, the Self-Defense Forces have quietly shifted their stance toward the understanding that Article 9 is too vague to be practical or needs to be revised because the very existence of the Self-Defense Forces contradicts it. This latter position is shared by people across the political spectrum, although they have very different ideas on how to revise the document (Hook and McCormack 2001).

Katō assured the dinner party that all current members of the Self-Defense Forces "had been raised in the democratic spirit of postwar Japan and nobody wanted a war but rather the recognition of the Self-Defense Forces as a military." Consequently, all of them seemed to appreciate Prime Minister Koizumi Junichirō's initiative to seriously discuss the revision of Article 9. According to Katō, "Now, the Self-Defense Forces' legal status is unclear and we are basically operating in a gray area." Katō favored the defense clauses the Germans had included in their Basic Law as an ideal solution for Japan, sharing a notion of "normalization" that Ozawa Ichirō had promoted in 1993.[15] Germany looms large in the imagination of some Japanese officers (in addition to the United States, but far less prominently and only when it comes to issues of historical legacy and legislation). At a previous meeting with Commander Katō and other officers, as well as numerous times during my fieldwork, I was told that "the German military has been so much luckier than Japan's Self-Defense Forces." In a somewhat twisted configuration of ideas that are tied to the wartime German-Japanese alliance, Katō and some other officers viewed the Self-Defense Forces' situation in comparison to that of Germany as follows: The IJA—and thus by extension the Self-Defense Forces—had been blamed for the Asia-Pacific War. In Germany, the entire population had taken on the responsibility. The Self-Defense Forces still labored under this legacy. The German armed forces had fully "recovered." The Self-Defense Forces were the only military in the world that found itself unappreciated and in a legally fragile place and thus in an overall vulnerable position in Japan and internationally. Today the German armed forces might not be extremely respected by German civilians, but their legal position was secure and comparatively clear. The Self-Defense Forces were also under an enormously strict network of civilian control. The most disturbing facet in the minds of some Self-Defense Forces officers was that the upper-level military administration had no experience in and understood very little about military matters. No one spoke, however, of the fact that the German state had taken responsibility for Nazi Germany's wartime actions while the Japanese state had returned to an ambiguous position concerning Japan's role during the war.[16] Neither did anyone mention the broad debates about the German armed forces in the 1970s and 1980s that brought forth a major wave of reforms (Abenheim 1988; Kühne 2000; Frevert 2001).

Katō hinted at the need for the Japanese government to take a more critical stance concerning Japan's war responsibility, but then he pointed out that "the Taiwanese have never complained about their treatment in Japanese textbooks; only the Koreans have done so," suggesting that Korean concerns might be unjustified. This was the moment, however, when some of the other men chimed in, as if the commander had finally said something they could connect to and agree with. Asked about the reasons for this discrepancy, Katō suggested that during the Asia-Pacific War, the Taiwanese felt that the Imperial Army was not as bad as the Chinese Army. No one mentioned forced labor, sexual slavery, or war crimes. Rather, all the men at the table seemed to agree that since both of these countries had been colonies of Japan, one of them must have been misrepresenting the wartime behavior of the Imperial Army.

We eventually moved on to more pleasant small talk. The farewell upon our return to the base was loud and hearty. The following morning, I returned the uniform, the boots, the cap, and the helmet. I carried a regimental banner as a souvenir in my bag to the railway station. Ono, accompanied by the president of the Young People's Association, dropped me off at the local train station, just in time for me to get on the next train to the city and back to civilian life as I knew it.

CHAPTER 2

Postwar Postwarrior Heroism

Men are supposed to be responsible for protecting newborn
babies, women and aged mothers. Men in Japan, however,
are utterly incapable of accomplishing this mission because
they do not receive military training.

Prime Minister Hashimoto Ryūtarō, *Japan Times
International*, April 1–15, 1999:17

The disaster relief mission to Honduras went very well and
we got a lot of good press. But there is a downside to this
kind of success as well. People must not forget that we are
not a bunch of nurses! We are a military!

Lieutenant Colonel Saitō Hiroyuki*, December 1998

How do officers grow as leaders when there is no armed conflict to test
them? Roméo Dallaire (2003:30), commander of the U.N. mission to
Rwanda, answered this question as follows: "You train and train, and
then you train others." I ask this question more broadly: What is a
peacetime career in the Self-Defense Forces? How do Japanese service
members translate combat training that is directed at inflicting and
withstanding extreme forms of organized violence into risk-taking to
save the lives of others? And how do those men whose lives are permeated by military rules, values, and interests negotiate their masculinity
within a military organization that trains them for war, while limiting
their experience to operations that prohibit violence. If their masculinity as professional soldiers is defined by the actions they perform and
how they perform them, how do Japanese service members articulate
these actions, these experiences, these markers of their professionalism? In this chapter, I suggest that a broad variety of masculinities is at
work in the Self-Defense Forces—apparent in the organizational struc-

ture, actions, speech of their personnel, and representations in public relations material.

In Japan and perhaps elsewhere, in the absenc of combat, operations other than war assume the role of battle in constructions of heroism just as the rhetoric of the front experience and combat continues to permeate the "war stories" of Japanese service members. The following statements, made in 2004 by three GSDF service members in their twenties, poignantly capture the conflict between the perceived normality of the military and the notion that death constitutes a key component of military heroism.

> How I think about it? I am against it. Have you ever seen photographs of Iraq? Horrific.

> Frankly, there is no great cause behind the Iraq deployment! Just as America's dog, pitiful Japan kowtows to America. There is nothing else! It's not because I particularly like to fight but I would like to go [to Iraq]. Somehow I feel that in a mental state in which the bonds of life adjoin those of death there must be "something" to discover. I am tempted to volunteer. As a soldier, you must experience a battle once. . . . After all, I don't want to become a toy soldier!

> There are lots of problems associated with this deployment but personally, I would like to be sent to Iraq. I might die or get sick. . . . I do not want to live very long. I feel like everything or nothing. To return home unharmed would be best. But even if not, I wouldn't care. (Konishi Makoto, Watanabe Nobutaka, and Yabuki Takashi 2004:88–89)

A few months after Prime Minister Hashimoto Ryūtarō from the conservative Liberal Democratic Party got carried away and made the comment in the epigraph above, Lieutenant Colonel Saitō Hiroyuki* insisted on imposing Hashimoto's terms of militarized masculinity onto the Self-Defense Forces. At the time Saitō was in charge of military planning for the entire GSDF and had just returned from the Self-Defense Forces' first international disaster relief mission. From his perspective, the operation in Honduras was a success for the GSDF, but he also pointed out that for these new missions in faraway countries the Self-Defense Forces would need more female personnel, especially nurses, because sick and injured women, children, and elderly people were more comfortable with women. Saitō was pleased with the generally positive tone of media reports in Japan, particularly those within the Nagoya area, from which most members of the Honduras mission had been dispatched. Yet in the same breath he expressed his dissatisfaction with the way the Self-Defense Forces presented themselves to civilian society at home. In

Saitō's view too much emphasis was placed on humanitarian missions and community work projects, and he was concerned that a respectability based on such an image of the military would do nothing to improve the military's public profile. Media reports and the bulk of Self-Defense Forces' recruitment and public relations materials alike would misrepresent "the military, and not accurately reflect what service members primarily train and exist for, namely the defense of Japan." I examine how the Self-Defense Forces' public relations apparatus crafts their image by employing popular culture in chapter 4. Here it suffices to point out that whereas Prime Minister Hashimoto declared the protection of women, children, and the elderly to be truly male and masculine tasks, Lieutenant Colonel Saitō felt that the military should not be measured by its men's capabilities for doing just that.

Perhaps Hashimoto's comment about caring men and military training could have been made by any statesman caught off-balance on rearmament fantasies. Certainly, some soldiers in any given U.N. operation would understand Saitō's concerns about nontraditional military roles.[1] Considered together, however, their claims about the connections between gender and the military highlight the many facets to constructions of "militarized masculinity." At first glance, the politician Hashimoto and the military man Saitō merely referred to an essentialist relationship between manhood and the military and declared defense matters to be a male and masculine activity. Both men claimed that the kind of manhood that service members of the Self-Defense Forces are expected to embrace is distinctive from other types of manhood and requires a distinctive sort of man. And, perfectly in tune with Judith Butler's (1995:24) suggestion that gender is not a disposition but an accomplishment, both men assumed a militarized manhood that is trained, practiced, and achieved in the Self-Defense Forces. Military establishments all over the world invest a great deal of energy in creating the illusion that military tasks are inherently male and masculine ones. Hence, even if militarized gender "is assumed in relation to the ideals that are never quite inhabited by anyone," in Butler's formulation, the very performance of militarized gender is precisely that "which produces retroactively the illusion that there was an inner gender core" (Butler 1995:32). In the military more than anywhere else, sanctioned manhood is out in the open, its meanings constantly spelled out, its purposes frequently repeated. Perhaps no other organization drills into its members with more vigor what kind of men they must be. Hence, if gender is always only imitated, as Butler suggests, then the military must be understood as one of the very centers of these imitations.

Cynthia Enloe's (2000) assertion that military manipulations privilege masculinity by manipulating the meanings of both masculinity and femininity is also true of the Japan Self-Defense Forces. In contrast to the idea that masculinity depends primarily on an other constructed as feminine (Goldstein 2001:251), however, I suggest that men in the Self-Defense Forces measure their masculinity primarily against that of other men, not against women. Hence, the sense of community and comradeship of men in the Self-Defense Forces is not rooted primarily in the marginalization of women. Rather, the Self-Defense Forces' organizational identity and the militarized masculinity of their service members are informed by past and present militarisms and have been molded by the until recently near-hegemonic position of the "salaryman," or white-collar worker, as the ideal representative of Japanese masculinity, the legacy of the Imperial Army, and the tens of thousands of American troops stationed on Japanese territory. For the Self-Defense Forces in present-day Japan, as well as for individual service members, the gendered figures of the salaryman, the Imperial soldier, and the American soldier loom large. For service members, however, there is no easy identification with one of these configurations of masculinity. Rather, each configuration embodies desirable and undesirable features and thus moments of identification and dissociation. These tensions within masculinities effectively emphasize the Self-Defense Forces' and individual service members' efforts to achieve a militarized masculinity that is geographically located and historically grounded within the geopolitical space of Japan, East Asia, and the world. And they facilitate the positioning of the Self-Defense Forces within a historical timeframe, by creating an organizational history and securing its future through the continuous redefinition of the service members' respectability vis-à-vis their civilian male peers, the Ground Self-Defense Force's relationship to the legacy of the Imperial Army, and the proximity to the U.S. and other military establishments.[2]

The assumption of the characteristics of one gender configuration—the salaryman, the Imperial Army soldier, the U.S. soldier—over those of another may seem easy to the outsider, but for service members this process entails intense conflicts that involve institutional as well as individual decision-making. One gender configuration is not more real (or artificial) or more hidden (or overt) than another. Rather, institutional procedures provide the conditions under which a different configuration comes to the fore at a particular moment while others recede into the background. These transfigurations are facilitated (and at other times impeded) by written and unwritten rules—a carefully protected set of public relations and marketing strategies that prescribe as well as document every single step in order to both protect a sense of military identity among the troops and represent the Self-Defense Forces in the best light to the Japanese and/or the international public. Subsequently, instead of one homogenous and stable gender mode, the habitus that is expected from and accepted among service members has been multifaceted, unstable, and amorphous.

The anxiety about how to properly perform militarized masculinity, indicated by Hashimoto's and Saitō's comments, as well as by numerous service members in conversations with me, is by no means unique to the Self-Defense Forces, although Japanese service members often appear hyper-aware of their camouflaged gender identity. As the types of valorized soldierhood multiply, armed forces in democratic countries the world over have increasingly allowed for the integration of different sexes and genders and have become increasingly inventive about what roles to take on in an effort to maintain their legitimacy in a post–cold war world. They also have invested in aggressive public relations efforts in order to convince an increasingly critical public of their necessity and usefulness (Burk 1998a). These broader changes have destabilized the sense of proper militarized masculinity that once centered firmly on the combat soldier. Every move Japanese service members make attests to this instability. One young male officer candidate, for instance, imagined that he would enjoy the celebrity status of male military heroes in Hollywood movies, while a middle-ranking male officer, close to retirement at the age of fifty-one, expressed a more modest quest for public approval and the recognition that "any other working man in Japan can expect."[3] Another older male major smiled sheepishly when telling me about his prayers for no war to happen until his retirement. A new male recruit refused to acknowledge that the Self-Defense Forces are a military organization in the first place. Another officer candidate was proud of being posted to the prestigious Northern Army in Hokkaido, which gained its reputation during the cold war for its proximity to the former Soviet Union, for having the newest weaponry on its bases, and for offering the toughest training, which supposedly produces the best combatants. One captain was proud of his status as "the mother" of the squad, while another fretted that the men in the Self-Defense Forces were "not properly initiated into the concept of self-sacrifice for the sake of the nation."

As they are frequently transferred, officers in particular shift from one configuration of self-presentation to another when being reassigned from a field post in Kyushu or Hokkaido to a desk post in Tokyo or abroad, and in the process transgress geographical, cultural, and linguistic boundaries. These transgressions entail negotiations of the shape and position of militarized manhood by individual service members as well as—in often contradictory ways—by the armed forces as an organization. Service members do not passively internalize these configurations of militarized masculinity. They are aware of the instability of the hierarchy that connects them, and they contest, debate, and resist it. An officer recalling his special forces training, known for its brutality, might cry on a public relations video, for example, highlighting the enormous strain on the service members undergoing that training (video screening on open house day, GSDF Fuji School, 2003). A service member who helps prepare Sapporo for a mass sports event evinces different qualities than one who guides children to a first-aid tent in a remote village after an earthquake. And a JDA division head carries himself differently at the center of the military command in Tokyo than when he is out for a drink as the commander of a base in rural Shikoku. With these processes in mind, the following analysis focuses on locations where negotiations of masculinity and professionalism intersect and crystallize: the entry into the Self-Defense Forces; the less spectacular but numerous local missions that include community projects, large-scale events, and disaster relief; combined exercises with U.S. Forces, Japan; and international peacekeeping operations.

INDIVIDUALISM AND THE "SALARYMAN"

The "salaryman," or white-collar employee, has played a major role in the formation of masculine identity among Japanese service members. Until the recession of the early 1990s, the salaryman was an important prototype of post–World War II Japanese masculinity. Introduced to western readers by Ezra Vogel in 1963 (1971 [1963]:9) as *the* Japanese masculine stereotype, white-collar workers in large corporations and the government bureaucracy personified economic security and social status. During the 1990s, even when the luster of economic success began to crumble, the image of the Japanese man held by people in and outside Japan was still "a workaholic who toils long hours for some large corporation, goes out drinking with his fellow workers or clients after work, plays golf with them on weekends, rarely spends time at home with his wife and children, and does hardly anything around the house, such as cleaning or changing diapers" (Ishii-Kuntz 2002). Parts of that image began to disintegrate as more and more white-collar employees found themselves without a job and increasingly became victims of a stalling economy (Osawa 1996; Dasgupta 2003).[4] During his heyday, and to some extent even today, the salaryman has been glorified in popular media and advertising in and outside Japan as the "company warrior" *(kaisha senshi)* and his masculinity militarized as "corporate warrior-like masculinity" *(kigyō senshiteki otokorashisa)* (Yamasaki H. 2001:52). These "company warriors" give their best for the company and sacrifice their health and their family life, from which they are usually alienated. Product advertisements targeting male white-collar workers have created images of the ideal man that are one-dimensional and ahistorical. Through their military references to battle, victory, defeat, and death in relation to the white-collar employee's total devotion to his company, these advertisements fashion the white-collar worker as a peacetime incarnation of the warrior.

The "samurai spirit" that is frequently evoked to make the contemporary salaryman a "company warrior" is decisively premodern and thus remains unrelated to unpleasant memories of aggression and defeat in more recent Japanese history. According to the vulgarized and commercialized version, the object of the warrior's devotion and the tools of the trade may have changed, but he remains true to the samurai spirit. The present-day samurai fights his battles at work, not in the field. His loyalty is tied to the company, not the clan. His masculine spirit, however, remains the same.

In the post–World War II era, wartime products whose marketing had tied the sexual potency of the soldier to the military capacity of the empire (Frühstück 2003) were replaced by a new generation of energy-enhancing products for the successful salaryman, with ads that preached virtues explicitly associated with soldiering and prioritized self-discipline and self-sacrifice (Rohlen and LeTendre 1996:60). Advertisements for new health drinks and other nutritional supplements promised to remedy fatigue and reinforce one's "spirit" *(seishin)*. By the early 1960s—just as the salaryman was emerging as the hegemonic masculine ideal of the new era—such energy-enhancing tonics as Guronsan from Chūgai Pharmaceutics, the energy drink Ripobitan D from Taishō Pharmaceutics, and Esukappu from Esuesu Pharmaceutics came on the market (Cwiertka 1998). Several decades later, in 1989, the energy drink Regain was introduced for the same target consumer group. Advertisements for these products generally represent Japanese men as salarymen, portraying them in work- and company-related contexts, without sharing significantly in domestic work or child rearing (Roberson 2005). They also maintain a distinct rhetoric of combat. Regain, for instance, is promoted with the slogan, "Can you fight for 24 hours? Businessman, businessman, Japanese businessman?" (Steger 2002). And the motto for Ripobitan D is still "Fight!" or "Faito!" (see figure 4). Yet another salaryman image was used to illustrate an article on positive thinking titled "'Positive' Sells Now" (" 'Pojitibu' ga ima ureru"), published in the February 8, 1999, issue of the weekly magazine *Aera* (p. 34). In the illustration, the salaryman's head is surrounded by female figures in cheerleader costumes and the slogan is again "Fight." In a similar vein, morning exercises for employees in some companies continue to resemble the morning routine of a military base and begin with the exclamation of "Fight!" (Kondo 1990:78–104)—a cry that conveys the militarization of everyday life.

The salaryman has increasingly become an ambiguous figure, hailed in mass culture for his willingness to work himself to death *and* ridiculed for his ignorance and powerlessness in family matters. In service members' narratives, however, the imaginary salaryman/warrior emerges as everything service members believe they are not or do not want to be. Opposing the sociocultural milieu that has created a highly militarized image of the salaryman, individual service members commonly refer to the salaryman with loathing. As representatives of actual soldierhood, service members do not have much sympathy for salarymen's claims to militarized masculinity. Service members do not acknowledge any of the warriorlike features ascribed to salarymen in advertising or evoked in corporate training sessions meant to increase team spirit.

Privates in particular paint a far less heroic picture of these salarymen and sharply distinguish their own masculinity. They disparage salarymen as unmanly, selfish, and weak, and consider their professional lives to be "monotonous," "boring," and driven by profit-making. It is precisely the desire to be different from salarymen that motivates many men to enlist in the Self-Defense Forces. Ōmiya Hiroshi, a veteran and the author of *The Weird World of the Self-Defense Forces! (Soko ga hen da yo Jieitai!* 2001), vividly describes this decision: Ōmiya joined the Self-Defense Forces, quit, tried his luck as a salaryman, and after a couple of years rejoined the Self-Defense Forces because he could not stand the life of a salaryman. To him and other service members, salarymen seem a colorless, faceless, and conformist mass that stands in stark contrast to their own individualism and independence of spirit, albeit

FIGURE 4. The November 30, 1998, issue of the weekly news magazine *Aera* featured a full-page advertisement for the energy-enhancing drink Ripobitan D, which appealed to both the salaryman-as-combatant (with the battle cry, "Fight!") and the salaryman-as-family-man (with the image of a baby).

within the boundaries of the military. A twenty-five-year-old recruit who had graduated from a university told me that he had worked as a salesclerk in a fishing equipment shop for several years and eventually quit to enlist in the Self-Defense Forces. He was bored with the day-to-day routine of his sales job, he hated being inside all day, and he could not stand the idea of doing the same thing every day for the next thirty-five years or so. The irony of his comments, considering that he had just spent the entire morning repeating the same few movements during mortar training, seemed to escape him. During the previous few weeks, he had also had to get up, put on his military uniform, and eat and go to bed at the exact same time every day (with about 800 other men of his regiment), and—if he did indeed make the Self-Defense Forces his lifetime career—he would continue to do so for most of his working life.

For civilians, donning a military uniform may connote giving up one's right to act as an individual and thus be equated with giving up one's identity. By contrast, from the perspective of Ōmiya and other young service members, military uniforms allow them to become individuals. The uniform can say things they do not have to say themselves, and, as Paul Fussell (2002:198) suggests, "one of its functions is precisely to assume a character not [their] own." Besides, a uniform provides its wearer with a definite line of demarcation between his person and the world.

> It is the uniform's true function to manifest and ordain order in the world, to arrest the confusion and flux of life, just as it conceals whatever in the human body is soft and flowing, covering up the soldier's underclothes and skin. Closed up in his hard casing, braced in with straps and belts, he begins to forget his own undergarments and the uncertainty of life. (Hermann Broch, cited in Fussell 2002:14)

Whereas the outside observer imagines military service as the loss of freedom and a life of obedience and subordination, young, often socio-economically underprivileged recruits see it as the opposite: liberation from societal expectations and boredom, from the doubts of choosing a profession, and, above all, from the anonymity of the masses. In spirit, at least, joining the Self-Defense Forces also means liberation from a sense of alienation in the present-day world, in which nothing significant ever seems to happen. In the words of an enlisted service member speaking about her male comrades, "Many men who join the Self-Defense Forces do so because they want to get away from real life" (Bandō 1990:287).

The notions of individuation and individuality also appear as important frameworks for a person's choice of the branch of service. Asked about why he joined the GSDF after graduating from college, Lieutenant Colonel Asakawa Itaru*, an aviation officer, explained that when he first joined the GSDF, he perceived both the ASDF and the MSDF as dominated by machines. In his account, only in the GSDF did the individual man and what he could become really matter:

> I felt that the main attraction of these two branches of service was the opportunity to deal with airplanes or ship machinery, while the individual human being hardly matters at all. There are planes, ships, and missiles. People are merely attached to them. My interest in national security was not so much a material or physical matter but rather a mental or psychological one [seishinteki na mono]. I felt that mental defense was more important than material or physical defense.

Asakawa articulated an attitude that other service members share. While to many service members the salaryman's daily routine seems unadventurous and his life inconsequential and predictable, the routine of the Self-Defense Forces offers challenging exercises that both allow and demand a person to "explore one's limits," "get to know oneself," "grow as a person," and "stand on one's own feet," according to several enlisted men. These challenges are primarily of a physical nature, but service members believe that overcoming physical limits can translate into overcoming mental ones and that skills learned in the military can be retooled for use in other jobs (Oka Yoshiteru, Sankei Shinbun, August 4, 1998). Service members from new recruits to generals express a wish in choosing the military, to do something exciting by working outdoors, engaging seriously in sports, or participating in strenuous field exercises and dangerous operations. They are interested in "discovering [their] true strengths" in both physical and mental terms.

By their own reckoning, their individualism carries a moral superiority. They see their willingness to "sacrifice [themselves] for their country" as superior to the salaryman's sacrifice for his company. Indeed, from a service member's perspective, the salaryman's pursuits seem selfish. As one new recruit expressed it: "Salarymen's lives seem so similar to one another and completely devoid of any surprises. Even though basic training was tough and Self-Defense Forces routines can be pretty rough, at least I wanted to do something special, something different." Another service member recalled that he did not really know anything about what service members do, but just could not imagine himself in front of a desk in an office for the rest of his life.

The rhetoric of loathing for the salaryman within the Self-Defense

Forces goes back to the days of their foundation.[5] During the 1950s and 1960s, a salaryman's comfortable lifestyle was not an option for most men who enlisted in the Self-Defense Forces. Many of these men came from socioeconomically underprivileged rural areas. For these men, the sense that touches of heroism, self-sacrifice (for the good of the whole society), adventure, and action were inherent in their work allowed a romanticization of their military lives and a self-perception of a masculinity superior to that of a salaryman. For them, the attractiveness of a salaryman's life lay in his middle-class, white-collar existence, but they also were repulsed by its very ordinariness. Another aspect of belonging to the Self-Defense Forces, namely the relative job security as a state employee, remained, however, almost unmentioned in these service members' narratives about their motivations to enlist.

As their careers advance, significant numbers of officers begin to recognize that despite their emphatic rejection of a salaryman's life (however unrealistic their understanding of that life might be), their professional lives have become very similar to those of salarymen. Most officers spend many hours with clerical work despite being primarily interested in working in the field and with other men. As if to minimize this, some stressed how glad they are to be able to leave their offices at 5 P.M., "in contrast to salarymen, who have to prove their loyalty with a company until midnight." Not a single officer I talked to seemed particularly unhappy about his job at the JDA, but when I asked them what they preferred doing, all replied that they found being on a base with the men much more satisfying than doing mostly desk work at the JDA. They described their frustrations with resigned comments, such as: "After all the training, I ended up living like a salaryman." Others believed that because the Self-Defense Forces are "not respected as a military, working as a service member comes down to being a salaryman." A colonel in his early forties, Tanaka Kinuyo* recalled how he had wanted to become a pilot. Once he graduated from the NDA in the mid-1980s and began to move up through the ranks, however, "desk work seemed to explode compared to work in the field."

It is not always clear, however, whether the "salarymanization" (*sarariiman-ka;* Endō 1993) really bothers all officers who say so. Perhaps that claim is a rhetorical facet of self-stylization among Self-Defense Forces officers that goes hand in hand with the self-perceptions of some service members as "citizens in uniform" that Ute Frevert (2001) has described in service members of the German Bundeswehr.[6] In Germany, the conscription system was introduced in 1956 and an alternative community service added in 1961. By the 1980s, those who refused to do any kind of service were criticized, while conscripts doing community service were welcomed as "heroes of the everyday" (Bartjes 2000:132). Today, two-thirds of German civil servants perform jobs once classified as women's work, and thus civil service offers opportunities to destabilize gender roles. Even representatives of the conservative Christian Democratic Party welcome the new trend toward civil service as a desirable indicator for a new "ecology of the social" and a "culture of helping" (Bartjes 2000:142). In postwar Germany, the citizen has become a model for the soldier instead of the soldier a model for the citizen, as was the case during the first half of the twentieth century (Bald 2000:110). With the Self-Defense Forces, however, the situation is more complex, for it remains a constant struggle for service members to differentiate their professional lives from those of salarymen.[7]

Written and unwritten Self-Defense Forces rules push service members toward *looking like* salarymen or at least blending in with salarymen and mainstream society as much as possible. As Major Kataoka Hiro*, at one point head of the GSDF public relations division in the JDA, emphasized—a major component of desired volunteers is their "normality": "We search for normal citizens. We don't want freaks or radicals no matter whether they are from the right or the left." Dress, hairstyle, and other aspects of physical appearance are all managed in a specific but not particularly rigid way. The publicity machinery of the Self-Defense Forces has further appropriated the salaryman configuration in order to emphasize the "normalcy" of its men (see figure 5), picturing the Self-Defense Forces as an organization populated by ordinary men, who could *almost* as well be found in any other male-dominated Japanese company, government agency, or organization. The qualifier here is the sense that they work for a very special organization.

As an unstated rule, service members regularly change into their civilian clothes whenever they leave base. When, for example, I met three officers for lunch directly across the street from the JDA, they changed into business suits just for our 90-minute meeting. Personnel and graduate students from the NDA who wear their uniforms for classes appeared in casual clothes indistinguishable from those of other young and middle-aged men and women whenever I went out to dinner with them in Yokosuka, Tokyo. The efforts to blend in with civilian society are most apparent in large cities where anti-military feelings are assumed to be particularly strong, and one rarely sees Self-Defense Forces uniforms. Considering that Japan is a relatively "uniformed society" (McVeigh 2000a), where

防衛ってなんだ！

ーオレも読むっス！！ー

ーサラリーマン金太郎ー

グラビアとCD-ROMで、警察予備隊発足から有珠山災害派遣までの半世紀の歩みを特集。
CD-ROM（Windows®対応）には動画を合計28分収録！！（裏表紙側をご覧下さい。）

FIGURE 5. The cover of the 2001 defense white paper features Salaryman Kintarō and is a hot pink color, as a way of attracting a more youthful audience. Here the hero of a bestselling cartoon series that had been adapted for television and screen snarls in the guise of a salaryman, "What do you mean, defense!? I must read this as well!!" The image hints at the transformation of Kintarō from a former motorcycle hooligan into a salaryman hero, suggesting that the Self-Defense Forces offer the opportunity for a similarly radical transformation.

people including male white-collar workers, female clerks, bank employees, elevator operators, taxi drivers, school pupils, and many others wear a uniform, the Self-Defense Forces' hesitation to wear their uniforms off-base is noteworthy. While, according to their supporters, school uniforms stand for "youth, diligence, cleanliness, truth, goodness and beauty" and are believed to have a positive effect on students (McVeigh 2000a:54), Self-Defense Forces uniforms originally carried negative associations with violence and war, as well as with the U.S. military. In the aftermath of the occupation era, wearing a military uniform made some soldiers uncomfortable because the original Self-Defense Forces uniforms looked similar to the uniforms of the U.S. military. One woman's son was suspected of being the offspring of streetwalker who catered primarily to the U.S. military and was harassed on the street. Twenty years later, this man's mother still remembered the many times she and her son had cried about that accusation (Sase 1980:58).

The Self-Defense Forces have made an effort, however, to redirect these associations—both to war and to the U.S. military—by adjusting their uniforms and overall appearance. In contrast to middle school and high school uniforms for boys, whose rigid designs were originally modeled on European army uniforms, Self-Defense Forces clothes seem rather loose and relatively unrestricted. The recently introduced custom of wearing baseball caps, which now substitute for conventional berets, further indicates the attempt to design a look that makes service members resemble civilians in casual dress. Today, first-year cadets are the only ones who have to wear uniforms off-campus. Wearing the uniform is supposed to help instill pride in being a service member and facilitate the creation of an identity as such. Some cadets believe, however, that they must wear their uniforms in order to be prevented from doing anything strange, such as returning to their parents or hiding at a girlfriend's place (Ishikawa M. 1995:104–105). In contrast to their fathers' generation, which faced a fairly hostile social environment, present-day cadets no longer expect to be attacked on the street when recognized as service members. But, uneasy about wearing their uniforms off-campus, some cadets confide that they will rent a room in Yokosuka, where they change into their personal clothes before going off into the city. Sometimes they are mistaken for railway employees, whose uniforms—in the eyes of un-accustomed viewers—look similar to those of cadets, but they want to avoid "sticking out" and being easily identifiable as NDA cadets. By contrast, when I traveled to a base on the outskirts of Nagoya in the winter of 1999, the sergeant who met me in front of the railway station was in fatigues, and nobody on the street paid much attention. On another occasion, when I took a break from fieldwork at a camp in the summer of 2001 and went by bicycle on a short sightseeing tour of the vicinity with two sergeants, both of them remained in their uniforms. Other service members report that in remote areas of Kyushu or Hokkaido, for example, where the Self-Defense Forces' presence is often of considerable economic benefit to the region, they have been encouraged on the street by old men and women to work hard. In the city of Nazaki in Hokkaido, for instance, which has roughly 26,000 inhabitants, service members and their dependents comprise a sixth of the population; their combined salaries total half of the city's budget (Endō 1993:33). Service members believe that the fact that their income taxes alone are a considerable economic boon for the town contributes to them being tolerated.

Beyond the dress code, most service members' physical appearance does not reveal their involvement with the military when wearing civilian clothes. While other armed forces strictly prescribe the length of hair and the range of acceptable hairstyles, similar rules do not apply as strictly to Japan's service members. Sometimes one sees the crew cut so characteristic of some other armed forces, however, among those service members who serve in urban areas, considerably longer hairstyles are far more common. Service members seem unaware of any particular restrictions except those against tattoos, dyed hair, body piercing, and full beards. The same goes for body build. Some service members described being ridiculed for being short and slim when they first joined the Self-Defense Forces, but on my numerous visits to bases I came across hardly any efforts, so prominent in some other military establishments, to increase service members' body mass. During their years at the NDA, cadets have to engage in sports club activities, which range from the less popular judo, karate, and mountaineering clubs to the very popular baseball and tennis clubs.[8] Privates and sergeants speak of the primary task of their training as "steeling their bodies." Both classes of service members, however, report that later in their careers, the emphasis in training is much more on perseverance and cardiovascular training than on muscle building. This emphasis can be attributed in part to unsatisfactory sports facilities on many bases, which leave few options for enhancing physical fitness besides jogging and golf, as opposed to, for example, lifting weights or working out on machines. More generally, muscle building is not high on the fitness agenda of Japanese men, and overly muscular bodies are not considered particularly desirable in wider Japanese society, where lean features are the ideal for both men and women (L. Miller 2003). Asked about the benefits of physical strength in soldiers, some were quick to explain their belief that physical strength was important for soldiers but that "as Japanese" they would particularly excel as soldiers with the "spiritual strength" to persevere. This appeal to "spirit" carries a reference to that other military establishment with whose legacy service members to this day grapple—the Imperial Army.

THE SHADOW OF THE IMPERIAL SOLDIER

Self-Defense Forces service members cannot help but participate, passively or actively, in a mostly quiet but persistent debate about the Self-Defense Forces' roots in the Imperial Army. They do so precisely because their intrinsic connections to the Imperial Army affect the kind of manhood they aspire to, their sense of self-respect, the ways they relate to the Japanese state and the Self-Defense Forces as an organization, and their perception of their role in Japanese society. This participation is most immediately apparent in their use of language. Blending in with wider society affords frequent code switching from a distinctly military to a civilized language. Among themselves, service members use the language of all military establishments. When talking to outsiders, however, they use a special lan-

guage constructed almost entirely after World War II. This special military
language was created in order to break tradition and disrupt connection to
both the old imperial structures (Humphreys 1995) and language adopted
from the German military (Low 2003:83). New terms for ranks, branch of
service names, unit designations, and the like have been coined for the Self-
Defense Forces. Other terms derive from American military vocabulary.
Various metaphors and euphemisms are intended to move the Self-Defense
Forces closer to civilian organizations (Hook 1996:152), and they are similar to the invention of new terms in the armed forces of Germany. In official language, for example, service members are not called "soldiers"
(heishi, senshi or *gunjin)* but simply "special public servants" *(tokubetsu-
shoku kokka kōmuin)* or "members of a group or unit" *(taiin)*. Consequently, when JDA publications refer to other countries' soldiers, *"heishi"*
as in *"Beigun heishi"* (American soldier) or *"Roshia-gun heishi"* (Russian
soldier) is used, while Japanese soldiers are consistently referred to as
"taiin" (group member). This distinction unintentionally highlights the
problematic status of service members being both similar to other civil servants (and salarymen) and yet special and different from them. The same
logic applies to military equipment, rank, and unit names. Hardly any use
is made of words like "war planes," "fighters," or "combat planes." Instead, they are called "special planes" *(tokubetsu hikōki)*. Rank is usually
referred to by numbers such as *ittō rikusa* (first rank land help) for an army
colonel, *nitō rikusa* (second rank land help) for a lieutenant colonel, and
santō rikusa (third rank land help) for a major. An infantry unit is termed
a *futsūka* (general unit).[9] This conscious distancing of the Self-Defense
Forces' language from that of the Imperial Army is also expressed by references to one's place of deployment simply as a workplace *(shokuba)*
rather than unit, battalion, brigade, or division. Using language evocative
of everyday experiences may also serve to make the military community
more comfortable with what they are doing. Carol Cohn (1987:704) wrote
of U.S. defense intellectuals' language that it is packed with euphemisms
that are "fun to say"—"racy, sexy, snappy. You can throw them around
in rapid-fire succession. They are quick, clean, light; they trip off the
tongue. You can reel off dozens of them in seconds, forgetting about how
one might just interfere with the next, not to mention with the lives beneath
them." Japanese military euphemisms, by contrast, are bulky, lengthy, and
have a bureaucratic, objectified sound to them. They are slow and easily
twist the speaker's tongue. They are complicated and not easily understood
by civilians, thus somewhat defeating the purpose of their invention—to
signal a clear rupture between the IJA and the Self-Defense Forces.

Cohn (1987:705) made another important point about the use of a civilianized language for an organization charged with state violence: "It is simply learning a new language, but by the time you are through, the content of what you can talk about is monumentally different, as is the perspective from which you speak." Speaking this kind of expert language, then, "offers distance, a feeling of control, and an alternative focus of one's energies; it also offers escape" (Cohn 1987:706)—in this case, escape from thinking of oneself as a potential perpetrator of war and violence. Although they already have a mandated distance from combat, the Self-Defense Forces have not compromised another important function of an expert language: exclusion or the denial of a voice to those outside the professional community. Japanese civilians without ties to the Self-Defense Forces would not know what any of the special terms mean.

Service members seemed highly aware of the existence of this official language, and some expressed resentment toward having to use it. By and large, however, they have internalized intricate code switching concerning their language, their clothes, and other facets of their behavior. Still, there are corners of their existence where the IJA soldier lingers.

The figure of the imperial soldier is on service members' minds whenever they engage in international operations, precisely because these operations are loaded with symbolism that enhances Japan's postcolonial image. As Colonel Osaki Tetsu* explains: "For us, international deployments in the context of peacekeeping or disaster relief missions are important not only in order to accumulate experience but also to convince neighboring countries formerly under Japanese colonial rule that we have nothing in common with the Imperial Army."

In Osaki's and other officers' accounts, the hope of performing well abroad is intertwined with the desire to shed guilt by association and bury the Self-Defense Forces' ties to their imperialist predecessor. As Colonel Teraoka Nobuhiro* remarked: "It is terrible to say this but the ideal situation for the Self-Defense Forces' reputation and our alleged connection to the Imperial Army would be a natural disaster somewhere close, here in East Asia. That would give us the opportunity to show to the Japanese population, to our neighbors, and to the international community that we *have changed*—that we are not their fathers' (and grandfathers') army anymore." Colonel Teraoka expressed his hope that through increasing engagement in international missions, the Self-Defense Forces would be recognized as different from the IJA and would

cease to be suspected of being likely to commit the atrocities its predecessor did. After Japan's first international disaster relief mission to Honduras in November and December 1998, and newspaper reports in
Japan acknowledging its success, one senior officer involved in the planning of the mission, claimed, "Now everything will change!" He imagined that deployment abroad would display, in the eyes of the Japanese
and Japan's allies, the Self-Defense Forces' capabilities as a functional,
experienced, trustworthy, and technologically up-to-date organization
more effectively than relief missions on Japanese soil ever could.

In Teraoka's and other officers' imaginations, the "imperial soldier"
provides one cornerstone of their gender identity as service members. He
represents an important configuration of militarized masculinity with
which service members grapple, but he is not archetypal in the sense that
George Mosse (1996) ascribes to the manly ideal ostensibly born during
the Napoleonic wars in Europe. Neither is he marginalized like the failed
and unhealthy masculinities that emerge from Angus McLaren's (1997)
examination of the trials of masculinity in Europe and North America.
Where Mosse finds that throughout the modern era a "hegemonic masculinity" reasserts itself in the western world, the imperial soldier serves
as both an ambivalent and ambiguous configuration of militarized masculinity. Enhancing the Self-Defense Forces' reputation as an establishment of superior masculinity and progressive modernity vis-à-vis the
masculinity of the imperial soldier, which is tainted by war and defeat,
the militarized masculinity of the hero at home and—to a lesser degree—
abroad, converges where risk-taking, violence, military professionalism,
national identity, and pride meet. The imperial soldier is rhetorically mobilized so that service members can both differentiate *and* parallel the
risks they are willing to take on disaster relief or peacekeeping missions
abroad with the violence associated with their predecessors.

In these schemes, imperial soldiers represent attack, aggression, war,
destruction, death, and even massacres for some. These notions are recast in terms of risks specific to the Self-Defense Forces. Service members
see themselves as committed to taking risks—whether at a natural disaster site on behalf of civilians or at a post-conflict site in order to prevent further conflict and maintain peace alongside soldiers from other
countries. Since the immediate postwar era, Self-Defense Forces service
members like Inoue Eishun* have been called in to re-erect buildings destroyed by the bombing of Japan's cities and rebuild roads crushed by
natural disasters—tasks that could not be more different from those of
the IJA. Inoue emphasized the differences among service specialties: "We

in the engineers' corps never felt useless or underappreciated. The guys from the infantry did. They were frustrated and got quite bitter but we engineers were right there where the action was, rebuilding Japan." Looking back on a remarkable military career that started somewhat against his will, Inoue is perhaps more reflective than most first-generation Self-Defense Forces veterans. His father, an IJA officer, did not return from the Chinese front. He had been set on a career in engineering from his childhood onward, but when he was ready to enter a university his mother presented him with his father's will, which read: "By all means, our son must become a military officer." At first devastated by his father's demand, he entered the NDA, studied engineering, and later joined the GSDF engineer corps, thus to some degree satisfying both his father's and his own wishes. Even after his retirement from the Self-Defense Forces as a three-star general, he has maintained close ties to military think tanks and policy makers. For Inoue, the IJA is his father's army and thus by definition a force from a different age with very little connection to the Self-Defense Forces. In fact, he noted with some pride, he was "one of the first high-ranking officers in the GSDF to suggest a complete reform of the Self-Defense Forces at the end of the cold war," which, for the GSDF, was marked by the disappearance of Russia as a threat to the nation's security.

Not all officers approach the history of their profession in such an uncomplicated manner. Admiral Hirota Wataru*, for example, said he would never forget how two young men had pulled him off a train and beat him up when he was commuting in his NDA uniform in the 1960s. Feeling vaguely apprehensive that he was to personally pay for the war his father's generation had fought and lost, he can understand that some service members have found an odd resolve in comparing their own misunderstood existence to the members of the IJA and Imperial Japanese Navy through the notion of the "heroic victim," a figure that has dominated much of Japan's post–World War II consciousness (Orr 2001; Watanabe Morio 2001; Standish 2000). These service members see themselves as belonging to a "community of suffering" (Kühne 1996b:189). Realigning themselves with the sense of suffering and sacrifice of the wartime generation entails embracing helplessness as well as forgiveness rather than examination, responsibility, and truth. The sense of suffering and sacrifice is also recast as being misunderstood, underappreciated, and disliked despite the service members' commitment to the Japanese population's safety and security. Those service members who have felt most underappreciated as protectors of the Japanese population have typically assumed that large parts of the Japanese population are pacifist and adamantly anti-military. In a restaurant near a base in Tokyo, service members I interviewed lowered their voices when they told me that the local population would not react well if they knew that my lunch companions were service members. "Many of them are communists," one major explained.[10]

The symbolic relationship between service members of the Self-Defense Forces and the notion of the imperial soldier also rests on the tension between efforts to dissociate by demonizing the Imperial Army and the desire to re-create a military tradition and uninterrupted history that allows service members to identify with and be proud of their predecessors. In the lives of service members, acts of conscious dissociation from the Imperial Army compete with moments where similarities and continuities are acknowledged and embraced. Moments of ambiguous and ambivalent attraction alternate with those of repulsion on the individual and the institutional level in the headquarters in the capital and the offices of rural units.

Differences between the three branches of service aside, Morimoto Jun*, a soldier scholar and instructor at the Staff College in Tokyo, concedes that some service members imagine the imperialist past as a simpler time when the soldier's place and status stood unquestioned, his role was unmistakably clear, and the masculinity he aspired to was singular. But for most, imperial nostalgia ends there. Reflecting on the dominant attitude toward Japan's role in World War II in the centers of military learning, Morimoto explained that during the late 1950s and the 1960s, Imperial Army veterans were first excluded and then selectively integrated into the Self-Defense Forces, creating a continuity that seemed necessary at the time to build a functional military. He saw the main impediment to viewing the Imperial Army as a model for the Self-Defense Forces as the IJA's failure in war making, their core expertise: "That is the reason why it has been impossible to positively relate to the Imperial Army and craft both a positive military history in which the history of the Self-Defense Forces could be incorporated and a model of soldierhood that service members could embrace and identify with."

Dismissal of the IJA as a model may be far from complete and consistent, but it does stand firm in the GSDF precisely because the IJA failed at defending the homeland. Moreover, the IJA was charged with war crimes and sexual slavery, a legacy that has haunted the GSDF. Hence, most service members' relations to IJA veteran organizations are cool or nonexistent. Colonel Tsutsui Kiyoshi*, for example, feels a distinct lack of connection to Imperial Army veterans and thinks that his apprehension might be representative of the officers' class: "Conversations with Imperial Army veterans about the Imperial Army's war crimes always cause tense exchanges. Every time I tell them that I consider war crimes a sign of a lack of discipline among the troops, most Imperial Army veterans become really angry." There is another important aspect to Tsutsui's position. Tsutsui and the Self-Defense Forces at large must acknowledge the IJA's war crimes in order to claim they are radically different. There are others who point to a tragic systemic failure within the IJA. According to Colonel Fujiwara Toshio*, "They were convinced that they could rely on their discipline. Stories about how brutally they had been treated by their superiors were legendary. Some hated their superiors so much that they shot them in the back during battle." To this day, IJA veterans have little interest in talking about battle memories and instead exchange stories about how they struggled to survive life in the military (Buchholz 2003:287). Some, like Colonel Katō Seigo, insist that "the Imperial Army had its good sides too. It provided a good education for men who under different circumstances would not have been able to afford it."

Yet even officers who occasionally articulate conciliatory comments feel uneasy about relations with Imperial Army veterans. Some Self-Defense Forces veterans noted with concern that some men within their ranks had connections to the revisionist Society for History Textbook Reform, that other service members had visited the Yasukuni Shrine, which houses the spirits of convicted class-A war criminals, and that yet others idealized Mishima Yukio and had ties to right-wing organizations.[11] Especially on the base in Ichigaya in the middle of Tokyo, it is easy to get drawn into politics. One veteran indicated, however, that in general politically motivated recruits soon quit. For them, the everyday dirty work of the Self-Defense Forces is just "too down to earth and has nothing to do with their ideas of how cool it would be to wear a uniform and all that. We are, after all, farmers in uniform (*gunfuku o kita nōmin*)" (Nezu 1995:87–88; see also *Shūkan Kinyōbi* 2001).

Yet heroism is a narrative construct, so current Japanese service members' "war" stories remain firmly entrenched in the rhetoric of previous war stories, of the front experience, the glorifying, the ennobling, and most of all the *inner* experience once ascribed to Imperial Army soldiers. Today, of course, international missions involving saving rather than taking lives serve as the core narratives about militarized mascu-

line identities. Beyond basic training, and possibly special forces training and missions in Japan, the wish to push their limits as men and as
service members is thus often projected onto operations abroad. Framed
as eye-opening experiences in one way or another, these missions are
narrated by soldiers and officers in terms of individual masculinity, military professionalism, and national identity. They double as front experience and are narrated within the rhetorical framework of heroism
and sacrifice that was enthusiastically promoted during the first half of
the twentieth century (Ohnuki-Tierney 2002; Kushner 2006) and was
retooled for the rebuilding of Japan immediately after World War II
(Griffiths 2002). Much like the idealists in the Imperial Army who
imagined that war would transform them and their society (Ohnuki-
Tierney 2002), Self-Defense Forces members volunteer for international missions because they long for an *authentic experience* of their
own. The desire to capture some kind of genuine experience is evident
in the relative unimportance they attach to the purpose of mission and
their specific job in the mission.

According to the ideology of their time, members of the Imperial
Army fought in combat, killed, and died for the "Greater Japanese Empire" (Dai Nippon Teikoku). In the Self-Defense Forces, the will to sacrifice one's life has been transformed into the humanitarian notion of performing a host of tasks for the public. This redefinition of inflicting
violence underpins military conduct. In lieu of a battle cry, for example,
officers are told to "value and respect their lives and the personalities and
lives of others" (Oka 1998:146). As another example, the peacekeeping
law demands that Self-Defense Forces withdraw if a violent situation
emerges and carefully restricts their use of weapons.[12] Although service
members' militarized masculinity is still established in actions that involve some risk to their safety and well-being, the emphasis is on saving
rather than violating others. MSDF captain Abe Susumu* felt that the
importance of this kind of risk-taking *experience* could not be exaggerated. He spent six months as a peacekeeper in Mozambique during the
1993–95 U.N. intervention there and described the experience as both
deeply disturbing and formative. Abe related that the dysfunction of the
local administration and the poverty as well as the disastrous hygiene
conditions in Mozambique highlighted Japan's achievements and made
him proud of his country. "The difference between life in Japan and the
pitiful condition of a third world country like Mozambique," he said,
"made me understand that there is a Japan worth defending." Together
with other participants, he was celebrated as a hero, and his photograph

was displayed in the local Self-Defense Forces headquarters of his regiment. He was also promoted faster than his comrades (Akiyama 2003; *Securitarian* 2003b). Service members like Captain Abe are held in high regard as men with *real experience*. He and his comrades do not imagine an international mission as the best alternative to the front experience of combatants but rather as a kind of combat.

Abe's militarized manhood was proven not by killing and dying, but by his success in performing an occasionally dangerous job that he felt local men could not or were unwilling to do. Clearly, his handling of these tasks reconfirmed his efficient and effective manhood vis-à-vis the local men, with whom he found it difficult to work. In the light of public attitudes toward peacekeeping in Japan, Self-Defense Forces service members translate their experience into stories of success and heroism, and so Abe's memories were also shaped by the experience of his return to Japan. Abe composed his return to Japan within a framework of patriotism and a sense of purpose. He said that he had always thought of the emperor in a rather disparaging manner. But in a moving statement, he told a group of fellow service members and myself how honored he had nevertheless felt about being greeted by the emperor when he returned to Japan from the peacekeeping mission. He could remember every word the emperor said to him and reported: "I felt as if I had been touched by something higher. It was this very brief encounter with the emperor that made me realize and feel something like my national identity as a Japanese; what it really meant to be a soldier and my responsibility of guarding my country for the first time in my life."

A higher level of efficiency also worked as a marker of superior masculinity for Major Takashima Kazuo, one of 500 service members who had been deployed in Iraq in late July 2004. He knew that the scale of Japanese activity there was modest. His unit oversaw the refurbishment of one school and was working on five others. It also built two stretches of road; pumped up to 100 tons of drinking water a day, mainly in rural areas; and supplied medical equipment to hospitals. Major Takashima and his comrades struggled to adapt to local conditions. "Japanese society is very strict about time. Sometimes they [the Iraqis] don't come [on time] . . . so we set the appointment ahead," he explained (James Drummond, *Financial Times*, July 21, 2004).

Indeed, for many younger Japanese service members, the opportunity to participate in a peacekeeping operation is an important motivation for joining the Self-Defense Forces. They experience a peacekeeping mission as a badge of honor and as proof of their special capabilities and efficiency. They also enjoy certain privileges during such missions. Forty-five service members who joined the U.N. armed forces in the Golan Heights, working together with one thousand troops from Canada, Poland, Austria, and Slovakia, shared their rooms with only one other service member—a considerable improvement over their living conditions at home. They also made 12,000 yen per day, a considerable amount of money; could frequent a bar called Fuji House, which had thousands of Japanese records available for Karaoke; and used bathtubs on a daily basis (Oka 1998:289–291).[13]

For a variety of reasons, however, peacekeeping operations raise frustrations for soldiers. Fighting armies tend to view rescue and peacekeeping missions as emasculating, demilitarizing, and frustrating, and some military observers suggest that for fighting armies, operations other than war could undermine the readiness of the armed forces to win a war (Bacevich 2005:57). During Operation Restore Hope in Somalia from December 1992 to May 1993, for example, U.S. soldiers were discontented because they felt that they were *not* supposed to do the actions for which they had been trained and had joined the military. The experience provoked one participant to exclaim that, "I joined to defend my country" and that "soldiers should not be the world's police or Red Cross. I am an infantryman." Another participant worried that if the United States kept up their peacekeeping efforts, they would "be expected to do humanitarian acts for everyone" (Miller and Moskos 1995: 615–637). For Japanese troops, peacekeeping operations also can be dissatisfying because they emphasize aspects of the armed forces that are not central to their self-perception, as Lieutenant Colonel Saitō suggested in the epigraph to this chapter. Restrictions under which the Self-Defense Forces are allowed to operate are another source of such frustrations and put additional stress on participating service members. In 2003, Captain Okada Shun* was posted to the Golan Heights for six months. He remembered his participation in this peacekeeping mission as both emasculating and challenging to his nationalist pride as a Japanese man.

> I was simply frightened when I was off duty and unarmed. I was very self-conscious every single minute, knowing that I had no appropriate weapon on me to defend myself if anything happened. I also felt ridiculed and pitied by men of other units of the U.N. forces, who shook their heads over us Japanese because they thought that we did things rather strangely.

In his view, both effects were due to Japan's International Peace Cooperation Law that regulates Japan's participation in peacekeeping operations and designates only marginal roles for the Self-Defense Forces. In contrast to peacekeepers from other nations, for instance, Japanese peacekeepers are lightly armed for self-defense purposes only when on duty, the captain explained. Moreover, the Self-Defense Forces must immediately withdraw should a violent situation arise.

Like the prestigious international peacekeeping missions, domestic and international disaster relief missions provide important sites for grounding militarized masculinity. These missions involve physically strenuous work, a positive collective experience of the interdependency and functionality of a unit, the victims' gratitude, enormous media attention in Japan, a sense of usefulness as the only Japanese organization prepared to move in after a large-scale disaster, and thus a positive impact on service members' sense of purpose and recognition. According to General Hirota Wataru, it was international peacekeeping and large-scale disaster relief missions that reassociated militarized masculinity primarily within the GSDF. He noted that throughout his professional life, the Air Self-Defense Force had always been the service branch with the cleanest reputation and the most glamorous image. Then the GSDF began to go abroad on peacekeeping missions and were dispatched after the Kōbe-Awaji earthquake had occurred and, "suddenly, the GSDF became the cool guys." Quite a few NDA cadets and new recruits would corroborate Hirota's initial view of the GSDF, noting that they chose the ASDF over the GSDF, not only because of their fantasies related to flying, but also because the Imperial Army did not have an air force and thus the ASDF does not suffer from the dark associations that encumber the GSDF and (to a lesser degree) the MSDF (Komachi 1998; Oka 1998).

Pride over participation in a prestigious mission can reach far beyond the individuals directly involved, extending to the entire regiment and the local community, who envision the disaster relief operations as making them respectable individuals, men, and heroes. As already indicated, today, young recruits are often drawn to the Self-Defense Forces because of the opportunity to participate in disaster relief and peacekeeping missions. For them, the image of the IJA soldier has begun to pale. Increasingly, they substitute an image based on the U.S. soldier, which also carries loaded gendered meanings, albeit different ones from those of the IJA soldier.

OCCIDENTALISM, PROFESSIONALISM, AND THE AMERICAN MAN

The primary mode of direct encounter with the U.S. military is through combined exercises in Japan and the United States, which function as important lenses for negotiations over valorized configurations of military manhood and its universality. Such encounters with the U.S. military shake service members' carefully nurtured notions of the military hero as a helper and savior rather than a warrior—especially their sense of professionalism, functionality, and efficiency—and thus the concept of "the American soldier" in Japanese service members' imagination is just as fraught with contradictions and tensions as "the imperial soldier." Identification with the American soldier is far from being automatic or consistent, ranging instead from desirable to impossible to, most often, highly problematic. The American soldier is identified with aggression and violence, but—in the eyes of Self-Defense Forces service members—his modernity releases him from any similarity to the imperial soldier. Typically imagined as a Caucasian male, the American soldier personifies what some service members perceive as a more desirable military and what others view as a permanent emasculating threat. The coexistence of these sentiments can be traced to Japan's defeat and the post–World War II occupation era, when the notion that Americans would teach Japan democracy (and other things, like English) took on an overpowering quality (see figure 6). A sense of rejecting any such subordination lingers within citizen movements from those on the left that demand the removal of U.S. bases in Okinawa to radical right wing organizations such as the Association to Honor the Spirits of the Fallen Heroes (Eirei ni kotaeru kai), a revisionist group affiliated with the Japan Association of Bereaved Families (see figure 7).[14] These two sides' political goals and the Japanese state they envision differ radically, but they share a sentiment that has been expressed by one Japanese citizen as follows: "May Japanese people [one day] be able to control this country" (*Kono kuni o Nihonjin ga tōji dekimasu yō ni. Nihon kokumin;* votive plaque at Yasukuni Shrine, May 2003).

For Japanese service members, the image of the U.S. military is juxtaposed with their own perceptions as a military that helps local schools build their sports grounds, reconstructs remote roads washed away by typhoons, sorts through rubble in search of survivors after natural disasters, and disinfects streets to prevent epidemics. The conviction that these tasks can be carried out successfully *only* by the Self-Defense Forces

FIGURE 6. The story Hirakawa Tadaichi tells in this English conversation book from 1946, in which a U.S. soldier teaches a Japanese boy English, leaves no doubt about the superiority ascribed to American militarized masculinity in the immediate postwar era. The title, *Come, Come, Everybody*, was borrowed from the theme song of Hirakawa's English conversation radio program.

[NOTE: Joe T. Hirakawa, known as "Uncle Come Come," graduated from the University of Washington before World War II, majoring in drama. His English radio program caught the attention of millions of Japanese. The official title of the program was "English Conversation" ("Eigo Kaiwa"); it first aired on NHK on February 1, 1946, and ran until February 9, 1951. After a break of about ten months, the program was revived as "Kamu Kamu Eigo" (Come Come English) by a network of private-sector radio stations on December 25, 1951. The last edition of the program was broadcast on July 30, 1955. The success of the program is usually ascribed to Hirakawa's excellent pronunciation, which he mastered while living in the United States, as well as his acting background.

FIGURE 7. In a 2001 brochure, "Let Us Break Out of the Mind Control of the Tokyo Trial" *(Tōkyō zaiban no maindo kontorōru kara nigedasō)*, the right-wing Association to Honor the Spirits of the Fallen Heroes (Eirei ni kotaeru kai) suggests that the Japanese population has not yet overcome American indoctrination—embodied by an image of General MacArthur of fifty years ago (Eirei ni Kotaeru Kai 2001:6).

lays claim to the warrior ideal so prominent in the U.S. and other present-day military establishments' imagination.[15] In the imagination of service members, the configuration of U.S. soldiers blends images of those U.S. soldiers actually in Japan with representations of American men in popular culture.

Established on July 1, 1957, U.S. Forces, Japan (USFJ)—with its army, air force, navy, and marine corps elements—consisted of approximately 44,590 military personnel in 2003. They have been stationed in Japan pursuant to the U.S.-Japan Treaty of Mutual Cooperation and Security of 1960.[16] U.S. service members cannot of course be defined as a singular, monolithic gender and stable mode of military professionalism. Japanese service members today, however, do not focus on the diversity of configurations of masculinity within the U.S. military (Enloe 2000) and instead highlight the Caucasian male combat soldier. This homogenization of U.S. militarized masculinity into a single entity has several important effects: it facilitates Japanese service members' claim to a masculinity quite different from the traditional, war-making armed forces; it furthers the stereotype of Japan's uniqueness; and it encourages the establishment of a single normalized military rather than a more comprehensive understanding of the diversity of military establishments in other parts of the world.

Popular memories of the occupation period may have helped to create male subjects' feelings of inferior status in the postwar global order (Yoneyama 1999:190).[17] Within the walls of Self-Defense Forces bases, however, the sense of subordination has had its own repercussions. For older generations of service members, the American soldier has primarily been a reminder of Japan's defeat in 1945. This sense of subordination initially manifested itself in the postwar years when the U.S. military began to train Self-Defense Forces service members. Retired Major General Yamamuro Kintarō*, for instance, remembered how he and his comrades had struggled to learn all the new English terms but soon realized that "the training itself was more or less the same" as that in the IJA. Born in 1917, Yamamuro had attended the Imperial Army Academy for Accounting (Rikugun Keiri Gakkō). Posted in supply units, first as a member and later a commander, he had been lucky enough to mostly avoid the front lines. He experienced the defeat in one of Japan's colonies, returned to Japan, and soon thereafter joined the Self-Defense Forces. Worn by the war years and recovering from a romantic relationship he had left behind, he did not join the Self-Defense Forces with great enthusiasm. However, he felt useless otherwise, having spent his entire life in the military, and he sensed that the Self-Defense Forces was his only chance to rebuild a life for himself and his wife in Japan. He had an impressive career as the commanding officer of some of the most prestigious units within the Self-Defense Forces. As one of the first officers to be sent to the United States in order to study at a military academy there, he had felt both privileged and burdened, and his relationship with the United States and the representatives of the U.S. military remained ambivalent. He vividly remembered how intimidated he had felt by the experience of being such a poor, undernourished Japanese man among all those other officers. He still felt miserable whenever he remembered an instructor speaking of the American decision to drop the atom bombs on Japan even though the instructor had criticized that decision.

Other service members also felt conflicted about the transition from the Imperial Army to the Self-Defense Forces under U.S. control. In their eyes, at least, American soldiers seemed striking and rich, and some found it humiliating that their former enemies were supposed to show them how to make war. Some young Japanese recruits tried to joke about that, saying that "it was great. Just like joining the military of a

foreign country," but none of them managed to crack the slightest smile
(Sase 1980:61). These moments of paralysis and emasculation mirror
more well known images, such as that famously represented in the photograph that shows General MacArthur in a military uniform next to the
much smaller figure of the Shōwa emperor in a frock.[18]

The first generation of Self-Defense Forces members has long since retired, but to this day service members are keenly aware of both similarities and differences with the U.S. military. Today, service members use
the notion of an American military manhood as a foil against which they
measure their own organization, their level of professionalism, and their
range of valorized configurations of masculinity. The American soldier
serves as the link to the international security world. Much as "interna-
tionalist women" view Caucasian American men as "linked to a kind of
transnational social upward mobility" and as fetish objects onto which
Japanese desires for inclusion into "global society" are projected (Kelsky
2001:156, 188), service members see the USFJ and the imaginary U.S.
military more generally as promising entry into the international arena.
American soldiers thus represent a military norm, and therefore service
members accord American military men the authority to "pass" into the
international sphere of respected and fully legitimate military organizations. Moreover, in service members' eyes, the U.S. military features as
the "western military." In contrast to Japanese troops, young officers
note with envy the seemingly uncomplicated status of the U.S. military
in wider society, indicated, they believe, by the U.S. military man's swag-
ger and other physical expressions of confidence.[19]

Thus, Self-Defense Forces service members imagine U.S. troops to be respected at home and extend that understanding of the U.S. military's reputation to the international arena. They feel the lack of such respect in Japan
and suspect that that lack of respect might affect their reputation abroad
as well. As one GSDF officer, Colonel Mishimata Keizō*, remembers the
time when he was posted to the Japanese embassy in Washington, D.C.:

> At official functions, American officers seemed so proud of their status
> as military men and happy to show off their wives as well, whom they
> always brought along. We had to spend quite a lot of money on my
> wife's formal dresses. She had never been to any such parties before we
> lived in the U.S. In Japan, the wives are not invited, and we men usu-
> ally show up in regular business suits in order to blend in with civilian
> participants.

Young Japanese officers' views of U.S. officers merge with military figures crafted by the Hollywood movie industry, simply because most mil-

itary visualizations in Japan's popular culture represent the U.S. forces (Kiyotani 2002). Moreover, most Hollywood movies represent special forces, which tends to exaggerate a narrowly defined and exclusive configuration of warrior-type masculinity within the U.S. military. This selective fictional representation further distorts the perception of the U.S. military as the one and only, and normal, "other." Hence, when asked about their personal military role models, younger Japanese service members tend to mix real-life figures with fictional ones and name not only U.S. military men but also depictions in popular culture. In 1999, for example, three officer candidates I interviewed admired and wished to one day be like General Norman Schwarzkopf, Vietnam volunteer Chris Taylor (Charlie Sheen's character in Oliver Stone's 1986 film *Platoon*), Captain Karen Walden (played by Meg Ryan in Edward Zwick's 1996 film *Courage under Fire*), or Captain John Miller (Tom Hanks's character in Steven Spielberg's 1998 film *Saving Private Ryan*). Here, too, it is the action, the authentic experience, the opportunity to prove themselves that draws Japanese service members to the protagonists in these films. Most middle-aged service members, who were perhaps less in tune with present-day popular culture, denied having any model or personal military hero. Very few seemed to admire their commanders or some other superior, and nobody actually named a particularly accomplished comrade or commander among the Self-Defense Forces.

Except for the German military, whose legacy some officers occasionally compare to their own situation, most service members do not have a sense of the significant differences among military establishments in the western world. This vague picture of the international military landscape enhances their tendency to view their own organization as unique, especially among middle-aged and older service members. This uniqueness resonates both with the official self-representation of the Self-Defense Forces administration and the broader discourse of the uniqueness of Japanese culture (Kiyotani 2002:83; Befu 1990; Mouer and Sugimoto 1995).

The continued presence of the U.S. military on Japanese territory complicates Japanese military masculinity, particularly around American bases in Okinawa. U.S. Forces, Japan are dispersed among 91 facilities located on Honshu, Kyushu, and Okinawa, but 75 percent of all USFJ personnel are stationed in Okinawa (Bōeichō 2000a:219; Ishikawa 1995b). The U.S.-Japan security alliance ties the Japanese and American troops closely, and in rather unique ways, to one another. The USFJ embody the more powerful partner in this intimate bilateral security alliance and forces Japanese service members to adopt and adjust themselves to American ways, codes, and equipment. Ironically, the association with the U.S. military through a security alliance that puts Japan in a position subordinate to the United States carries prestige for Self-Defense Forces service members, primarily in the context of combined exercises. Since the first U.S.-Japanese combined exercises in 1984, such exercises have been held every year in both Japan and the United States. In fiscal year 2004–5 alone, the Self-Defense Forces were involved in sixteen instances of U.S.-Japan combined exercises, including integrated command post exercises and various kinds of field training for the GSDF, mine-sweeping and anti-submarine training for the MSDF, and rescue and air defense combat training for the ASDF. In the GSDF's exercises alone, roughly 5,000 service members train annually with Americans in combined training situations (Bōeichō 2001a:332, Bōeichō 2005:501–502). (A smaller number of service members have trained with South Korean and Russian troops as well.) Service members who have participated in such combined exercises comment on the high level of respect they have for the USFJ and occasionally call them "truly professional" for how seriously they take their performance in training situations. One major described such a combined exercise as a culture shock: "I knew instantly that I had a real (honmono) military in front of my eyes. American soldiers run from morning to evening, because they think that the basic ability to fight lies in a strong body. You hardly ever see Self-Defense Forces service members run" (Oka 1998:88). This major also discerned a different sense of safety among Japanese and American military personnel. During combined exercises in which he had participated, he recalled how two American soldiers wanted to give up because of the cold. "We would have told them to get inside to get warm," he said, but there "is no such sense of sympathy among American commanders." Even if these two soldiers would have suffered permanent effects from being out in the cold for too long, he was sure that letting them warm up inside would have been considered a greater potential damage to the morale of the American troops. "In the Self-Defense Forces, where the safety of service members is a primary concern (anzen dai'ichi no Jieitai)," he emphasized, "this is unthinkable" (Oka 1998:89–90). Ambivalent about his perception of American professionalism, his comment was as much one of astonishment, admiration, and relief that training matters in the Self-Defense Forces were not handled quite as ruthlessly as he felt they were in the U.S. military.

This major's perception is also interesting in light of the increasing concern for the safety of troops in the western world. Writing about the effectiveness of the officers' corps, Andrew Bacevich (2005:57–58) notes that since the early 1990s, the "spirit informing U.S. military operations was not audacity but acute risk aversion" and that "to minimize the prospect of U.S. losses, the armed services relied whenever possible on air power," which in the long run "eroded the collective ability of the officer corps to stay the hand of the advocates of intervention." From a humanitarian perspective, Roméo Dallaire (2003:517) sides with Michael Ignatieff in arguing that "riskless warfare presumes that our lives matter more than those we are intervening to save." Yet in the eyes of Self-Defense Forces service members at least, their concern for the safety of their troops both during exercises and missions is a major point of diversion from the U.S. military. For a long time, the concern for troop safety had been informed by the desire to differentiate the Self-Defense Forces from the IJA. More recently, though, it has been driven by political concerns in the wake of Japan's involvement in the Iraq war. Upon his return to Japan from his stint in Samawa, Iraq, in November 2004, Lieutenant Colonel Shimada Shingo said that he was "filled with the feeling of satisfaction" and relieved that all troops up to that point had "returned home safely" (November 27, 2004; Agence France Presse/Channel NewsAsia International).

Some observers were sure that the death of a single service member in the line of duty in Iraq would have unleashed a major backlash against that deployment as well as the Self-Defense Forces more broadly. In the same vein, a service member's wife spelled out what many other military wives must have thought: "My husband did not join the Self-Defense Forces to make war." As military wives, they cannot publicly oppose the deployment of troops, but in private they worry about the deployment of troops to Iraq. Since the war in Iraq turned into a kind of guerrilla war, another wife contemplated that once Japanese soldiers were deployed there, the situation in Iraq might suddenly transform into a battlefield for Japanese service members. One wife recalled such a situation during military action in Cambodia, in which a thirty-three-year-old Japanese man had died, prompting his father's suicide.[20] That woman was also afraid that if Japan supported the U.S. military in this way, Japan would be the next target for terrorists. For her, acts of terrorism showed the limits of the U.S. military might. She was convinced that "Japan must pursue a non-military path. Why imitate the U.S.," she asked, "considering that it has failed? We must not only think about what we can win but also about what we might lose"

(*Shūkan Josei* 2001:208–209). Perhaps this woman's lack of appreciation for the romantic conglomerate of warrior masculinity, patriotism, and Japan's military posture in the world can be explained as a wife's fear of losing her husband in a war she does not consider to be Japan's business. But she is not the only one who sees the U.S. military as a frightening force.

Occasionally service members take an outright negative view the American type of military professionalism and warrior masculinity. They perceive U.S. troops as perpetrators of reckless behavior on Japanese and particularly Okinawan territory, citing car accidents, violent crimes, and rapes, for which these troops have not, or only superficially, been held accountable in Japanese courts.[21] Part of the blame for this behavior has always been placed on the Self-Defense Forces shoulders. In August 2004, however, the crash of a U.S. Marine Corps helicopter onto a university campus near Futenma Air Base in Okinawa prompted immediate protests against the U.S. military. Putting their finger on the unequal power relations between service members of the USFJ and those of the Self-Defense Forces, some demonstrators also turned against the Self-Defense Forces. Self-Defense Forces service members were seen deferring to the Americans running the crash site. The "Go back to Japan!" shouts of some demonstrators (James Brooke, *New York Times*, September 13, 2004)) brought into focus not only the fact that U.S. soldiers occupied and controlled the site (and, by implication, Okinawa) but also the days of the IJA, which had abandoned the Okinawan population, coerced many of them to commit suicide, and retreated to the mainland during the last months of World War II.

Back on the maneuver ground, the status imbalance between U.S. and Japanese service members surfaces in a more subtle manner but one that is nevertheless irritating to Japanese troops. At first Adachi Keitarō*, a GSDF major, had only praise for the American service members with whom he had trained, but then he suddenly peppered his assessment with a rare outburst of sarcasm:

> U.S. soldiers are true professionals of war. They even leave the training area behind like a battlefield. We have to clean up for them because the Self-Defense Forces cannot afford to be accused of endangering civilians who might find cartridges or other dangerous pieces of weaponry and injure themselves. Nor can we risk that troops who find such things commit suicide with equipment that belongs to the Self-Defense Forces.

The concern with lost bullets, cartridges, and other Self-Defense Forces equipment is drilled into service members from their first days of training. One NDA cadet remembered the loss of a bullet that prompted a search by the entire platoon on the vast training ground. Their instructor, she recalled, continuously yelled at the cadets, and it took them a while to understand what the fuss was all about (Sekizaki 1995:178).

Militarized masculinity, as we have seen, is similar to other gender configurations in other social spaces: It is crisis-bound, malleable, and constructed. Japanese service members constantly oscillate between the two positions epitomized by Hashimoto and Saitō's comments. Every day they negotiate their roles and gender identities in and outside the Self-Defense Forces, and between their ostensibly masculinizing existence as service members and the (equally) ostensibly emasculating roles they perform as such service members. In their struggle to achieve a militarized masculinity and create new forms of military heroism, they re-create and fixate on other men's masculinities: They attach nostalgic sentiments to a dramatically distorted image of an IJA soldier, seeing him as a monolithic form of unproblematic military masculinity; they long for an equally unrealistic notion of the U.S. soldier, whose masculinity they imagine to be unbroken and widely respected; and they establish themselves as superior in relation to the salarymen, who for a while seemed to embody in the popular imagination the "samurai spirit" much more perfectly and smoothly than Japan's current-day soldiers did. Some service members might well subscribe to the idea that in contrast to killing and dying for the emperor, risking one's life for civilians is a more real heroism, but for most the struggle continues as the norms of masculinity in the Self-Defense Forces remain defined by contradicting desires and any notion of military heroism is tempered by the pressures to be *like* other military establishments and *not to be* a military at all.

CHAPTER 3

Feminist Militarists

Men think it's a big deal if a woman joins an all-men group,
but it isn't really. Once you are in the water, there is no difference between men and women. Once you dive, it gets dark
and you cannot see much. That can be scary, and you have to
get used to it.

Tamura Satomi in Nogan 2002:37–39

Female service members *(josei jieikan)* like Tamura Satomi, quoted
above, employ certain identity strategies when they negotiate a specific
set of tensions that characterizes their military experience: tensions between the Self-Defense Forces' public face and internal gender politics,
between the expectations of their families and their own aspirations, and
between their attempts to establish themselves as professionals equal to
men and their "refeminization" in popular media.[1] Female service members in Japan, especially officers, share that struggle in an organization
that uses them for self-promotion and at the same time marginalizes
them within its ranks. I will argue that in contrast to male service members, female service members' militarized femininity is less molded by
historical female warrior figures, who largely have been forgotten (Frühstück 2007a; Wright 2001), than by their male peers, their families, and
representations of female soldiers in popular media. Despite these differences, for women too, the military profession permeates their sense of
self more thoroughly perhaps than in any other profession, leaving them
with a distinct understanding of who they are and who they want to be
as women and as service members. In the process, they are molded into
"feminist militarists" (Gusterson 1999:19)— military women for whom
the experience of exclusionary practices helps raise their consciousness
and contributes to their determination to struggle against discrimination
and for a more complete incorporation into the military. Female service

members struggle to balance these tensions and to withstand the pressures associated with them. I will describe in this chapter how some female service members subscribe to the contradiction between womanhood and motherhood and their integration into the military. Yet others see the expanded military participation of women as evidence of women's achievement of equality. For many, however, this contradiction differs little from the pursuit of a career in any male dominated realm. Many ascribe specific meanings to their lives by holding on to the dictum to "not give up without a fight" (Nakamura Tomi*). As I will show, their male peers, as well as the mass media, measure them against the foil of a normative ideal type and find them to be transgressors.

THE ULTIMATE CHALLENGE

The integration of women into the Self-Defense Forces has been a strictly regulated process. Unilaterally driven by the needs of the military rather than by attempts to create equal career opportunities for women, the hesitant integration of women has proceeded within narrow limits that are informed as much by the slow transformation of gender relations in Japanese society at large as by the necessities of legitimization specific to the armed forces.

The difficulties of fully integrating women into the armed forces are not unique to the Self-Defense Forces. Around the world, debate about this issue has centered on the supposed contradiction between warmaking and women's physical and mental "nature." Opponents have constructed "combat" as a place that reveals the last truths about and boundaries of gender. In their minds, combat makes visible "gender-specific capabilities": the physical and psychological weaknesses in women, men's instinct to protect, and the challenge to male comradeship posed by the presence of women. But, more important, these arguments have continued to be made in nonfighting militaries, such as the Self-Defense Forces, and despite the fact that current-day combat is largely a technological affair rather than a matter of physical prowess. In the U.S. armed forces, which have one of the largest percentages of women service members among NATO member countries (see table 1), female officers have been strongly behind the demands for this kind of equality for women. Depending on rank, social background, and ethnicity, however, other female service members do not necessarily want to be involved in combat areas even if they want that option (Miller 1998). Since the 1980s, the debate in the United States, for instance, has been dominated by the exclusion of women from combat. Such exclusion was justified by the supposed necessity to protect women and by the assumed lack of women's physical capabilities. The ban on women from combat was lifted in 1991 and substituted by the Ground Combat Rule, according to which women should be excluded only from direct combat on the ground. During the administration of George W. Bush, the notion of the need to protect women reemerged. However, instead of being tied to the physical integrity of women, it was now associated with that of the nation: The female soldier who engages in combat or is captured by the enemy endangers national security because the rape of a female soldier is more demoralizing to the nation than the death or injury of a male soldier. Subsequently, the efforts to achieve full equality in the U.S. armed forces practically came to a halt (Seifert 2003:33–34). However, for female soldiers in the war in Iraq, which lacks a defined front line, direct combat has become a reality despite the Ground Combat Rule (Ann Scott Tyson, *Washington Post*, May 13, 2005).

In Germany the exclusion of women from the armed forces was also argued on the grounds of protecting women and their "nature." Eventually, what forced the opening up of the military was a verdict of the European Court, which ruled in 2000 that women's exclusion violated the equality rules of the European Council. Subsequently, Article 12a of the German Basic Law, which prohibited women from using a weapon in the name of the state, was amended. Since 2001, all areas of the armed forces have been open to women. Ever since, the integration of women has been almost exclusively debated within the armed forces, whereas the wider public has remained disinterested (Seifert 2003:39). German female soldiers themselves are somewhat more ambivalent about the full integration of women than their American peers. In a recent poll among German soldiers, 84 percent of female soldiers, but only 60 percent of male soldiers, agreed that a complete opening up of the military to women was desirable. Men who viewed the integration of women skeptically primarily doubted the physical capabilities of women, were concerned about sexual problems that occur when male and female soldiers live together, and suggested that there might be a decrease in combat capability because of the participation of women (Seifert 2003:40).

Members of the Self-Defense Forces have articulated similar objections to the integration of women. In Japan, the first women to become eligible to enlist in the new national military after the Asia-Pacific War were nurses. They were later admitted to clerical positions in the GSDF in 1967, and in both the MSDF and the ASDF in 1974 (*Securitarian*

2002u). Colonel Mukasa Noriko, for example, entered what is today the Higher Nurse Academy (Kōtō Kango Gakuin) within the Self-Defense Forces Central Hospital, in 1967. At that time all female service members were nurses, she recalled. Continuing in the spirit of earlier generations of military nurses who had been eager to contribute to the nation alongside men, women like Mukasa considered themselves service members first, then nurses (Frühstück 2007c). Her attitude changed in her late twenties, when she began to work in the Sapporo Hospital. There was a shortage of personnel, and during night shifts she had to attend to the obstetrics division of the hospital. Her regular contact with new life, she remembered, made her glad that she had chosen her profession. In August 2001, she became the director of the Higher Nurse Academy within the Self-Defense Forces. She described her goal as instilling, in both students and instructors, a sense of "sincerity, modesty, and dignity as members of the Self-Defense Forces." She made teaching the primary passion in her life and was very aware of her responsibility as the first female service member to direct the instruction facility of the hospital (*Securitarian* 2002p).

A first breakthrough for women was prompted in 1974 by the shortage of male recruits. In the course of Japan's rapid economic growth it had become increasingly difficult to recruit enough men to join the ranks. The Self-Defense Forces personnel offices began to promote the idea that the military offered a number of roles that could be filled just as well by women as by men but—much as the German political elite—held on to conventional notions of women's nature. On May 9, 1974, Prime Minister Tanaka Kakuei of the governing Liberal Democratic Party spelled out a policy that initiated an effort to integrate women into areas within the Self-Defense Forces other than nursing. The Self-Defense Forces engaged in intense discussions about all the tasks that could be achieved just as well by women. "Women [would] not be used at the front lines but in the area of communication and clerical work where lots of tasks fit their nature. We will open these positions to women" (Nakayama 1998:52–53). In subsequent years, other positions considered "suitable for women" were opened to them; for example, in 1978 women were granted access to training as medical doctors and dentists (Taoka 1991).

The Equal Employment Opportunity Law of 1986 served as the next significant integrative impetus. As an arm of the Japanese government, the Self-Defense Forces were to comply with laws that concerned equal opportunities for women in all areas of the employment and career process. Subsequently, between 1986 (GSDF) and 1993 (MSDF and ASDF), almost all branches of the Self-Defense Forces opened their doors to female recruits. In 1992 the NDA opened its doors to the first 39 female cadets. When the Self-Defense Forces began to participate in a long-term peacekeeping operation in the Golan Heights in January 1996, female service members from the GSDF joined a deployment for the first time, becoming members of the 45-person transport contingent (*Securitarian* 2001h). By the year 2000 all restrictions for women had *de jure* been lifted. Today, quite a few of the more than 10,000 female service members are high-ranking officers, and a few dozen have participated in prestigious international peacekeeping missions; others have been serving as pilots and commanders in contingents that are primarily male.[2] In 2002, for instance, several female service members participated in the peacekeeping mission to East Timor, and in 2003 in the humanitarian aid mission to Iraq (Bōeichō 2003 and 2004a:200–201). Hence, for the Japanese security state this shift allowed the Self-Defense Forces to present themselves as perfectly in step with other governmental institutions that established anti-discrimination policies.[3] The Self-Defense Forces have since undergone several waves of adaptation and mutation, as an apparent setback (the erosion of an overwhelmingly male military culture) has been parlayed into a further strengthening of the Self-Defense Forces as a modern institution that provides gender equality to a higher degree than certain segments of corporate Japan.

The integration of women stagnated, although, according to public relations officers, it became an important instrument for "deepening the understanding and appreciation of the Self-Defense Forces" *(kokumin no rikai)* within the Japanese population and for pursuing the "normalization of the Self-Defense Forces" *(Jieitai no futsūka)* as a workplace like any other—an issue that I examine in chapter 4. The overall number of women in the Self-Defense Forces has not risen above the 4.2 percent mark achieved by the early 1990s, placing Japan at the lower end of integrated forces in NATO (see table 1). During the 1990s, however, the educational level of female service members improved and contributed to providing women with a greater diversity of roles. In 1990, for instance, 98 percent of the 5,000 women in the Self-Defense Forces were high school graduates; the average age was 18.5 years. By 1999, the number of female personnel had reached 9,059, only 51 percent of whom were high school graduates who had enlisted as privates. Another 35 percent belonged to the sergeant class, and 14 percent were officer class service members, who are by definition NDA or university

TABLE I
Percentage of Female Service Members in the
Armed Forces of NATO Member Countries

Country	Percentage of female service members
Latvia	20
Canada	16.9
Hungary	16
United States	15.5
Slovenia	15.38
France	12.8
Czech Republic	12.21
Spain	10.7
Lithuania	9.07
Netherlands	9
Britain	9
Portugal	8.4
Belgium	8.3
Norway	6.3
Germany	6
China	4.8
Japan	**4.2**
Italy	1
Poland	0.47

SOURCES: Committee on Women in the NATO Forces
(www.nato.int/issues/women_nato/perc_fem_soldiers.jpg;
accessed January 12, 2006, Spakowski 2003:188)

graduates. Roughly two-thirds belonged to the GSDF (Kikuchi 2000:65). In 2005, there were 10,898 female service members, 7,276 of whom were members of the GSDF (JDA Public Information Division; email from January 22, 2006). Moreover, female service members are concentrated in only a few specialties, such as communication, intelligence, accounting, medicine, and general duties units (Takayama 1997).

According to the Committee on Women in the NATO Forces, Latvia's military has the largest percentage of female service members with 20 percent, followed by Canada with 16.9 percent, Hungary with 16 percent, the United States with 15.5. percent, Slovenia with 15.4 percent, and France with 12.8 percent. The armed forces with the smallest groups of female service members are Norway with 6.3 percent, Germany with 6 percent, Italy with 1 percent, and Poland with 0.47 percent.[4]

In the United States, the high number of women in the military is often interpreted as a marker of equality and a progressive society, but the overall picture is more ambiguous. As Cynthia Enloe has suggested (2000:xi), thoroughly patriarchal regimes occasionally "subvert the orthodox sexual division of military labor in order to maintain [themselves] in power." After all, apartheid-bolstering South Africa had 11 percent women in its 1980s military and the post-Communist Russian armed forces had 12 percent, a rise of 1 percent from the 1980s Soviet army. Today, the post-Communist armed forces in Latvia, Hungary, Slovenia, and the Czech Republic are among the countries with the highest percentage of women (see table 1).

Similarly, there is no single motive for joining the armed forces. In Japan, female service members across generations demonstrate a broad range of motives to join the Self-Defense Forces, but privates and sergeants in particular emphasize the desire to be challenged in a manner they do not expect from a civilian job. Similar to male privates who cringe at the thought of living a salaryman's life, female privates today perceive the Self-Defense Forces as a workplace where women with just a high school education can do something quite different from a boring clerical job in a corporate office. The ambivalent attitude toward low-level white-collar jobs, which I described from the perspective of male service members in the previous chapter, was even more pronounced among female service members. Sometimes it seemed that the dismaying prospect of the alternative, a boring and subordinated life as an "office lady," who "never gets to do anything but make copies and tea for male coworkers and superiors . . . and is pressured to quit once married and/or pregnant," was their main motive for joining the Self-Defense Forces (see figure 8).

Lieutenant Colonel Kuroyanagi Hiroko (Mineo 1998:232), for instance, remembered the 1970s as a time when it was difficult for female university graduates to find an interesting job. When she joined the Self-Defense Forces in 1977, she had been aware of their lowly image, but for her that poor image represented an additional challenge rather than a drawback. The tenuous job security of the public sector also attracted her to the military. Just as many of her female and male comrades, she knew nothing about security and defense when she joined (Mineo 1994:232). Similarly, a college graduate from Kanagawa prefecture did not know much about the Self-Defense Forces and worked for a trading

FIGURE 8. A female NDA cadet digs trenches during a maneuver on the Mt. Fuji Self-Defense Forces Training Ground, July
22–23, 1998. (Photograph by the author)

company for two years before she decided that she "wanted to do something different *(kawatta koto)*." In her mind, the Self-Defense Forces
were a closed society, and she imagined that by entering this closed society she "would find [her] own strength" (Bandō 1990:284).

Among female officers, the desire to pursue an interesting career,
one that would be closed to them in the civilian world, is even more
pronounced. Major Matsubara Yukue* had wanted to become a diplomat but failed the exam for the Ministry of Foreign Affairs. Discouraged, she consulted one of her college teachers and eventually decided
to join the Self-Defense Forces, in the hopes that she could pursue a
diplomat-style career as an officer. Similarly, when Sekizaki Yōko considered taking the NDA entrance exam, she also was attracted by the
idea of becoming "a kind of diplomat" and thought she had found her
ideal university:

Before I graduated from high school . . . I surprised my teacher by entering "National Defense Academy" in the survey about my future plans. He asked me how I wanted to realize my dream of becoming a diplomat. I said that I would join the Self-Defense Forces, become an officer, and then go into the Ministry of Foreign Affairs hoping that I would be posted abroad. I knew then that I would not be able to become an ambassador by taking that route but I could get pretty close to something like that (Sekizaki 1995).

Sekizaki, who had been studying for the entrance exams, knew that her parents worried about sending her off to a university, possibly far away from home. At the NDA, she would not have to pay fees for the education she received, and the academy even promised a future career. She imagined that these features would take a great burden from her parents' shoulders. Her father had expected Sekizaki to attend a regular university and was surprised to see her apply to the NDA. Her mother said that if she truly wanted to work in "a male society on equal terms," then she probably had made the right choice. It was only after Sekizaki received the notice of acceptance that her mother became doubtful and tried to discourage her from going to the NDA, suggesting that it was "too early to decide one's life at the age of eighteen." At that point, however, Sekizaki had already made up her mind, flattered by the friendly acceptance note that read, "Congratulations on passing the exam! The National Defense Academy awaits you with sincere anticipation." She also enjoyed the idea of belonging to a kind of elite as a member of the first class that officially integrated female cadets. That feeling was reinforced on the day she arrived at the NDA and, together with every other female freshman, she was surrounded by media cameras, which made her feel instantaneously famous (Sekizaki 1995).

While some female service members joined the Self-Defense Forces because they wanted to work for the benefit of other people *(hito no tame no shigoto),* similar to their male comrades, many female service members have been introduced to the Self-Defense Forces by their service member fathers or brothers (*Shūkan Gendai,* November 24, 1990; *Shūkan Shinchō* June 3, 1995). Female privates as well as sergeants often have a relative, a friend, or an acquaintance in the Self-Defense Forces, come from the lower socioeconomic strata, and gain acceptance or even support when they announce their intention to join the Self-Defense Forces to their parents, family, and friends. The familiarity with the professional environment of the Self-Defense Forces through a father, brother, or other relative contributes to that acceptance. Growing up, twenty-two-year-old Takenoshita Hisako had never thought twice about her career choice. Whenever she had seen a plane as a child (her father was a military pilot) she had always looked up and cried out, "That is my father." When she passed the exam for the MSDF School her mother was so happy that "she cried and shouted '*banzai*' at the same time" (*Josei Jishin* March 6, 2001). In 2001, she and her father became the first father-daughter pilot pair to serve on the same MSDF base.

Major Fukuzawa Kazue*, who had an officer brother, recalled that her decision was motivated by the photographs of him in uniform that hung on the walls of her parents' house. Growing up she thought that perhaps the Self-Defense Forces would be an interesting career for her as well. She found NDA brochures at the job search counter of her college, and the description of the officer candidate education—dormitory life, good facilities, strict schedules, summer breaks, travel overseas—looked exciting to her. So she joined "for the hell of it," thinking that it would be something different and that spending a year or two at the NDA would not hurt. A week later she packed her belongings and was ready to return home. She had found that life in the Self-Defense Forces "just did not fit [her] personality." Her parents, however, refused to send her the money for the train ticket, and since she did not have any money of her own (because she had spent all her savings on a college graduation trip), she could not leave. It was her parents who had encouraged her to splurge on the trip because they thought that once she took up a job she would never again have so much time to travel. When she phoned her parents to tell them that she wanted to return home, they practically "begged [her] to stay on at least for one year."

> They had been so proud of me joining the Self-Defense Forces in the first place. My picture had been in the local newspaper as the first woman in my hometown to join the Self-Defense Forces and they would have been very embarrassed if I had quit so soon. So I decided to continue at the officers' candidate school and at the same time look for a job. But soon I got so busy with training that I had no time to do so and ended up staying on.

Major Fukuzawa's trajectory at the NDA is fairly common. Every year, incoming cadets, as well as new recruits all over Japan, report that the first few weeks are the most difficult. Expectations of a strictly merit-based system, as well as lofty ideas about getting to know and challenge oneself and of training to help other people, all pale once the day-to-day routine of life at a military academy or of basic training begins to encroach on the participants' sense of self and independence. In recollecting her first days, thirty-year-old Tamura Michiko, who had been in the

Self-Defense Forces for ten years, said: "The worst was that we had to adjust the length of our skirts and sew the name tags onto our equipment. I wondered angrily why men's pants came in the right length while we had to adjust our skirts ourselves" (Bandō 1990:285). Another female service member found it difficult to properly make her bed. "Two of us would do one bed together and then the instructor would let a 5 Yen coin roll on the bed. When it didn't roll properly, we had to start all over again" (Bandō 1990:285–286). The separation from parents, family, and friends—for many a first—contributes to anxieties surrounding the new rules, the new lifestyle, and other adjustments.

Female privates without long-term career aspirations believed that a couple of years in the Self-Defense Forces would provide an opportunity to think about what they really wanted to do with their lives without just wasting time with odd jobs. A twenty-seven-year-old woman from Tokyo remembered that the Self-Defense Forces was her mother's idea; her mother had imagined that she would acquire all kinds of qualifications and take the public servants exam (kokka shiken) while working in the Self-Defense Forces (Bandō 1990:284). Other women, like their male comrades, cherish the chance to engage in sports more seriously than they might be able to do otherwise. Being a service member, Private First Class Himeta Mitsu* pointed out, worked well with her amateur soccer career, which involved a lot of practice and frequent games on weekends. Corporal Hori Mine* was drawn to the Self-Defense Forces mostly because she wanted to practice martial arts, which she knew she would be able to do at the Asaka GSDF base in Nerima ward, Tokyo. Emphasizing how dear the martial arts were to her, she wondered aloud whether she would have married her husband—also a service member— had he not also had an interest in the same kinds of sports. Twenty-eight-year-old Sakaki Noriko* from Nagano prefecture was another one of these hopeful women. She had not planned to attend a regular university but wanted to play sports seriously. The Self-Defense Forces seemed a good place for her to do that. By the time she began to attend the officers' course, she also had graduated from a private evening university.

Some of the female service members had seen Self-Defense Forces recruitment posters that aggressively advertised gender equality and the notion that women can have a "real career" in the Self-Defense Forces, one involving skilled labor and a merit-based promotion system. The promise of gender equality at the workplace contributes a great deal to the attractiveness of the Self-Defense Forces as a professional environment for women. According to a group of female privates, women who enlist in the Self-Defense Forces imagine they will be working with men "as human beings"—that the military hierarchy will override the gender hierarchy found in the corporate world (see also Hiiragi 1998:46). They imagine that precisely because the Self-Defense Forces has well-defined job roles and because military rank is ostensibly objectively awarded, gender in the military will matter less, if at all, than it does in the civilian workplace.

PIONEERS AND LONERS

No matter what their primary motives to join the Self-Defense Forces, women's commitment to a military career requires a considerable amount of independence and produces a sense—particularly among female officers—that they are pioneers and necessarily loners, who struggle to keep up with their male peers in a masculinist, potentially hostile world. Once in the military, female service members are under tremendous pressure to give in to conventional gender roles through a combination of expectations, assigned tasks, and the dynamics of power relations within the military. Similar to the fluid processes of identification and dissociation with gender configurations among male service members, such as the salaryman, the U.S. soldier, and the IJA soldier, which I analyzed in the previous chapter, female service members transition through various gender constructions in coping with the pressures. These constructions are modeled on a normative male soldier configuration and consist of three overlapping phenomena: the explicit and self-conscious denial that their femaleness matters at all, paired with the commitment to perform (just as well) as a man would; the trivialization of gender discrimination and sexual harassment as an intrinsic element of their profession against which each has to struggle on her own; and a rejection of the rules of conventional femininity. As feminist militarists, they become increasingly isolated from women outside the military, with the effect that they cannot recognize their problems as ones shared by women in other places (Enloe 2000:xiii).

Female service members like to insist that in their everyday lives the fact that they are women takes third or fourth place after being a service member of a certain rank in a specific regiment and unit. Asked about gender differences and instances of discriminatory treatment, Captain Kuragi Suzuyo* held on tightly to her conviction that the Self-Defense Forces were not ordered by gender. She blurted out, "I hate feminists!" In Kuragi's mind, feminism stood for the essentialist position that women are necessarily different from men, thereby justifying woman's different treatment within and outside the military. Perhaps Kuragi felt so strongly about suppressing the gender issue altogether because she thought it was too much of a burden to be the only female officer and often the only female service member in many professional situations. Kuragi seems to see herself caught in a quandary common among female soldiers who trivialize gender discrimination and sexual harassment elsewhere (Sasson-Levy 2003:93): If she acknowledged gender discrimination and became hurt or annoyed, she would confirm the very discourse that defines her as a sex object and as weak and vulnerable. Trivializing such incidents, then, is a strategy to prevent the aggressively marginalizing effect of gender discrimination and sexual harassment from fully unfolding. Moreover, if female soldiers like Kuragi had a clear understanding of themselves as victims of sexual aggression, they would position themselves within a discourse of victimization. In their eyes, victims are defenseless and vulnerable and have no place in the armed forces, among self-described defenders of the weak. For Kuragi and her female peers, it is clear that women who confirm their status as victims through their behavior will not be accepted as equal in the armed forces. Thus, there is an intrinsic contradiction between the discourse and the role of the victim and participation in the armed forces as a full member. Female soldiers who experience gender discrimination and sexual harassment are at the center of this contradiction. Ignoring such incidents, Orna Sasson-Levy (2003:93) warns, is interpreted by the perpetrators as silent acceptance and establishes it as military norm.

In describing the highs and lows of their careers, their plans for the future, and their attitude toward the military, however, female service members recalled incidents that indicated a gender bias. While some female service members emphasized that there were many "good, supportive men" in the Self-Defense Forces, others described themselves as quite isolated and saw themselves confronted with ideas about women that each felt she had to fight on her own.

Female service members on the officer's track had an especially critical view of the gendered order of the Self-Defense Forces, partly because they had more long-term experience in the Self-Defense Forces, considered their military career a priority, and encountered more formidable obstacles to the successful pursuit of their careers. After graduating from the NDA or another university, a female officer begins her career with gender-specific rules. Former NDA cadet Sekizaki Yōko found her initiation into the GSDF at the NDA in 1992 particularly repressive and the male hostility fierce when she first entered. The older cadets simply said that they did not want women at the academy. They saw that several new sections had been built and old buildings renovated at the NDA and on bases all over Japan in order to accommodate female cadets and service members, and they concluded that the female cadets were receiving special treatment. The women's bathrooms and dormitory rooms turned out to be much nicer than the older facilities for the men. Physical punishment became illegal when women were first admitted, and the older students resented having been treated much more harshly than the younger, female students (Sekizaki 1995:179).[5]

These resentments from male cadets have mostly ceased, and the number of female cadets at the NDA has tripled since 1992, when the first female cadets were admitted. Today 150 women attend the NDA together with 850 men, but a quota still limits the percentage of female cadets to five per class.[6] Because of the quota regulation the female candidate pool is much more competitive. In 1999—after ten years of recession—2.9 percent of male candidates but only 1 percent of female candidates were accepted to the NDA (Bōeichō 2000a:275). For them the world of the military did not feel like one in which they were privileged in any way; in fact, it seemed harsh and restrictive. Sometimes, Sekizaki thought of the day when she left the NDA in the following terms:

> On June 21, 1993, I stood in front of my unit commander and announced my retirement from the NDA: 'Platoon 323, second year cadet, Sekizaki Yōko retires.' . . . When I received the retirement papers from the chancellor, my one year and three months at the NDA were over. Until that moment I had hardly thought about what I had learned, what I felt, and why I wanted to quit the NDA. No, I could not think about all that. The sense of defeat among my fellow cadets, especially among the women, was strong. All of us had suffered in the same ways. Because I escaped, things will not change. . . . I live a brighter life now, but whenever I think of the NDA I feel like a bird that escaped its cage (Sekizaki 1995:171–172).

Sekizaki's retirement, she reflected years later, was not a sudden decision. Every month cadets left for different reasons. It bothered her that she had no time to think. She started to injure herself, and once she fainted during an exercise and was diagnosed with stress syndrome. More injuries followed. She wanted to join the ASDF but was sent to the GSDF instead. Her parents told her that she had changed and was not her old self anymore. Eventually, she decided to leave (Sekizaki 1995:182).

Although the majority of women who join the Self-Defense Forces overcome the feeling of being suddenly imprisoned within a few weeks, female service members' daily routines continue to be disrupted by frequent moments of frustration because of a solidly institutionalized gender inequality. Aggressively recruited by a male-dominated organization under public scrutiny to comply with gender equity demands, older instructors and commanders admitted that many women were, if anything, more serious and determined than the average male private. Yet these realizations did not necessarily keep these superiors from holding contradicting views about women's talents and physical capabilities, which were based on their general preconceptions of gender differences. However, both female service members and their commanders noted that women were rarely short on stamina and did not easily give up, even though women might be weaker and possibly slower. Still, women were sometimes looked down upon by their male superiors and peers because of their supposed physical shortcomings and coerced into assignments that reinforced conventional notions of feminine roles at the workplace, despite the fact that the Self-Defense Forces is not involved in fighting operations. "The Self-Defense Forces must be an equal opportunity workplace," wrote Shikata Toshiyuki (1998:37), a military analyst and retired general, "but the feminization [joseika] of the Self-Defense Forces would mean trouble." Lieutenant Colonel Kataoka Hiro*, at one point a personnel officer, shared Shikata's concerns. "A few female service members," he was certain, "are good for morale because men compete more fiercely in the presence of women. Too many women, however, would be destructive to unit cohesion." Neither Shikata nor Kataoka explained exactly what kind of trouble they imagined would occur if more women joined the Self-Defense Forces.

Male service members who were firmly against the participation and integration of women, or who wanted to limit women to clerical jobs, held dear a number of ideas about women that supported these older men's position. Most persistent was a conviction that women are physically weaker than men and thus weaken the overall performance of a unit. Female service members conceded that they were not as strong physically as their male peers, but some also noted that lifting most heavy equipment, for example, takes several people, that it cannot be done by just one or two supposedly stronger men. Tamura Satomi of the MSDF makes a similar point in the epigraph to this chapter. In 2002 Tamura was an instructor at one of the MSDF schools and the first female service member to specialize in underwater maintenance—an enormous achievement in the branch of service that is most notorious for its informal exclusion of women. When she was still in high school, she read a newspaper article about the Self-Defense Forces a job there struck her as one for which enthusiasm mattered. In high school she had belonged to a swim club, and the fact that all the other club members were male had never bothered her. Once in the Self-Defense Forces, she was frustrated by her initial lack of physical strength compared to her male peers and she realized that she had to work much harder than the men, but at some point she made the decision to succeed. Her line of work, she said, was as much about mental strength as it was about physical strength.

Other objections to the integration of women were that they might not be able to fully perform their duties during their menstrual periods and might take a menstruation leave of absence. Like other female employees in Japan, female service members have the right to take time off during their periods. A relic from the protection of women in the workplace in the 1920s, the menstruation leave of absence is—like other such measures—a mixed blessing for working women.[7] Designed to protect women at the workplace, it essentializes these women by claiming their "special," "physical" needs. At the same time, these policies maintain and reinforce a notion of male bodies as normative, omnifunctional, healthy, and stable. Asked about what she thought about this objection against the integration of women, Captain Fujii Setsu* laughed out loud before responding that it was "total nonsense." She and other women, she explained, regulated their cycle with the pill so that no such complications occurred when they participated in exercises.[8] Female service members also dismissed the idea that they cannot urinate in the field as yet another excuse to keep female service members at bay.

A number of young officers blamed senior personnel for pampering their female comrades. Women were apparently allowed to remove weight from their backpacks on long marches or received other kinds of help never offered to male soldiers. Younger female service members did not necessarily object to that assessment. Some felt that they were treated equally or even better than men. Commanders, however, they pointed out, were sometimes nicer to them because they considered them "just girls" and thus somewhat less than full service members. This different treatment typically was perceived in only positive terms among women who did not plan to have a long-term career within the Self-Defense Forces. Private Kawasaki Mizue who had been training in the artillery corps, by contrast, had mixed feelings about getting a break: "Even though I tried to do my work as best as I could, my commanders never reprimanded me or pushed me to work harder. It was obvious that they thought whatever I am capable of doing would be fine because I am just a girl after all" (*uno!* 1997:163). Kawasaki was sure that compared to her boyfriend, also a private, she had considerably fewer opportunities to excel and prove herself (*uno!* 1997:163).

Until a few years ago, similar forms of gender discrimination and sexual harassment provoked little more than willful ignorance on the part of the military administration. Major Aramata Haruko*, who had been the only female officer in an entire regiment, remembered how she struggled when a female private under her command tearfully told her about being continuously harassed by a male peer. All Aramata could do was console this private and try to get her transferred to a different camp. "I had learned my lesson on speaking up about sexual harassment early," Aramata said. During her time in the essentially all-male regiment, a JDA official had come to carry out a survey on sexual harassment. Told that the survey was anonymous, she responded truthfully and described several instances of sexual harassment in her own career, ranging from nude photographs used by male colleagues as computer screen savers, to being pinched on her behind by male colleagues or being verbally insulted with sexually explicit comments and jokes. Soon afterward, she was called to the commander's office. Apparently, as the only female officer in the regiment, she was the only person who had responded negatively. The results had been shared with the commander. The commander was furious and scolded her for "damaging the reputation of the whole regiment." She stood her ground, but later whenever she had to deal with sexual harassment she did so quietly, circumventing the official route of complaint through her superiors.

Based on my interviews, it seems that NDA cadets and younger officers today hold fewer misogynist attitudes than enlisted service members and their older peers. Opinions on the integration of women seem to be positive more often among officers than among enlisted men and more positive among recruits and younger men than among middle-aged and older ones. After all, sexual harassment and gender discrimination within the military came under public scrutiny only during the second half of the 1990s. Several high-profile sexual harassment cases shook the Japanese corporate world and began to concern the Self-Defense Forces as well.[9] In 1999 the large-scale *Questionnaire Survey on Sexual Harassment among the Employees of the Defense Agency (Bōeichō shokuin sekushuaru harasumento, ankēto chōsa' kekka no gaiyō)*, conducted by the JDA Bureau of Personnel Training, revealed that Aramata had not been alone in her experience.[10] Interestingly, according to the questionnaire, men and women more or less agreed on what constituted an act of sexual harassment; the actual experience of sexual harassment, however, was unevenly distributed. About 60 percent of female service members who reported experiencing sexual harassment had endured jokes with sexual connotations, been touched, or been subjected to comments on their looks, age, and marriage prospects. Of the surveyed women, 72 noted that they had been raped and/or assaulted *(gōkan, bōkō)* in comparison to 7 men who said the same of themselves. Another 182 (or 18.7 percent) of women responded that they had been "coerced into a sexual relationship" *(seiteki kankei no kyōyō)* in comparison to 14 men.[11] The bottom line was that among all government facilities, sexual harassment was "most seriously a problem in the defense bureaucracy" (Bōeichō 1999). The survey results contributed to the JDA's increasing attention to complaints about sexual harassment among the ranks (*Shūkan Yomiuri* 1999b; *Shūkan Hōseki* 1993).

Subsequently, the JDA introduced formal instruction on how to deal with sexual harassment or related issues and implemented policies to do so. A shift in attitudes and responses to reported cases seems to have occurred as well. In 1999 the head of the public relations office of the GSDF reported that he had just fired a service member for sexual harassment. In 2001 a sexual harassment case at the NDA was handled with great care and thoroughness. Apparently, a group of male cadets had entered the women's section of a dormitory and attempted to peek through a window into the female cadets' bathroom. Subsequently, the NDA administration had all male cadets fingerprinted in order to identify the perpetrators and then expelled them from the NDA. Similarly, when a high-ranking officer from the JDA apologized in 2001 to the governor of Okinawa after the well-publicized assault of a civilian Okinawan woman by a service member (*Japan Times,* March 18, 2001), this reflected (and may have further heightened) an awareness of sexual harassment among Japanese troops. This apology was particularly critical, as the Self-Defense Forces have always been concerned about their reputation in the shadow of the U.S. Forces, Japan and generally have made a point of differentiating themselves from the U.S. military by their flawless conduct in the public eye.[12]

It remains to be seen, however, whether the change in awareness in the military administration will have an impact on practices "in the field." In another survey published by the JDA three years later, female service members still identified a "lack of understanding of the necessity to treat women in the Self-Defense Forces equally" as a primary cause of their job dissatisfaction (Ioka 2002a:17). These institutional barriers are exaggerated by the fact that female service members must break with social conventions to pursue a military career. One reason active female officers may have been reluctant to speak about disadvantages and unequal treatment is that such experiences could be interpreted as a personal failure and thus as an acknowledgment of victimization and defeat, rather than as a reflection of any shortcoming in the internal gender politics of the Self-Defense Forces.

BREAKING WITH CONVENTIONS

Female service members experience their aspirations for a career in the military as a break with social conventions that would have them become primarily wives and mothers. As they pursue their training and their careers, female service members' professional lives continue to constitute a balancing act between their military careers and their families' expectations, as well as their hopes to start their own families. Although male privates often have stepped into the shoes of a father or brother, they seem to pay less attention to parental approval than do women. Numerous young men reported that their parents were against them joining the Self-Defense Forces but that they respected their choice. Yet others "did not really have a conversation about joining the Self-Defense Forces with their parents." They just *told* them what they would be doing. Female officers' families, however, are rarely supportive of their daughters' decision to pursue an officer's career long-term. This facet of female service members' lives also reinforces their militarization, which seems more comprehensive than that of their male peers: Breaking with social conventions means that instead of having a connection to the world outside the military in their partners, as their male peers do in their typically civilian wives, the partners females select are in the military as well.

In addition to the concern that a daughter would be "totally taken away by the Self-Defense Forces and become an entirely different person" (*uno!* 1997:163), parents share certain kinds of objections to a daughter's career as an officer in the Self-Defense Forces. One objection is that a service member's work is considered potentially dangerous, less because of the possibility of a military conflict (even though that fear has recently increased) than because of the physically demanding training and the need for many of them to handle weaponry and heavy machinery. The higher the rank, one female officer said, however, the less physically strenuous the work, and so the less it matters in terms of physical strength whether one is a man or a woman. Another parental objection is related to the status of the Self-Defense Forces as constitutionally illegitimate and their reputation as "a bunch of men incapable of doing any work other than a soldier's" and as a rough environment unsuitable for a young woman.

Mothers of female officer candidates and officers in particular worry that their daughter's profession will move center stage in her life and that her ambitions to start a family will move into the background or out of the picture entirely. Off base, working women are expected to be attentive mothers and efficient housekeepers, mostly without much help from their male partners. Even though the average age of marriage rises continuously, and more and more Japanese men and women remain single or at least childless, their parents still imagine the bourgeois nuclear family as the true core of a woman's life, as Major Matsubara Yukue's statement indicates (Frühstück 1999a, 1999b, and 2002):

> On top of the really tough basic training and the officer's training thereafter, in addition to all the uncomfortable situations that came about because of my being always the only female officer in the cafeteria, among the troops, in the class room, and in the field, on top of all that I had to deal with my mother's negative attitude. My mother was against my military career and did not get tired of pushing me to take a year off and try the exam for the Ministry of Foreign Affairs again. I know that even now that she sees my success she still is against my officer's career, even though she has stopped saying so. I guess she has resigned herself to the fact that this is my work now. Recently, however, she asked me to at least marry a civilian.

The worries of officers' parents are not entirely groundless. Statistical data are hard to come by, but my interviews and conversations with personnel officers and other service members revealed that it was rare for male officers to remain unmarried; in contrast, female privates typically married male service members and quit when they had children. According to a small-scale survey of 273 female service members in a GSDF training unit, more than half had a boyfriend, almost all of whom were service members as well (*uno!* 1997:165), while most female officers who were around thirty years old remained unmarried (see also Hiiragi 1998:48).

Female privates tend to be pragmatic and conservative in their expectations of romance and marriage. Those women who pursued an early marriage assumed that their husbands would bring a stability *(antei)* to their life that they could not achieve on their own, no matter how much money their husbands made or whether they retired or continued working after getting married. Women tended to have a fairly favorable opinion of their male colleagues as potential marriage partners. "The range of men is broad enough for a woman to make a good choice. There are cool guys *(suteki na dansei),*" one female private pointed out, "for whom the women compete, and whoever is first wins the guy. When women are not into competing for men, marriage gets delayed" (Bandō 1990:287; see also Frühstück 1999a). But there were also criticisms about male service members. There are some "real assholes" *(hontō ni aho da wa),* said Fukugawa Keiko*, a retired service member.

In contrast to these individual impressions, few female privates had strong opinions on whether service members were preferable to civilian men as husbands, but they agreed that once in the Self-Defense Forces— after graduating from high school—female service members no longer have many opportunities to meet, let alone date, civilian men. Some had never had a civilian boyfriend. Most female privates left no doubt that they planned to marry at some point and imagined that in addition to the sense of stability and security, an early marriage would also offer an escape from the dormitories on base and a bit of individual freedom. Female service members preferred the privacy of an apartment to group life on base, where they—in contrast to their male colleagues who can move off base as soon as they turn thirty—share a room with up to five other women as long as they are unmarried. As already noted, most female privates planned to quit when they got married and had children, as they were convinced that it is best for a child to be taken care of by the mother. Very few of the unmarried female privates imagined that child care would be or should be shared with their husbands. When two service members are married to one another, it is in most cases the woman who retires from her Self-Defense Forces job, but there are also couples who continue working. One female service member said that she wanted to continue working after marriage and that she would go on being single until she "found a man who accepted that" (Bandō 1990:287).

Maintaining a steady relationship is difficult for female service members on the officers' track. At the NDA and on bases throughout Japan, premarital relationships among service members in the same unit *(tainai renai)* are kept secret. According to Fukui Hide*, female cadets at the NDA, where intimate relationships among cadets are prohibited, made sure to never be seen in a friendly private conversation with a male cadet. Such relationships do exist, though, and cadets claimed that everybody knew about them but just ignored them. Officially, couples can be transferred to separate bases, but during my seven years of research I met quite a few couples who were on the same base or on bases close to each other. Both female and male officers noted that one of their primary criteria for a desirable partner was a high level of understanding and tolerance for the hardships of their profession. An officer's lifestyle considerably restricts the opportunities for meeting and socializing with people outside the military. Transfers to bases all over Japan every two or three years, several week-long absences during maneuvers, absences during weekends, and an early start to the workday all count against the conventional rhythms of a relationship, in which it is commonly assumed that the woman takes care of the home life. Officers' wives typically move with their husbands until the children graduate from elementary school and then live separated from their husbands for long periods of time, but for many female officers an equivalent flexibility from a male civilian partner seems out of reach.

But would they even want a civilian partner? For some, the unappealing vision of a life as an "office lady," which they sought to escape by joining the Self-Defense Forces, goes hand-in-hand with an unfavorable view of civilian men as potential partners. Asked about matchmaking arrangements with men outside the Self-Defense Forces, one female service member explained that she imagined that civilian men, who did not use their bodies all day as did women in the Self-Defense Forces, would be weak, and she refused to meet any. Another female service member recalled an experience that confirmed that assumption: "During field training we carry about twenty to thirty kilograms as if it were nothing. I met this guy and he complained about how heavy his five or six-kilogram bag was. I just thought, "Give me a break" [*chotto ne*]" (Bandō 1990:286). In other words, while socializing with civilian men symbolically underscores for male service members their own special militarized masculinity, for female service members it raises latent suspicions about their commitment to their profession and thus is not a desirable connection to the outside world, with its picture of weakness and subordination.

According to Colonel Katō Seigo and Sergeant Terasaki Makoto, most service members' wives are full-time housewives, who typically take responsibility for educating the children, and for re-creating a new home every few years, when the family moves again. Most female officers thus assume that a civilian man will not understand their profession and will not be willing to follow them on their transfers. Many fail at finding a civilian partner who is willing to put up with the unusual work patterns and times. Even marriage between two officers may involve living separately in ever-changing locales.[13] Yet, despite these difficulties in balancing a family with a career in the Self-Defense Forces, female service members sometimes give in to the parental pressure to start a family. Major Kajimoto Masako*, for instance, recalled that her parents relentlessly pushed her to marry and have children. Even though at that time, she said, she had no desire to start a family, she married a fellow officer and had two children. Her assessment of that decision was—rather typically for female service members—pragmatic rather than romantic: "He is a fine enough man but I would not have married him if my parents had not insisted that they might die soon and that they wanted to see a grandchild before they did so. They are still alive and well. I feel that they robbed me of my career."

There is also the problem of having and raising children while pursuing a military career. Once on maternity leave, Major Kajimoto had begun to think about giving up her career altogether, partly because taking care of two infants while working on a base full time just seemed too daunting. "Now that you are here," she said to me when her husband left the living room to get more coffee, "he plays 'good dad,' but when we are by ourselves he does not lift a finger for the babies or in the household." Besides, she explained, there were also financial concerns:

> It really does not make much sense to work and spend almost my entire salary on daycare as we do now. Whenever one of my children is sick I have to stay at home anyway and my colleagues punish me for it by pressuring me to quit. It already started when I got pregnant the first time. They commented on my big belly and how inappropriate it was for a pregnant woman to wear a uniform. I tried to ignore them but it was hard.

The negative attitude of Kajimoto's colleagues is significant, not only because the Self-Defense Forces explicitly promote themselves as an organization that does not pressure women to quit when they marry and have children, but also because the Self-Defense Forces produces special uniforms for pregnant soldiers (Kikuchi 2000:96).

Lieutenant Tsutsui Eri* had a more balanced arrangement with her husband: "Whoever can leave work without disrupting efficiency at the workplace stays on base or stays home with the child." However, she too found it hard to withstand the pressure from her colleagues. As children and household matters are still broadly conceived of as women's responsibilities, the fact that this lieutenant even considered the possibility of her husband staying at home when the child was ill is exceptional in a (military) culture where most male service members expect their wives to take over all the housework (Ishii-Kuntz 2002:197). Some female service members with children feel the unspoken accusation of neighbors and acquaintances that they are not caring appropriately for their children. Lieutenant Commander Takemoto Miho, for example, was constantly asked why she had to be away for weeks on maneuvers despite having children. Only when she could not restrain herself, she said, did she respond that she was paid as much as a man and thus was also expected to work as much as a man (Mineo 1998:239).

In these ways, pressures from their Self-Defense Forces superiors and peers reinforce the concerns of parents and the community about female officers' career pursuits. Female service members find themselves caught between the marginalizing currents within the Self-Defense Forces and a largely apprehensive family response to their choice of profession. This precarious position is even further undermined in the wider public arena of mass media.

REFEMINIZATION VS. HYPERMASCULINIZATION

Representations of female service members in Japanese mass media, particularly in popular weekly and biweekly magazines seem to inadvertently subscribe to the notion that womanhood and military must not go together. These representations range from suggesting that women's expanded military participation is a symptom of the militarization of Japanese society to implying that military service is evidence of women's achievement of equality. The mass media solves the tension between these positions by employing two alternative techniques of normalization: "refeminizing" female service members through of sexualization, or hypermasculinizing them by representing them with conventional masculine gender markers such as big muscles, stern faces, and crew cuts.

In recent popular weekly magazines, female service members commonly have been the objects of a sexualization that takes its clues from heteronormative soft porn.[14] Magazines such as *Gendai Shūkan, Shūkan Bunshun, Josei Sebun, Shūkan Yomiuri, Shūkan Shinchō, Shūkan Hōseki,* or *uno!* represent female service members in clothes and poses common for tabloid depictions of female bodies.[15] They report in a more or less sensationalizing manner about female service members in the contradictory way so common in Japanese and other countries' mass media reports on women with exceptional careers (Auslitz-Blesch 1989; Vogel 1997; *Flash* 2003a–2003c). Articles on female service members, police-women, and women in similar traditionally masculine professions emphasize in positive terms their exceptionality, which primarily manifests itself in their choice to work in an extremely masculinist environment. At the same time they recoup the conventionality and ordinary femininity of these women by including photographs of them in provocative poses—preferably sparsely dressed or in girlish clothes, thus containing the transgressive potential of these women's career choice. I refer to these procedures as "refeminization" that—concerning female service members—serves as a subtext to the discourse of normalization, which affects the Self-Defense Forces as a whole. The effort to refeminize female service members is underscored with additional information about the featured women's family status, and details about their bodies, such as their height, weight, and waist measurements. Typical articles have titles such as "Eight female service members exposed down to their waist: Their true strengths and their capabilities concerning charm and beauty" (*Shūkan Gendai*, November 24, 1990); "War and peace for nine beautiful female service members: My case" (*Sapio*, August 28, 1996); "The combat organization Self-Defense Forces: Here one finds everything women desire" (*uno!* February 1, 1997:161–165); "For a wife, take a 'cannon ball beauty'" (*Scholar*, November 15, 2002); or "Sexual harassment en masse in the Self-Defense Force" (*Shūkan Yomiuri*, November 28, 1999); "I want to meet the heroines of the sky" (*Flash*, May 13, 2003); or " 'Top gun' . . . This is how beautiful Japan's first female instructor is" (*Flash*, June 10, 2003).

Private Satō Yūka, for example, is shown in the weekly magazine (*Shūkan Bunshun*, December 16, 1999) poker-faced and saluting in uniform as well as flirtatiously smiling in a kimono with artfully done hair. According to her profile, she belongs to the GSDF, works on a base in Kumamoto, is 159 centimeters tall, and weighs 52 kilograms. She counts music, flower arrangement, kendo, and calligraphy among her hobbies. Her boyfriend is also a service member. Before joining the Self-Defense Forces she was a high school student and "wanted to challenge herself under difficult conditions" instead of becoming just another clerical worker. Asked whether she is proud of representing a profession whose purpose is "to contribute to Japan's security," she responds that she is not quite sure what that means. She does, however, appreciate the gratitude that Self-Defense Forces troops encounter during and after disaster relief missions. Asked which weapon she would like to try out, she responds that she is most interested in driving a tank. However, she cannot think of a military model she aspires to imitate. All of the other twelve short portraits show female service members between the ages of nineteen and thirty-four. Next to the small photographs of these female service members dressed in camouflage fatigues and saluting or pointing a machine gun at the reader, are large photos featuring the same female service members now dressed in bikinis, swimsuits, sports outfits with short pants or short skirts, or conventionally feminine dayclothes.

The June 1993 issue of *Denim*, another popular magazine, features several "female beauties in uniform," including a policewoman, a sentry, and several female service members. These women are also represented both in their uniforms at work and in suggestive settings and poses. In one photo, platoon leader Abe Mutsuko lies on her back on the beach in a bathing suit, coyly running her hands through her long hair; clad in a bikini with flower design, platoon leader Takayoshi Yori, who also happens to be Miss Kōchi, crawls in the sand. The accompanying article again emphasizes both their exceptional profession and their ordinary femininity.

In *Shūkan Gendai* (November 24, 1999, 221–228), another weekly magazine, female service members are also pictured in bikinis or swimsuits, but not nude, despite the cover headline that promises just that. Primarily enlisted service members in their mid-twenties in bikinis and bathing suits crawl provocatively on leopard print scarves. Private Satō Terumi, for example, lies on such a wrap, looking longingly up at the reader (see figure 9). One learns from her profile that she is twenty years old, 153 centimeters tall, with a waist of 57 centimeters. As if relieved, the author acknowledges that she is a typical "girl of today," who likes to play in the hip district of Shibuya and in Tokyo Disneyland with her boyfriend. She joined the Self-Defense Forces following the recommendation of her father. In the Self-Defense Forces, she felt she had found the right atmosphere "to test her limits" but was bothered by "the lack of private time." To the question of what she likes to do most, she replies, "Doing nothing and going to a spa." One does not learn anything about Satō's unusual work, supposedly the occasion for the photograph series in the first place. *Shūkan Gendai* (November 24, 1990) features Takashiro Fumi, a twenty-three-year-old staff sergeant. In addition to her body measurements, the magazine reports that Takashiro's dream is to marry a rich man, live in a house with a swimming pool, spend her honeymoon in Hawaii, and participate in the Honolulu Marathon in order "to create memories." Next to photographs of women in bikinis and swimsuits, there are again smaller photographs of them in uniform that—much as in the article in *Shūkan Bunshun*—illustrate that "nobody would believe that these bodies in swimsuits belong to the same women as those in combat uniforms."

When the transgressive potential of such female lives is not contained through such contrasting representations, it is dramatically exaggerated in hypermasculine representations. While the techniques of refeminization work to make female service members look cute and sexy, those of hypermasculinization suppress these features and overemphasize those commonly associated with a masculine physique. Reminiscent of the violently powerful female figures in popular comics and animated films, these gendered representations in the mass media often cast female service members as extremely ambitious to the point of being dangerous to work with (*Friday* 1996; Kikuchi 2000:70). Although the identities of female figures in popular cultural productions constantly change (Napier 1998 and 2001), the hypermasculinization of female service members in the mass media is primarily suggestive of a permanenet loss of (proper) femininity. "Two Women Who Tackle Men" reads a headline in the popular weekly magazine *Shūkan Shinchō* from thirty years ago, on February 10, 1977. At a time when female service members other than nurses were still rare, several pages of photographs show female service members playing American football, repairing a plane, sitting on their beds laughing, and working at office desks with male superiors hovering over their shoulders. At that time, female service members other than nurses were still rare. The article warns readers not to spar with these women, thinking they are "just women"— that a man could get hurt doing so. The text describes the two service members as special and yet normal women. Serious about sports, they trained first together with male service members and later on their own. They ostensibly "forget that they are women" and, the reporter concludes, the "only difference between them and men is that they wear bras during training." Twenty years later, in 1996, *Friday*, another popular weekly asks, "If you are not tough and kind you are not a woman!? The girl power of the members of an army tank unit and a university baseball team" (*Friday*, October 4, 1996).

The military journalist Kikuchi Masayuki (2000) speculates that the phenomenon of tomboyishness among female service members—and, one might add, the perception of this among men—may be a recent phenomenon because almost all roles within the Self-Defense Forces have been opened up to women. Kikuchi suggests that the new variety of jobs

新隊員に射撃訓練の基本を見せる

「最初はどうなる事かと心配だったけど、一生に一度の経験ができて本当によかった」撮影が終わると、全員が顔を上気させて感想をもらした。ついさっきまで戦闘服に身を包んでいた同じ婦人自衛官とは思えない。

一般婦人自衛官を採用したのは昭和42年の陸上自衛隊が最初。海上、航空は7年遅れの昭和49年にスタートさせている。この23年の間に彼女たちの意識も大きく変わり、今回のような企画が成立したわけだ。

婦人自衛官数は陸海空あわせて約5000人、そのなかで最も多いのが陸上自衛隊で約2900人。陸自ではスタート時こそ通信、会計の2職種しかなかったが、現在は航空、

FIGURE 9. In illustrated articles about female service members in popular weeklies magazines, their profession typically plays a subordinate role. As in this example from the weekly *Shūkan Gendai* (November 24, 1990), the emphasis is on presenting female soldiers as perfectly *normal* women, and thus women who can be sexualized.

FIGURE 10. The caption for this illustration in a book called *Here We Go—Women Soldiers (Ganbare josei jieikan)* reads, "Are female officers dangerous?" The size and the antics of the much larger female figure indicate that the answer is "yes" (Kikuchi 2000:70).

within the Self-Defense Forces, in combination with the challenging task of combining family and children, may well have produced a kind of "super woman officer" *(sūpā fujin jieikan kanbu)*. The illustrations in Kikuchi's book hypermasculinize female service members as physically huge Amazons with crew cuts (which no female service members actually wear) and angry faces, physically indistinguishable from males—thus emphasizing what the military ostensibly does to women, and perhaps indicating a deeper anxiety about the potentially emasculating effects of the integration of women into the armed forces (see figure 10).

Caught in the tight framework of parental and wider social expectations to live normative lives, the pressures from military superiors, and the hardships of their profession, the women who pursue a career within an organization of a highly ambivalent status appear determined, individualistic, and conscious of their professional and gender identities as fluid, unstable, and malleable, just as their male peers are, even though the points of reference for their identity constructions differ considerably. They continuously negotiate the assumed contradiction between womanhood and their integration into the military. They see the expanded military participation of women as a symptom of and evidence for women's achievement of equality and themselves as both active and passive agents of this process. But some current female service members remain skeptical about whether their integration is indeed spurring the transformation of the Self-Defense Forces or is simply causing their own transformation, from unassuming, adventurous, courageous young women into feminist militarists. It becomes clear that the military not only taps into the symbolic gender order in Japanese society but also contributes to its construction. The Self-Defense Forces, in any case, are keen to prove their transformation by excessively employing female imagery in their public relations efforts—the object of analysis in the next chapter.

CHAPTER 4

Military Manipulations
of Popular Culture

On January 26, 2004, the director of the JDA announced the historic deployment of the Self-Defense Forces to Iraq. The night before, at a promotional event for his new hit single, the singer Izumiya Shigeru suddenly sang a part of the song, "Let's Join the Self-Defense Forces" and ended with the line "Let's go to Iraq," instead of the original "Let's join the Self-Defense Forces, let's join," apparently in anticipation of the JDA director's announcement and in support of the operation.[1] The original tune, "Let's Join the Self-Defense Forces" had been recorded by Takada Wataru in 1969 as an ironic, anti-war song, which bitingly mocked the Self-Defense Forces. In a move of self-censorship by the National Broadcasting Corporation, the song was immediately banned in the wake of the Vietnam War, an incident that became increasingly emblematic for the relationship between the Self-Defense Forces and Japanese popular culture. Since the 1960s, a number of animated films and television series have produced memorable visions of the Asia-Pacific War, such as the atomic bombing of Hiroshima portrayed in *Barefoot Gen* (*Hadashi no Gen,* 1983) and the final days of the war as seen by two children in Kōbe in *Grave of the Fireflies* (*Hotaru no haka,* 1988) and other productions (Tomino, Ueno, Ōtsuka and Sasakibara 2002; Natsume 1997; Yasuhiko 2005). More recent video games, animated films, and comics offer a violent and militarist world to draw from (Kohler 2004; Schodt 2004 (1996):115–116; Nakar 2003; Napier 2001, 2005), but most producers of popular culture in Japan have been wary of addressing the Self-

Defense Forces in their work. Whether in cinema, video games, animated films, or comics, glorifying representations of Japan's military present have been conspicuously subdued in Japan's popular culture.[2] This is similar to most European countries and Germany in particular, where—some scholars argue—a peaceful popular culture has furthered the establishment of peaceful and anti-militarist societies (Kühne 2000; Maase 2000).[3] As Donald Richie and Joseph Anderson wrote in 1959, public sentiment in the mid-1950s was such that no film that favored the Self-Defense Forces and rearmament in any way could have been successful at the box office; hence none was made (see Tsutsui 2004:96). William Tsutsui (2004:96) points out that the Godzilla film series has been a well-known exception to that rule. But even in the case of Godzilla, only the most recent films in the series have been made with the support of the Self-Defense Forces, which provided access to the GSDF Fuji School in the hopes of having some impact on the "peaceful" representation of the Self-Defense Forces (Ōmori 1998). These recent Godzilla films have featured the Self-Defense Forces as a "noble guardian spirit of Japan's past, present, and future" (Tsutsui 2004:103, 104).

While popular culture has been hesitant to feature the Self-Defense Forces because "their function is not quite clear," as the comic artist Matsumoto Reiji (1998) noted, the Self-Defense Forces' public relations apparatus has long acknowledged the power of popular culture. This chapter discusses how the Self-Defense Forces tap into Japan's popular culture and try to fill a void of military representation by employing the techniques and strategies of popular cultural production in their public relations, image-making, and self-presentation efforts. Like most armed forces in democratic countries today, the Self-Defense Forces engage in a variety of such efforts—efforts that are culturally and historically highly specific.

Similar to the ideologues of the first half of the twentieth century, the public relations experts of the Self-Defense Forces have become increasingly aware that the separation of the military from the civilian sphere, which characterized most of the postwar era, has become obsolete. Yet where the earlier ideologues aimed at placing the entire society in the service of war making, the Self-Defense Forces are striving to manipulate and align themselves with popular culture in order to redefine and actively claim their place in Japanese society. For the most part, they have symbolically "disarmed" the Self-Defense Forces; normalized and domesticated the military to look like other (formerly) state-run service organizations such as the railway and postal systems; individuated and personalized representations of Self-Defense Forces service members; and made conventional notions of militarism appear spectacular. The Self-Defense Forces have carried out these attempts almost in a vacuum, given the lack of representations of the Self-Defense Forces in Japanese popular culture.

International and particularly U.S. criticism of Japan during the Gulf War in 1990–91 for providing enormous financial support but no soldiers triggered new aggressive efforts of self-presentation to increase the Self-Defense Forces' legitimacy and public approval in Japan and abroad.[4] The beginning of the 1990s marked the most dramatic shift in the Self-Defense Forces' public relations policy: away from a strategy of relative nonengagement with public opinion that had been characteristic of the cold war era to one of active attempts to create and control the Self-Defense Forces' public image. Implying that as long as they kept quiet and invisible the Self-Defense Forces could avoid controversy and critique, Major Kaneda Akira* of the GSDF described the previous policy of nonengagement with public opinion with the proverb "The pheasant would not be shot but for its cries" *(Kiji mo ākazuba utaremai).* In 1993 the JDA established a Department of Public Relations within the Division of Personnel Training in order to train officers in a variety of public relations skills, such as content analyses of newspaper articles, family visits, and the translation of Self-Defense Forces slogans into fruitful interactions with the local population around bases. By August 1999 General Chiba Yūsuke* of the GSDF saw a dramatic transformation under way: "Until recently we have tried hard to keep a low profile to avoid bad press. Now we show it all! We are naked!" General Chiba's statement itself could, of course, be understood as part of the Self-Defense Forces' public relations effort aimed at strategic self-presentation and active control of their public image. But recent public relations efforts have been increasingly calibrated to appeal to different segments of Japanese society. These segments include military buffs and other friendly and supportive groups; men with a taste for adventure and those who find themselves at a dead end in their own lives; the hostile and the ignorant, including men, women, and children; ambitious young women and mothers of potential recruits; the educated and the not-so-educated; the teachable and the unconvinced.

Today, roughly one thousand service members are entrusted with public relations efforts within the JDA and in individual offices on bases across the country. The Self-Defense Forces' public relations activities are directed inward to protect the troops from internal frailties and doubts, increase morale, and help craft and maintain a positive military identity among the ranks, as well as outward to diffuse distrust and build appreciation in the wider Japanese society and the world. These efforts borrow technologies from advertising and marketing as well as popular culture to help convey the purpose of the Self-Defense Forces: in recruitment posters that feature pop singers, in comic series and animated film formats such as *Prince Pickles: The Journey to Peace* and *Defense 3* (the first JDA-produced three-volume series of animated video films directed at elementary and junior high school pupils), in abbreviated defense white papers that feature the encounter of the cartoon figures Ms. Future with Mr. White Paper, in the appropriation of popular cultural figures such as Salaryman Kintarō and through the technologies of mass festivals during open house days, which feature such diverse attractions as beauty contests, live firing exercises, and free rides on a tank.[5] These different forms of self-presentation attract and engage a wide array of people, ranging from the young beauty contest participants, who live near the bases, to mostly male military technology fans, who come to the live firing exercise; or from the very young readers of their comics, to the chance passers-by at a billboard with a Self-Defense Forces recruitment poster. These public relations efforts send competing and occasionally contradictory signals about the Self-Defense Forces' tasks and the character of their service members, at one time camouflaging their potential for violence by symbolically disarming them and at another showing off their military prowess. Collectively, the images that dominate public relations materials suggest that the Self-Defense Forces are necessary for everybody's safety and security; that their members are ordinary men and women capable of extraordinary acts; that they are powerful but carefully trained and contained; and that they can militarily defend Japan if they absolutely must (see figure 11).

I begin with an analysis of recruitment posters as manifestations of the self-presentation of the Self-Defense Forces that is directed at a large, anonymous public, which, holding a variety of views of the military, either seeks them out or ignores them. From there I draw two wider circles: to material that is specifically produced for children and young adults to convince them of not only the necessity but also the "likability" and "coolness" of the Self-Defense Forces; and to an examination of military events organized by the Self-Defense Forces to publicly celebrate themselves, such as anniversary festivities, open house days, parades, and live firing demonstrations—events that appeal

FIGURE 11. The 133rd issue of *Bessatsu Takarajima* (1991) on the Self-Defense Forces illustrates the widespread consternation over the military's image. The title on the cover promises, "The Self-Defense Forces naked! Strange and sad—the real condition of the world's third-ranking military." The back cover emphatically asks, "No enemy to fight—nothing that has to be protected—who made [the Self-Defense Forces] into this military!?"

to an overwhelmingly male segment of the population already sympathetic to the military. Collectively, these techniques of persuasion familiarize well-defined segments of the Japanese population with the Self-Defense Forces and, at the same time, assure service members of their professionalism.

PUBLIC RELATIONS POSTERS AND CIVILIANIZATION

We have seamanship, seamanship, seamanship for love!
We have seamanship, seamanship, seamanship for
      peace! [in English]
Japan is beautiful.
Peace is beautiful.
The Maritime Self-Defense Force. [in Japanese]

> Public relations video clip for the MSDF, posted on
> the JDA website in 2005
> (www.jda.go.jp/JMSDF/info/event/cm_p/16cm.html)

Since the end of the cold war, during which skepticism about the state's use of violence increased in many countries, military establishments the world over have found it necessary to intensify their ever-more sophisticated public relations efforts. The U.S. armed forces, for instance, advertise an array of benefits to service ranging from access to technology and speed to adventure, risk-taking, and the opportunity to finance higher education or achieve some measure of self-actualization. U.S. Air Force slogans recently on view in California, for instance, appeal to the fascination with the military capacity to produce speed, promising potential Air Force recruits to "Move at the Speed of Light." The U.S. Army addresses the human element with slogans such as "An Army of One," "Be All You Can Be," "The Uniform Didn't Change Me. Earning the Right to Wear It Did," and, most recently, "You always hoped he would end up running with the right crowd, but did you ever think he'd also be leading it?" The U.S. National Guard hopes to entice young men and women to "Be One of America's Most Powerful Weapons." Emphasizing their special qualities and capabilities, the U.S. Marine Corps prides itself on being "The Few. The Proud. The Marines." Taiwan, one of Japan's neighbors, combined similar self-presentational references in a number of posters displayed in 2005 in Taipei. The Taiwanese army promised, "Challenges that come at the ultimate speed. They belong to no one but you," "Join the volunteer army: The future is in your hands," and "Joining the Army brings smiles to people's faces: Confidence, professionalism, commitment!" Close to the other end of the spectrum is the German military, which promotes the "citizen in uniform" who is committed to defending the freedom and rights of the German population in hot and cold wars. For him—and, more recently, for her—military training not only produces effective troops but also functions as a kind of "experiential therapy in freedom and democracy" (Bröckling 1997:298). A recent German military promotion slogan in Berlin announced, "We Build the Future" ("Wir bauen Zukunft").

Even further removed from the aesthetizations of violence, action, and technology in U.S. recruitment materials, promotions from the Self-Defense Forces rely primarily on vague slogans; a decisively nonviolent symbolism; an unambiguously gendered imagery; a glaring absence of the references to the nation, patriotism, or other concepts once exploited by the Japanese state; and frequent use and appropriations of English phrases. In Japan, public relations posters—more than 100,000 copies of which are printed and distributed all over the country—address an anonymous wider society that happens to live or walk by billboards, where they appear next to information about garbage collection, fire exercises, festivals, obituaries, and other announcements of interest to the local community.[6] Constituting aesthetizations specific to the Self-Defense Forces, they are only slightly bigger than 1.5 feet by 1.5 feet. The frequent use of the word "nation" and of informal pronouns for "you," "pride," and "friend" in the 1950s and 1960s have, in recent decades, given way to more general messages about Japan's "youth," the "population," the "public," the "future," the desire to "protect," and, most prominently, "peace."

The concept of peace has been embodied mostly by female figures. Since 1992, professional models who are also well-known television personalities have been depicted standing clad in military uniforms proclaiming "Peace People Japan, Come On!" The phrase "come on" in this slogan is a word play upon the last name of Kamon Yōko, who is known for her songs accompanying animated films. In other depictions, female uniformed office workers plead, "Please bring one big dream to us," while female uniformed mechanics work "step by step" (in English) in order to become "Shining people at a workplace of which one can be proud." Next to a picture of a female member of the ASDF, which covers half of the poster, one finds the slogan "Believe. Turn Towards a Steady Dream."[7] One of the newest among several recently introduced phrases is the slogan "for the public." More assertive slogans such as "Can You Stand on Your Own Feet?" or the encouraging "There Is a You that Can Follow a Code," are set off by posters on which cute little dogs bark, "I love peace!" In 2003 a Self-Defense Forces poster targeted the high school student population by featuring the all-women pop group Morning Musume crying out: "Doing One's Best Feels Good— Go! Go! Peace!"[8] Another poster carries the appeal, "Young power that protects peace." The slogan beneath a child standing somewhat forlornly in front of a combat helicopter on a GSDF recruitment poster reads, "Always for our people" (in English) and a smiling young woman firmly says, "It is my path, so I decide it myself—You take a future in your hand [sic]!" (in English). Yet another recent poster features the slogan "We appreciate it—young strength. There is a future to which I want to connect. There are people I want to help. There is a land I want to protect" (see figure 12).

These new slogans and imagery represent quite a leap from earlier recruitment and promotion efforts. Throughout the 1970s, the JDA public relations officers envisioned male service members as the ones who would protect, and women, whether service members or civilians, as the ones who would be protected. More important, however, references to the nation, pride, and defense were rare and did not appear in combination with female figures (Satō Fumika 2000b:64–65). The slogans "The pride in protecting the country" from 1975 and 1976 and "The desire to protect the country" from 1977 were accompanied exclusively by male figures. When women were featured together with men, however, slogans referred to "tomorrow" and the "future," as in the phrases "Young power that protects the happiness of tomorrow" of 1969, or "Encounter with tomorrow" and "Let's talk about tomorrow," among others from the 1980s (Satō Fumika 2000b:64).

More generally, the language of military public relations posters is reminiscent of the forms of speech found in Japanese advertising for government agencies and large corporations. The December 1, 2000, issue of a GSDF base newsletter, for example, carries the headline "With the *Local Population* Into the 21st Century!" *(Chiiki to tomo ni 21 seiki e!)*, a slogan that could also be found on newsletters for a variety of institutions ranging from community centers to homes for the elderly (Frühstück 2002). Brochures published by and for individual bases, as another example, carry slogans such as "We Want *People Who Love Peace*—JDA" (Bōeichō 2000b); numerous GSDF publications promote the idea that "There Is *Somebody* to Protect—GSDF"

FIGURE 12. This 2005 recruitment poster for the Self-Defense Forces reads: "We appreciate it—young strength. There is a future to which I want to connect. There are people I want to help. There is a land I want to protect." (Photograph by Jennifer Robertson)

(*Mamoritai hito ga iru;* Rikujō Jieitai 1998a:cover) (all emphases mine). Acknowledging the vagueness of the latter slogan, the GSDF public relations division explains: "The 'somebody' of 'There Is Somebody to Protect—GSDF' represents the family one loves, the people of one's community, and the beautiful nature and culture of our country. The feeling that one wants to protect the people whom one loves represents the strong wish of the entire GSDF" (Rikujō Bakuryō Kanbu Kō-hōshitsu 2006: back cover). Similarly vague, the GSDF logo features two open hands that form a bowl containing an abstract human figure.

Nothing indicates that this is the logo of the military; it could be that of a soccer team or even a spa (Bōeichō 2001b:246). Here, too, a lengthy explanation attempts to clarify the concept behind the image: "The center symbolizes the people and the Japanese islands that the GSDF wants to protect. The hand to the left signifies 'sturdyness and strength,' the one to the right stands for 'gentleness.'" (Rikujō Bakuryō Kanbu Kōhōshitsu 2006: back cover).

The new preference for references to time (future) rather than nation (past) is further emphasized by the use of the English language. English words and phrases are commonly used in Japanese advertising. In military public relations efforts they signal the alignment of military recruitment efforts with advertising for other kinds of services and products. The use of English also helps remove the present-day military language from that of wartime Japan, a practice that permeates military life to its very core, as I have shown in chapter 2. Instead of *aikoku* for "patriotism," for instance, such materials use "the love of country," "the love of people," or "the love of peace," all in English as, for instance, in the MSDF video clip quoted at the beginning of this section.

Collectively, depictions of uniformed men and women in public relations materials individualize and thus humanize the military experience in present-day Japan, but the iconography of Self-Defense Forces recruitment posters also has been unambiguously gendered. Even though the notion of "pride" has recently returned to military posters, it is embodied not by the stern-looking young men of the 1960s and 1970s but by the cheerfully smiling women who appear in combat or dress uniforms in decisively civilian settings. As Satō Fumika (2000b and 2004) has shown, until the late 1960s, when the Self-Defense Forces began to accept female volunteers into positions other than nurses, not a single poster featured only women, and only a handful published by the JDA included a woman in a group of men. At that time, the Self-Defense Forces clearly and exclusively targeted men as potential volunteers. During the next twenty years, until the implementation of the Equal Employment Opportunity Law (EEOL) in 1986 and the subsequent active effort by the Self-Defense Forces to recruit more women into their ranks, women appeared on more than a third of all posters, but only a small portion exclusively featured women. Today, in contrast to the actual number of women in the Self-Defense Forces, women are vastly overrepresented in public relations posters—almost 80 percent of all such posters now feature women. I believe that the use of women in recruitment images is an attempt to garner legitimacy by demonstrating the Self-Defense Forces' efforts to comply with the EEOL, which was strengthened considerably in April 1999. The over-representation of women in these posters resonates with efforts directed at civilian workers; all government offices are trying to transmit the same message of equality to the public. The Self-Defense Forces thus suggest that they are like any other governmental organization; at the same time their images of women serve to manipulate notions of peace and pride. Female figures render harmless a notion of "pride" that might otherwise be associated with nationalism and imperialism. They are pro-moted as the peaceful gender: their smiling faces suggest that there are nice, pretty women even in the Self-Defense Forces, and that they would not be here if the military were a violent, strange, dangerous organiza-tion (see figure 13). This pairing of "woman" and "peace" plays on wartime propaganda that depicted men as combatants at the front and women as mothers, wives, and supporters at home. As I have shown elsewhere (2007b), these neat gender boundaries are highly ideological and, during the Asia-Pacific War, were continuously transgressed by both men and women. These boundaries have remained firmly en-trenched in postwar society, however, and the Self-Defense Forces' pub-lic relations apparatus has merely been exploiting them in recruitment posters.

Also characteristic of Self-Defense Forces recruitment posters is the rarity with which they feature men and women in uniform with the tools of their trade—weaponry. Instead, the young men and women on the posters are often dressed in civilian clothes and look like ordinary Japa-nese citizens. They do not reveal any special talents or characteristics that would make them particularly suitable for a military career. Their faces are attractive, clean, and relaxed, and they do not show any signs of strenuous activity such as digging trenches or firing weapons—the iconic indicators of military action on U.S. military recruitment posters. For the action, movement, fire, and dust of many U.S. recruitment images, these posters substitute a quiet, sunny, relaxed atmosphere reflected in the static poses of the models and their ponderous gazes, which are never di-rected aggressively at the viewer. Except for the occasional combat plane decoratively placed in the background, weaponry or soldiers performing potentially aggressive acts such as shooting rifles or firing tanks seldom appear. On the rare occasions when weaponry is depicted explicitly, the faces of young, smiling women always offset the image. In short, "pro-

FIGURE 13. Today, public relations and recruitment posters for the Self-Defense Forces typically feature young, cheerfully smiling women and decisively nonmilitaristic slogans such as "Peace People Japan—Come On!"

tecting peace for the public" is represented as a calm, happy, clean, and subdued affair, a message that further underscores the slogans on these posters, and one that stands in stark contrast to the reality of military training.

WORLD PEACE WITH PRINCE PICKLES

It is a wonderful village! This country is really wonderful! People's hearts are warm and agriculture prospers!!! And more than everything else, there is peace!!! This country doesn't seem to have a Defense Force, right? It's just like I thought, in a peaceful country a Defense Force is unnecessary!!

> Prince Pickles in *Prince Pickles: The Journey to Peace*
> *(Pikurusu ōji: Heiwa e no tabi),* Kuwahata and
> Tomonaga 1995:1

These emphatic words are spoken by Prince Pickles (Pikurusu ōji), the male mascot of the Self-Defense Forces who decorates some service members' business cards. Prince Pickles can be purchased as a plastic doll in different sizes, in tiny formats on a string to be attached to cell phones and bags, and as fluorescent stickers. He is also the hero of three cartoon volumes first published during the early 1990s by the JDA public relations division: *Prince Pickles: The Journey to Peace (Pikurusu ōji: Heiwa e no tabi), Prince Pickles's Self-Defense Forces Diary (Pikkurusu ōji no Jieitai nikki),* and *Prince Pickles's Self-Defense Forces Diary II (Pikkurusu ōji no Jieitai nikki 2).* Between fourteen and thirty-four pages thick, the cartoon booklets were part of a larger campaign aimed at aggressively establishing new images of the Self-Defense Forces in Japanese society. The campaign was orchestrated by the JDA and designed by Dentsu, one of Japan's largest advertising corporations with close ties to the government, which has also heavily invested in the production and marketing of cartoons. The use of Prince Pickles and his female counterpart Miss Parsley constitutes a larger-scale attempt to bridge the gap between the Self-Defense Forces and civilian society, this time by trivializing and infantilizing the Self-Defense Forces' tasks in comics for young readers, who are potential recruits.

Directed at the young, the story of Prince Pickles integrates the aesthetic elements of a fairy tale (the central figure is a prince; the characters' names are fantasy names; a contemporary lesson is to be learned) with the didactic goal of explaining the significance of the Self-Defense Forces in order to persuade the Japanese population to sympathize with and appreciate the military. At the beginning, Prince Pickles stands on the hills outside his father's castle and welcomes a wonderfully sunny day in Paprika Kingdom. Suddenly he hears rapid marching noises. A group of soldiers from the defense force (Bōeitai) approaches. Observing the tough training of the soldiers, Prince Pickles becomes outraged at the sight of a commander ordering a young man named Pepper to do a series of push-ups more quickly. The commander replies—making a point that Pepper later repeats—that the kingdom needs a well-trained defense force in order to maintain peace and "protect the country" *(kuni o mamoru)*. Prince Pickles remains unconvinced. He wanders about while contemplating his conviction that the kingdom could do without a defense force. There has been no war in a hundred years, and he is sure that peace will continue. The same evening, Prince Pickles is summoned to see his father, the king. "When I die," the king says, "you will follow me as the king of Paprika Kingdom. Until then, however, you will need to learn a lot, including the necessity of the defense force!" "Tomorrow," the king announces, "you will leave on a journey. While you travel you will learn plenty and hopefully find answers to your questions on your own." Prince Pickles wanders off. The last scene of the day shows him standing on his balcony, deep in thought (Kuwahata and Tomonaga 1995: 1–5).

A few days later, Prince Pickles's arrival is announced in Broccoli Kingdom. A young man, who introduces himself as Carrot, welcomes him at the gate. Prince Pickles explains to him that he has come to learn things about his own country. Carrot volunteers to give him a tour of the countryside where farmers work the fields. Carrot introduces Prince Pickles to the village head, Asparagus, and his daughter Parsley. Prince Pickles is immediately smitten by Parsley, who welcomes him, the Prince of "such a wonderful country," and offers to show him around. Prince Pickles now wears a superman-style coat, a kamikaze-style headband, and a sword.

Over dinner at the home of the village head, Asparagus asks Prince Pickles how he liked the village. Prince Pickles answers how wonderfully peaceful he finds it and how much he appreciates the absence of a defense force. An embarrassed Carrot responds that in fact there is a defense force nearby. "Next to us is the Evil Empire, which has a huge military," Carrot explains. Prince Pickles laughs out loud. To the startled faces of his hosts, he repeats that there has not been a war for decades. Later he shares his thoughts with Carrot: "You are scared, Carrot, right? Fears for

the future of the kingdom only scare our people. So let's bury them!!"
They go to sleep. The next morning, Parsley accompanies Prince Pickles
to the rice fields, where he learns that this year's harvest is expected to
be poor. Parsley tells him that the neighboring empire will most probably face the same problem, a situation that scares her because their need
may prompt them to attack. The story then cuts to the Evil Empire
(6–10), where a fat, mean-looking emperor named Gōma stuffs himself
with food and wine. His character as a despot, who suppresses his
people, is reflected in his subservient and anxious butler. Eventually the
butler tells his master that there will not be any food left for the winter
if he continues to eat so much now. Gōma gets angry and announces that
if they do not have food of their own they will have to steal it from somewhere else. He sends his docile servant over to Broccoli Kingdom to let
them know that there will be war if they do not hand over all their food.

The story cuts back to Broccoli Kingdom. Upon receipt of the bad
news, the ministers and the king of Broccoli consider their options. One
minister suggests that they ask Paprika Kingdom for help. Another remarks that the only role of the defense force of Paprika Kingdom is to
"secure their own borders." Yet another minister says that Paprika Kingdom must see that they do not have much choice and could be attacked
by Gōma's empire as well. Carrot eavesdrops on these consultations.
Alarmed by the situation, he jumps on his horse to ride over to Paprika
Kingdom and ask the king, Prince Pickles's father, for help. The king re-
fuses to help, reiterating that "the defense force is only for the protection
of our country" and that it "cannot be deployed for the sake of other
countries." A crushed Carrot returns home (9–14).

In the meantime, Prince Pickles has a picnic with Parsley. At the very
moment that he attempts to kiss Parsley, they hear the sound of marching. Gōma's military approaches. Prince Pickles cries out, "What is the
[Broccoli] Police Force doing?" Parsley is scared and helpless. Prince
Pickles asks Parsley to go to a safe place while he warns the village, but
she insists on coming with him. In the village they warn the field workers to hide women and children and tell the men to stay and defend the
village. To their surprise, everybody—including the men—flees. Parsley
cries out, "How can they give up their own village?!" Gōma's military
attacks Prince Pickles. Prince Pickles has superhuman strength but eventually is knocked unconscious. Parsley is carried away into the evil emperor's castle (20–27).

Carrot, his father, and other people from the village find Prince Pickles. The village and all the fields have been destroyed. Prince Pickles

learns from Carrot that his father had refused to help. He does not understand why his father did not send the defense force. The king of Broccoli explains to him that they used to have their own defense force, but since there had been peace for such a long time, they had kept only the border police force. The king suggests that their military weakness invited Gōma's attack (30). Suddenly it occurs to Prince Pickles that Parsley is gone. He gets on a horse and rides home to see his father and mobilize the defense force. During the ride he realizes two things: That in order "to protect what one loves one needs strength" and that "the defense force undergoes tough exercises for precisely this purpose."

In the next series of images, Prince Pickles argues with his father about the deployment of the defense force. His father insists that the defense force cannot leave the country. When they are told that Gōma's forces are about to cross the borders of Paprika Kingdom, the king changes his mind, makes Prince Pickles the chief commander of the defense force, and orders him to defend the borders of Paprika Kingdom (34). Prince Pickles proudly takes on the task and triumphantly emerges as a capable military leader.

Up to this point nothing has indicated to the reader that Prince Pickles is qualified for such a role, yet he and his troops hold back the attacking forces. At the moment Gōma's troops withdraw, Parsley emerges out of nowhere and rushes into Prince Pickles's arms. The troops cheer. Prince Pickles departs from the village to return home. Some men thank him and report to him that they will form the Broccoli Kingdom Defense Force, as they have realized that a country has to defend itself on its own. Parsley asks him to come again. He smirks and promises to return with a ring (42–43).

The last sequence again shows a quiet and sunny sky over Paprika Kingdom and the castle. Prince Pickles and his father watch the defense force exercises together. He tells his father that he realizes now that a defense force is necessary even in a country at peace. The cartoon ends with a little speech by the king, who once more spells out the moral of the story:

> The strength that is necessary to protect one's beloved parents, one's family, and one's sweetheart must be neither too big nor too small. One can maintain peace only if one knows the world, entertains good relations with other countries, and works on the protection of the country (Kuwahata and Tomonaga 1995).

In *Prince Pickles's Self-Defense Forces Diary II (Pikkurusu ōji no Jieitai nikki 2)*, the story continues. At the beginning, Prince Pickles explains that he has reevaluated his view of the Self-Defense Forces because of the attack on Paprika Kingdom and is now on his way to a study program in the Japan Self-Defense Forces in order to learn how to equip his own "little, independent Kingdom" with a defense force (1). At first the plot here seems less developed than in the first story. Each double-page spread describes a different aspect of the Self-Defense Forces. Instead of colored cartoons, here cartoon images of Prince Pickles and other figures, with whom the reader is already familiar, are combined with photographs of "real" service members. For example, Prince Pickles jumps over a wall with real service members; Prince Pickles stands in the snow and navigates a real rescue helicopter on snow and ice. Prince Pickles, now in a GSDF uniform, runs along with real soldiers during their field exercises.

The story in the second volume is written from Prince Pickles's perspective: Prince Pickles, who has come from "faraway Paprika Kingdom," begins his stint in the Self-Defense Forces. His study abroad turns out to be a succession of exercises. As he participates in the tough military maneuvers, his confidence in his physical strength wanes. The sight of attractive female soldiers makes him quiver with excitement. But he manages to succeed. Together with other soldiers, he helps to retrieve various objects from the bottom of the ocean in a region that has suffered damage from a typhoon (see figure 14). He is ecstatic when the victims thank him. In addition, he is sure that he "will never forget" how he participated in the exhibition at the Air Force Festival as a member of the Blue Impulse Team and feels that everything he is learning in the Self-Defense Forces has made him grow.

The story moves on to the contentious Japan-U.S. relationship that is—so the cartoon claims—"necessary for peace." The entire section on the Japan-U.S. partnership takes up the problem of intercultural communication and how the Japanese are at a disadvantage. Prince Pickles's name causes confusion. A blonde, blue-eyed soldier calls him by the name of Takuan or Horse Radish. He protests the misunderstanding and introduces himself in English. Then he is addressed as Oshinko, another word for "pickles" in Japanese—clearly a frustrating, if comical, experience for Prince Pickles and the Japanese.

Prince Pickles's first lesson emphasizes the Self-Defense Forces' role as a participant in a rescue mission. While learning how "Ground, Maritime, and Air [Forces] cooperate in order to protect Japan's peace with high-quality defense capabilities," Prince Pickles looks forward to Parsley's visit to Japan. Anticipating a date with her the next day, he browses the Tokyo-based leisure magazine Pia. Then a letter from his father arrives announcing the king's visit on the following day. Prince Pickles is

FIGURE 14. Throughout the *Prince Pickles* cartoon volumes Prince Pickles (here shown in volume one) frequently changes his outfit from the various uniforms of the Self-Defense Forces into fantasy costumes that emphasize his superhuman spirit and commitment to world peace. (Kuwahata and Tomonaga 1995)

unpleasantly surprised. He half-heartedly welcomes his father, and the tour of the base begins.

First, he shows his father the GSDF exercise ground, which is populated by soldiers in camouflage gear armed with guns and bazookas. Prince Pickles announces to his father, and the reader, that the GSDF's role is to defend and "protect the country's peace and security." His father adds that the Self-Defense Forces participate in peacekeeping operations as well, and Prince Pickles expresses surprise at his father's level of knowledge. The king says that talk about the Self-Defense Forces' reputation as a contributor to international peacekeeping operations has reached even distant Paprika Kingdom. The text explains that in order to build world peace, the Self-Defense Forces would like to help nations overseas as well. Prince Pickles reports that he has participated in such an international peacekeeping mission, sporting a blue United Nations beret.

It turns out that Parsley was on the same peacekeeping mission. As they had a quiet moment sitting on a stone together, surrounded by palm trees, she first told him that she had joined the mission as a volunteer to help, if only a little. But then she admitted that she had really joined to be with Prince Pickles. A confused and embarrassed Prince Pickles jumped up and, in lieu of proposing to her, asked Parsley to "work [with him] for world peace." In another large photograph, the reader sees a huge MSDF ship, and Prince Pickles in the corner of the image explains: "We don't have an ocean in our country but in Japan the MSDF is very important and responsible for protecting the surrounding waters" (shūhen kaikyō). The next image, a ship on top of a whale that is out of the water, seems to offset the seriousness and reality of the previous image. Here the story returns to the father's visit and the cartoon style prominent in most of the diary.

Prince Pickles, now in an ASDF uniform, explains to his father the role of the ASDF, namely to keep guard over Japan's airspace, contribute to transport efforts during peacekeeping missions, and help out during disaster missions. Prince Pickles introduces the king to an F4EJ combat plane pilot, and they take off on a short flight, in a demonstration of the impressive technology the Self-Defense Forces have at their disposal. Militarism manifests itself as technology and speed. When the plane lands, the king does not feel well and has to lie down. The woman who is taking care of him turns out to be Parsley. The king recovers; Prince Pickles takes the opportunity to tell his father that he plans to marry Parsley as soon as he is finished with his stint in the Self-Defense Forces.

This scene provides another opportunity for the king to emphasize the necessity to protect his country, Paprika Kingdom. Turning to Parsley he says, "This is a time when everybody has to think seriously about the preservation of peace, Parsley. Please help Prince Pickles to preserve world peace from now on."

Similar to recruitment posters and other public relations material that circulate in wider society, the Prince Pickles cartoon volumes carefully avoid direct references to the Japanese nation. Place names range from "vegetable countries" (the region around Paprika Kingdom) to "kingdoms" and "empires," as well as to "villages" and "land." National symbols such as a flag also are entirely absent from the cartoon iconography. Only the last images of the comic bring Prince Pickles back into the real world. Prince Pickles sits in the middle of a round table with Asian delegates on one side and Euro-American delegates on the other. Behind them is a world map with Japan featured prominently at the center. Prince Pickles explains that peace talks similar to those in Europe have begun in Asia. "In the vicinity of Paprika Kingdom," Prince Pickles goes on, "among the vegetable countries similar talks must be started and opinions exchanged." Interestingly, the map behind Prince Pickles shows Japan's neighbors on the continent. "Let's ask the king for advice," Prince Pickles thinks. "The first of such meetings," Prince Pickles imagines, "must include our Paprika Kingdom, our neighbor Broccoli Kingdom, the United States of Celery, and the Cresson Union."

Prince Pickles decides that a meeting of the vegetable countries is absolutely necessary to maintain peace. "Now that I have experienced life in the Self-Defense Forces, I too have to think more seriously about the preservation of peace. I definitely feel more confident about commanding the Self-Defense Forces of Paprika Kingdom," writes Prince Pickles to his father, who is apparently well and back home in Paprika Kingdom. Upon receiving the prince's letter, the king thinks that now that Prince Pickles has experienced all these important things in the Self-Defense Forces—tough exercises, disaster relief activities, peacekeeping operations—he has matured quite a bit and has started to talk with reason. "I am so pleased and will do my best as well," says the king as the cartoon ends.

The story of Prince Pickles is structured as a rite of passage. Its moral is threefold: Even in a peaceful country Self-Defense Forces are necessary; it is most appropriate to defend one's country on one's own; and protecting one's country is actually the same as protecting one's parents, one's family, and other loved ones. Consistent with other Self-Defense

Forces recruitment materials, patriotism is individualized, personified, and broken down into the love for specific individuals who need to be protected against an evil force whose identity remains unknown. Whereas within the Self-Defense Forces the mascots Prince Pickles and Parsley personify a male and a female member of the three services, in the cartoon Prince Pickles at first represents the prototypical young Japanese, or perhaps the Japanese public at large: peace-loving, well-meaning, naive, and ignorant. Only through his experiences in the cartoon story is Prince Pickles transformed into a peace-loving, well-meaning, and informed citizen who has overcome his naiveté, who understands that the Self-Defense Forces are necessary, and who gets married in the process, thus suggesting that knowledge and appreciation of the military can be or should become a normative element of growing up. This underlying message perpetuates a prominent line of discourse about both the (normal) state and (the normal state of) masculinity that has been pursued in international and conservative national media: Only a state with a military is normal and mature, and only a man with military experience is a real man.

The popular appeal of Prince Pickles, Parsley, and other figures in the *Prince Pickles* volumes lies partly in their cute looks. They have small bodies and big round heads dominated by big round eyes. The strategic use of cuteness serves as a tool for achieving a more sympathetic public response. During the 1970s, cuteness became a marketing tool for almost everything in Japan (Watanabe Morio 2001:137–138). As a sentiment, cuteness has been objectified, commodified, and commercialized to a considerable degree, affording it a significant communicative potency among social actors (Riessland 1997, Miller 2000, McVeigh 2000a:153–155). The JDA has tapped into that potential, as have numerous government agencies, corporations, universities, and other organizations in Japan, which all have their own mascots—cute fantasy figures that often appear in male and female pairs. In the realm of the military, the creation of Prince Pickles and Parsley constitutes an attempt to normalize the Self-Defense Forces, which intend to appear like other organizations and governmental agencies through this trivialization and infantilization.[9] As mediators of the normalization of and familiarization with the Self-Defense Forces, Pickles and Parsley join Pipo-kun and Pipo-chan, who represent the police as friends and helpers of good citizens; Yū-chan and Ai-chan of the post office, who look like squirrels; and the Kansai International Airport mascots Kan-kun and Kūkō-chan, who are shaped like little jumbo jets and come in blue and hot pink. But Prince

Pickles and Parsley also symbolically engage in the task of making something attractive, something that to many Japanese men and women has become commonplace: they are glamorizing peace, which emerges as a fuzzy notion roughly equivalent to the maintenance of the status quo.

With the publication of the Prince Pickles cartoon series and the subsequent publication of the defense white paper in comic format, the Self-Defense Forces also appropriated another late 1980s trend. During that time, government agencies and large corporations began to produce a new brand of adult comic book that addressed general information, politics, business, literature, documentation, and education. According to Sharon Kinsella (2000:71), this kind of comic was characterized by a political revisionism, apparent in the implicit encouragement of readers to rethink their (critical) views of large corporations, the Diet, and the military forces. It culminated in the production of *Manga History of Japan (Manga Nihon no rekishi)*, commissioned by the academic and literary publisher Chūō Kōronsha—a forty-eight-volume work that later was recognized by the Ministry of Education and Culture as suitable for educational purposes at state schools. Corporations also selected information comics as their medium of choice for communication and public relations messages, as did governmental institutions such as the Printing Bureau of the Ministry of Finance, which decided in 1994 to publish the *Environment White Paper* in comic book format. In each of these public relations comic books, company operations are presented not as profit-making enterprises, but as public services (Kinsella 2000:73, 77, 79–87, 95). Believers in the effectiveness of information presented in comic format argue that comics motivate people who have little time to read to do so. Comics work as the hook that pulls people in and gets them to read the text information (Schodt 2004(1996):297). Thus, in choosing comics to manipulate and re-create their image, the Self-Defense Forces has strategically adopted a format already normalized by other government agencies and large corporations. The story of the Self-Defense Forces mascots Prince Pickles and Parsley works to improve the Self-Defense Forces' visibility as an organization that operates both nationwide and internationally. Furthermore, it represents the Self-Defense Forces' public relations efforts to actively create and disseminate images of themselves suitable for mass consumption, specifically by young people.[10]

In contrast to recruitment posters and comics, as well as other textual and visual attempts to win over an amorphous public whose attitude toward the military is assumed to be a mixture of ignorance, disinterest, and hostility, the Self-Defense Forces also target segments of the public that are more accepting of a conventional, aggressive militarism. This radically different image of the Self-Defense Forces is partly enacted at open house days and anniversary festivals, but it is most prominent at the annual live firing demonstration.

CELEBRATIONS OF MILITARISM

Each year the Self-Defense Forces organize dozens of large-scale public events designed to showcase soldiers' workplaces and to display their skills, their new equipment, their achievements over the year, and—most of all—their humanity.[11] Self-Defense Forces events cover a broad range of entertainment efforts. Open house days, anniversary festivals, parades, and live firing demonstrations draw thousands to tens of thousands of people onto a Self-Defense Forces base or exercise ground that is normally off-limits to civilians. The Self-Defense Forces Music Festival, for example, is held annually in the Budo Hall in Tokyo and draws an audience of over 40,000. The festival features 1,000 service member musicians who play primarily marching music during a series of six concerts over two days. Scantily dressed female special guests from the pop music scene enliven their performance. Annual joint concerts with all three service branches in March feature classic music in the Suntory Hall in Tokyo or the Symphony Hall in Osaka and draw audiences of about 2,800 for each concert.

Individual bases open their gates for various self-celebrations as well: As its main attraction, the Iruma ASDF Festival in November 1998, for instance, featured a Miss Air Force Contest in which local civilian women were encouraged to compete. The participants were escorted to a stage by uniformed male service members and interviewed by a female officer. Lined up at center stage, the contestants were flanked by an equally formally arranged group of senior military personnel and representatives of a number of companies, who presented them with gifts at the end of the ceremony. At the annual parade at the GSDF Asaka base in November 1998, Prime Minister Obuchi Keizō spoke publicly about the necessity of tough training for the Self-Defense Forces in the light of the North Korean missile incident. At the NDA Open Door Festival (Bōei Daigakkō Kaikō Kinensai 46) on November 15, 1998, cadets staged a wide array of presentations and performances, ranging from an attack exercise simulation on the NDA's training ground to a judo competition, a flower arrangement exhibition, and a taikō concert. At the

Matsushima ASDF Festival in July 1999, visitors could have their photographs taken with a female model and the Blue Impulse Team framed in the background. The Fuji School forty-ninth anniversary festival on July 20, 2003, offered rides on a tank in Self-Defense Forces helmets and uniform jackets. Thousands of people lined up for that experience.

These events do not merely, like the posters and cartoons, represent and narrate the meaning, capability, and character of the Self-Defense Forces; they also create certain experiences for the audience and thus follow a specific choreography that reveals in yet another way how the military positions itself within a society whose security it is supposed to assure. The core elements of most of these events, and specifically of the base open houses, are modeled on the live firing demonstration held annually at the foot of Mount Fuji at one of the largest firing ranges on the main island of Honshu. It was first organized in 1961 primarily in order to introduce the latest weaponry and tactics to officer candidates. In 1966 it was opened to the public as an important part of the attempt to deepen the understanding and knowledge of the Self-Defense Forces in the Japanese population. Today it serves as the culmination of a week of demonstrations aimed specifically at military personnel, such as NDA cadets and service members who attend military courses. The last two demonstrations, held on a weekend in September, appeal to a larger audience and are the most elaborate and expensive of the week's events. Encapsulating the main characteristics of the most aggressive and bluntly militaristic of public relations efforts, this event has varied slightly each year. It offers yet another perspective on the larger public relations scheme of the Self-Defense Forces. It reinforces messages projected in other public relations efforts while also offering sharply contradicting ones about the military's potential, technological sophistication, and violent capabilities.

Each year the live firing demonstration draws over 50,000 witnesses. But this is not a random crowd; the audience is made up of people who are decisively supportive of conventional militarism and its displays of combat simulations. The majority of visitors are middle-aged or older men, some of whom wear a piece of clothing or a cap that indicates their appreciation of the Self-Defense Forces. Yet others have their small children and grandchildren in tow, some of whom are dressed up in military camouflage from head to toe. To receive a ticket, one has to fill out a form and provide one's name, address, phone number, and one's profession. Although in general anyone who provides this information and sends their application in early enough receives a ticket, one is in actuality giving military authorities an opportunity to check out one's identity.[12]

In this setting, "the public" is easily divided into several distinguishable groups. There are the members of the prefectural support associations, which include veterans, family members, and friends of service members. They come from all over Japan to see what their relatives and friends do, and they already understand and accept the work of the Self-Defense Forces. For them the live firing demonstration serves as a statement of allegiance and celebration, and their participation should be seen as partaking in a rite of solidarity. This sense of "togetherness" is also evident as friends and colleagues occasionally become reacquainted and attendees cluster together in small groups to eat and drink. The sense of commonality is closely linked to explicit messages, conveyed by the demonstration, of sharing in the mission and pride of the Self-Defense Forces.

Other members of the audience include government officials from around the country, especially those from locales near the military bases. Inviting influential and local opinion leaders, the organizers hope, will keep them tolerant of the noise and traffic caused by the activities of the Self-Defense Forces. More generally, their ambiguous status within Japanese society makes it necessary for the Self-Defense Forces to cultivate ties with hundreds of representatives of local governments on a long-term basis. The live firing demonstration provides the Self-Defense Forces with an opportunity to host these authorities.

Service members themselves attend the live firing demonstration either as formal guests, such as the heads of the three services, or as individuals, mostly in civilian clothes, wearing only a cap, shirt, or some accessory that identifies them as service members. They are mainly interested in seeing new weaponry in action, but they also act as experts or professional appraisers of the performers. At least in the eyes of those who actively participate, they help to turn the live firing demonstration into a test of professionalism. The presence of foreign commanders and officers also can be seen as part of the recognition that the Self-Defense Forces seek from other professionals.

Given the size of the crowd and the huge number of service members and weapons appearing in the demonstration, the whole operation is logistically complex. On the weekend I attended in 1998, an area measuring hundreds of square yards formed the maneuver area, serving as a stage for the demonstration, in front of the stands for important guests and benches and mats for ordinary audience members. Off in the distant hills a few miles away were the targets. A military band playing march music was stationed between the mats and the stage. Behind the stands a number of vendors' booths were set up selling drinks, snacks, and souvenirs. There, visitors could buy shoes, belts, and lighters emblazoned with the various unit emblems of the Self-Defense Forces, along with tie clips, Prince Pickles and Parsley dolls in various sizes, and telephone cards with pictures of weapons and vehicles—another way in which the Self-Defense Forces presents itself as accessible. Other booths offered videotapes of weapons or military vehicles and small plastic models of tanks and planes. This area also housed the public toilets, a small medical tent, and a communications tent.

A few minutes past 10 A.M., a fleet of buses with female tour guides brought dozens of invited guests to the stands. Twenty minutes later, a train of jeeps and limousines passed by the regular visitors' stands, bringing the most important guests to their centrally located stand. All these people were greeted formally by Self-Defense Forces personnel and shown to their seats. A single national flag flew above the control tent located to the side of the stands. Before the demonstration began, a military spokesperson, a woman, described the kinds of vehicles that would appear, the targets that would be shot at, and the weapons that would be used during the demonstration. At exactly 10:30, a male announcer took over. He stated that the demonstration was based on the cooperation of the GSDF and ASDF and that its aim was "to deepen the understanding of the Self-Defense Forces." He, too, went through the kinds of drills, equipment, and armaments that were soon to appear, and it was his voice that would later be heard shouting the commands for the soldiers performing in the demonstration. Aside from the initial female speaker, no female voice was heard until the demonstration was over and the visitors were ushered back to their transport. Not a single female service member participated in the actual live firing. In contrast to other representations of the Self-Defense Forces, this event seemed to reconstruct an obsolete world of the military and combat as a preserve of men.

The demonstration began with two yellow and green smoke grenades being set off on hills opposite the stands in order to define the boundaries within which the Self-Defense Forces are allowed to fire live ammunition. The first performance was by the ASDF. Two bombing runs—one of explosive bombs, the other of fire-bombs—were carried out by Phantom jets, closely followed by a number of helicopters swooshing down across the maneuver area. These runs excited several members of the crowd, but most watched silently, and some, including myself, covered their ears to shut out the deafening sound of the explosions. From this point on, the public address system repeatedly patched the audience through to what sounded like the communications network, so that it seemed as if we were hearing the actual orders of the commanders.

Then, two groups of six soldiers jumped out of planes, landing where the smoke grenades had been set off. They jumped in staggered form, allowing the crowd to watch for a few minutes as they parachuted down. Immediately after this, another group of paratroopers shimmied down the cords from large transport helicopters, while smaller combat helicopters at the side of the area supplied support fire. Subsequently, two large helicopters landed at the front of the stage. Several motorcycles emerged from one while the other disgorged some jeeps. Here and there people clapped their hands and called out in shouts of amazement.

The next segment of the demonstration was dominated by the GSDF. A number of armored personnel carriers rode up to the front of the stage, and out spilled service members, who ran up some embankments to shoot a variety of small arms at red and white targets. Immediately following them, two anti-mine missiles were fired out of jeeps. Three artillery pieces were presented, and the announcer explained that while these pieces could fire as far as thirty kilometers, on this day they would fire only five or six kilometers because of safety restrictions. After these guns were fired, a single large anti-aircraft missile was launched. Then four tanks appeared and shot at other targets. While some members of the audience seemed to hold their breath, others murmured "amazing" and "well done."

After a fifteen-minute break, the second part of the demonstration, which comprised a simulated battle, began. After a few new tanks were introduced and fired, several helicopters rose from the sides of the stands to fire a variety of missiles and machine guns at these targets as well. This was also the signal to begin an artillery and mortar barrage with the aim of providing support fire and smoke screens for the soldiers and vehicles that simulated fighting within the confines of the stage. Then, in quick succession, helicopters fired anti-tank missiles, tanks (going up and coming down from their firing stations) shot at diverse targets, and two tanks reversed very quickly and stopped about 25 meters from the first row of spectators. This time, the crowd reacted strongly to the aggressive display of power of the tanks—a combination of size, noise, smell, and smoke. Then two transport planes and two transport helicopters appeared over the audience's heads to drop dozens of paratroopers.

The finale was marked by a crescendo of activity. A number of smoke bombs erupted to create a backdrop of smoke a few hundred meters behind the stage. All the vehicles that had participated in the demonstration drove into the corridor created between this smoke screen and the front of the maneuver area; the helicopters that had taken part in the event flew above them. The sound was deafening. The demonstration, which had taken about an hour and forty minutes, was over. In quick succession, limousines and jeeps came up to the stands to take the invited guests to lunch at one of the nearby bases.

The first part of the live firing demonstration is what Don Handelman (1998:xxix) calls events of presentation, mirrors held up to the social order, reflecting and expressing what the state desires for society. The form, fantasy, and power of this kind of event derive directly from the social order. Local or regional civilian events are one example of such events of presentation, but the more significant instances are state-mandated occasions such as military parades. In this respect, the live firing demonstration is a variant of the annual parade the GSDF holds at the Asaka base or the similar, if smaller scale, performances at the NDA and on bases during open house days. The marching and performing troops as well as the authorities that review the parade embody the order of the state (Azaryahu 1999; Da Matta 1984:219). These individuals play a double role as both audience and performers; they are there to simultaneously watch the demonstration and to be on view.

For the rest of the audience, however, and for most of the demonstration, there is a strict divide between those who are qualified to be inside the order and the rigid hierarchy of the event and those who are outside of it (Da Matta 1984:218–9). This separation between the soldiers, the authorities, and the general audience was most evident during the first part of the live firing demonstration. The regular, undifferentiated audience sat separated from the others by ropes. The separation is established not only for practical reasons; it also carries messages about the loci of power and authority.

The live firing demonstration also contradicts the messages purveyed through the other public relations strategies and materials already discussed. Its messages are far from one-dimensional and clear-cut. The most explicit message of the live firing demonstration is the one announced over the loudspeakers at the beginning of the event: the intent "to deepen the understanding of the Self-Defense Forces." In contrast to public relations posters, which symbolically disarm the Self-Defense

Forces when addressing a wide, anonymous, undefined audience, or cartoons, which fictionalize and trivialize the military, this expressed purpose is not just an empty phrase invented by some public relations expert. Announcers guide the crowd's understanding of the live firing demonstration by providing an interpretive framework for what happens in the performance and for the general characteristics of the Self-Defense Forces. They furnish what seems to be rather uncomplicated data and information. For example, there are myriad explanations about specific weapons or vehicles including weight, power, range, and the place of production. This information forms part of a celebration of military technology and is associated with having the latest and most advanced equipment. Hence, only within the confines of a live-firing demonstration and thus in front of a sympathetic audience do the Self-Defense Forces ally themselves with other technologically advanced armed forces, for which the ability to produce speed emerges as a core characteristic in fighting a war and technological sophistication increasingly replaces brute force as the key to victory (Virilio 2002 [1991]).

While some of my analysis also applies to the annual GSDF parade on the Asaka base or to anniversary events on GSDF bases all over Japan, the live firing demonstration involves moments of spectacle that set it apart from such processions. The enactment of the combat scenarios reveals what remains carefully camouflaged in other public relations material. The show of fire power, which is the central element of the demonstration but entirely absent from material for consumption by wider society, takes on the character of spectacle, a dynamic social form that demands movement, action, and change on the part of the human actors at center stage and provides excitement, thrill, and pleasure for the spectators (MacAloon 1984b:244). Almost all of the presentations are accompanied by pyrotechnics that, like fireworks, combine exploding light, color, sound, smell, and even touch. The varied colors of the smoke bombs, dark gas fumes, and missiles become all the more impressive against the background of the rather subdued browns and greens of the stage, the soldiers' uniforms, and the vehicles' camouflage. A plethora of sounds and reverberations further amplifies the event's impressiveness: machine motors, airplane engines, the shouting of orders by commanders in the "patch-in" to the communications net, and most notably the firing of diverse armaments, including rifles, machine guns, cannons, airplane bombs, and missiles. Smells of sulfur and burned fuel that drift back to the crowd. The palpable vibrations of the armored vehicles that drive near the crowd further enhance the physical dimension of the demonstration. But through all of this the audience is aware that the performers are firing at nonhuman targets, adding an element of play, lessening the seriousness of the experience, and trivializing the potential for deadly violence.

There is very little space for improvisation or individual creativity in these demonstrations. Rather, the event is tightly scripted with the emphasis on its more dramatic aspects. The live firing demonstration offers a spectacularization of violence. It is this spectacularization that turns actions related to soldiering into entertaining displays.

By 1 P.M., about an hour after the demonstration had ended, service members set up an exhibition of tanks, mortars, and helicopters. Just as at the open house festivals on bases all over Japan, the public is invited to take a closer look at the helicopters and armored vehicles parked in the demonstration area. Positioned next to each vehicle or aircraft, large posters detailed its weight, performance capabilities, and place of production. Next to the larger vehicles, service members had set up metal steps so that spectators could climb on or enter into them. Some people climbed all over the weaponry; they felt the relationship between their own body size and that of the vehicles, and smelled the odors of these vehicles. The vehicle display was the site of much picture taking. Next to a Chinook C-347 Helicopter, for example, service members took pictures of children and adults donning pilots' helmets for the price of 300 Yen. This stage of the event also provided opportunities for people to speak to soldiers, who were assigned to stand next to the vehicles or act as ushers. Like open house festivals, this third phase of the demonstration is designed to bring the Self-Defense Forces closer to "the people" and—among other messages—show the crowd that soldiers are "real people." The overall mood of festivity is heightened by the fact that many people bring food and drinks and consume these refreshments during this stage of the demonstration. Thousands of people spread out private mats over the large ones provided by the Self-Defense Forces to create little territories within which they hold their picnics.

The public relations division invites media representatives from Japan's major newspapers and television stations to these demonstrations. Military photographers and journalists record the event for internal Self-Defense Forces use as well. Photographs of and reports on the live firing demonstration are printed in newsletters and magazines published by the JDA and exhibited during open house days; they also decorate the corridor walls of the NDA, the General Staff College, and other Self-Defense Forces institutions. The internal dissemination of the demonstration's images allows the event to transgress its spatial and temporal boundaries and to provide one of those self-defining moments that are a part of any organization's efforts of creating an organizational identity.

The live firing demonstration also allows the Self-Defense Forces to address certain issues, to redress some of the problems that are embedded in its ambiguous existence in Japanese society, to remind politicians that they are a resource that can be used in times of emergency, and to plead for support in political arenas normally closed to uniformed representatives. Similarly, the presence of foreign commanders and officers indicates that the Self-Defense Forces draw on other professionals for their capabilities in traditional fields of military expertise and performance.

The live firing demonstration most explicitly demonstrates the warmaking potential of the Self-Defense Forces. In contrast to more civilian messages that the Self-Defense Forces purvey in posters, in cartoons, and at other occasions of self-presentation, the live firing demonstration centers on the armed forces' potential for violent operations and constitutes what Michael Mann (1987) has called "mass-spectator militarism," or a fascination with all things military. The combination of picnic, festival, and open house that marks the last part of the day complements these processes. Here tactile experiences, shared food and drink, and the controlled breakdown of the boundaries between the audience and the performers work to domesticate and personalize the event. The troops and the weapons become objects that are both accessible and open to dialogue with invitees. There is fun in, but—in contrast to comics and animated films produced by the JDA—not fun made of the live firing demonstration, and the format does not invite questions from the audience. Finally, it contradicts the image of service members in other public relations efforts, as well as the service members' image as participants in peacekeeping, humanitarian aid, or rescue missions. Instead, this event stresses the conventional, modernist scenario of combat.

The Self-Defense Forces public relations apparatus orchestrates these three sets of public relations efforts—recruitment posters for the anonymous public, cartoons for children and youth, and live firing demonstrations for service members and sympathizers—to appeal to different segments of the Japanese population. It projects a series of civilianizing, familiarizing, trivializing, and spectacularizing messages about the military's capabilities, roles, and character. Some of these are mutually reinforcing whereas others radically contradict one another. None of these messages is more true than another: Combat simulations might look like

actual combat to the unaccustomed, but nobody dies. Live firing demonstrations and similar events center on a function of the military that generally has been regarded as its core function, the exercise of violence. Yet
no Japanese soldier of the Self-Defense Forces has actually exercised violence in the name of the state. Some public relations materials trivialize
the military, but several cohorts of soldiers have pursued whole careers
by doing exactly what recruitment posters and cartoons promise. Some
observers tacitly assume that the training for and prospect of combat is
what really holds the military together. Yet, during three and a half years
of deployment to Iraq—the closest Japanese soldiers ever came to war—
recruitment rates decreased, the number of suicides soared, and returnees
from Iraq primarily expressed relief that everybody survived the mission
unharmed.[13] The Self-Defense Forces public relations efforts, therefore,
do not simply cover up some hidden, real character of the military, usually assumed to be its willingness to exercise violence in the name of the
state. Rather, at a time of an ever-shrinking population of potential
(male) recruits, the Self-Defense Forces need to play all sides. They cannot hold on to the notion that combat is the core role of the military.
They cannot exclusively summon troops under the dictum of national
defense, because defense has not been necessary during the past sixty
years and because the "nation" has become a "zero sign, an empty con-
tainer into which diverse audiences can insert their varied fantasies, but
without having much substance" (Gerow 2006). They are uneasy about
their identity, an identity that is decidedly postmodern in nature—broken, bracketed, multiple. Thus it appears that the military needs to symbolically arm and disarm itself for public consumption in order to convince the fearful that they are protected and the peaceful that they need
not feel threatened.

   As with all advertising and public relations efforts, the big question is
whether these efforts work. Citing recent opinion polls about the increasing acceptance of the Self-Defense Forces and referring to the occasional recruit with a degree from one of Japan's most prestigious universities, public relations officers are convinced that their efforts are
fruitful and have improved their reputation since the 1950s. The military
historian Yoshida Yutaka (2002:7) has sketched military-societal relations in postwar Japan as follows: Since the defeat of the empire in 1945,
the Japanese population has hated the war and—by affiliation—the military. According to one of the first opinion polls about the armed forces
(conducted in 1956), 42 percent of respondents agreed when asked
whether the imperial armed forces had succeeded in training "proper

people" *(shikkari shita ningen);* while 37 percent disagreed. Concerning trust in the capabilities of the postwar military, public opinion was most negative in the 1970s. According to an international opinion poll conducted in 1970 of 6,000 youth on sex, war, and patriotism, among other issues, only 10 percent of youth from Tokyo agreed with 65 to 88 percent of young people in Manila, Saigon, Cairo, and Calcutta that having the biggest military possible was desirable. Of youth polled in Tokyo, 20 percent agreed with 56 percent of youth in Frankfurt, that it would be best not to have a military at all; and 70 percent of youth from Tokyo agreed with 65 percent of youth from Rome that keeping the military as small as possible was ideal *(Shūkan Asahi* 1970). In short, only German youth of the 1970s were more apprehensive of the military than their Japanese peers.

Based on recent polls and my conversations with younger service members, it seems that today the public relations efforts do at least provide new recruits with motivational narratives. By and large, service members across cohorts and gender note the lack of socioeconomic means that prevented them from pursuing some other career path or entry into a regular university as well as their initial lack of understanding of and interest in matters of national defense. Beyond that, however, their narratives are closely tied to the messages of the public relations activities I have examined above: gender equality, the desire to prove oneself, participation in disaster relief and peacekeeping, the wish to help people, and so on.

In addition, the fact that a major pop music group agreed to do a promotion for the Self-Defense Forces suggests that popular culture may now be willing to embrace a soft and fuzzy version of the military. The trend of an increasingly intimate relationship between the Self-Defense Forces and popular culture certainly constitutes a form of militarization, but it is a militarization that already has internalized the multifaceted character of the military as a group capable of caring, rescuing, and building, in addition to the much more remote possibility of one that would fight a war. As Aaron Gerow (2006) has noted with respect to recent Japanese military films, popular cultural production in Japan has reflected the nationalist turn in politics, but the nationalism in these works, as in the public relations efforts of the Self-Defense Forces, is warped and tortured, and confronted with a myriad of obstacles that force it to take convoluted paths, thus reminding us what nationalism has to erase in order to appear compelling and unproblematic.

CHAPTER 5

Embattled Memories, Ersatz Histories

May I pass the officer exam!

January 7, 2003

May I definitely pass the Ground Self-Defense Forces exam and be able to join the thirty-fourth infantry regiment!

February 11, 2003

May I become a noncommissioned officer candidate this year!

June 7, 2003

These prayers, written on wooden votive plaques, were scattered among several hundred displayed on the grounds of Yasukuni Shrine in the summer of 2003. The shrine—since the Asia-Pacific War a religious institution funded entirely by private donations—occupies a prominent place just north of the Imperial Palace in Tokyo. It is accessed through colossal gates of wood and metal along an avenue of majestic gingko trees. Visitors buy the plaques at the shrine, scribble their most heartfelt wishes on them, and hang them on one of the boards available for that purpose. Votive plaques at shrines throughout Japan carry prayers for health, happiness, success, luck, and peace. At Yasukuni Shrine, the relatively few votive plaques written by potential recruits and hopeful service members of the Self-Defense Forces hang next to others by civilians that express hope for world peace, success on school and university exams, recovery from illnesses, and other personal civilian matters.

The political significance of these plaques from potential and actual service members at Yasukuni Shrine rests on the fact that of the thousands of Japanese soldiers killed between 1853 and 1945, for whose souls the shrine serves as resting place, 1,068 were war criminals.[1] Visits to the shrine by representatives of the state are unconstitutional and thus remain a controversial topic in domestic and international debates over both the Japanese government's view of the Asia-Pacific War and the current proper relationship between religion and politics (*Yomiuri Shinbun*, August 18, 1999a). Some wish to restore government ownership of the religious shrine; others would like a nonreligious memorial to be built for Japan's military dead, so that those wishing to honor them would not have to go to Yasukuni Shrine. More recently, Koizumi Junichirō, prime minister from 2001 to 2006, acted more aggressively than most prime ministers (since Nakasone Yasuhiro) in making a point of visiting Yasukuni Shrine every single year during his tenure, in this way expanding his political capital on the right margins of Japan's political landscape. But even he refrained from doing so on August 15, when Japan commemorates the end of the Asia-Pacific War, until 2006, the year he stepped down.[2] On that day, the highly ritualized media spectacle whirls around a complex series of intertwined debates about whether a visit to Yasukuni Shrine by the prime minister and other members of government signifies an endorsement of Japanese imperialism; whether the Japanese state has appropriately and convincingly apologized and engaged in a satisfactory and coherent effort to gain the trust of its neighbors; and whether the roughly 200,000 visitors to the shrine on a day so loaded with historical symbolism signify a move to the right or represent the sentiment of only a slender margin of society.[3]

On August 15, the normally deserted parklike area around Yasukuni Shrine turns into an arena full of spectacle. In front of thousands of police, visitors drift in and out of the shrine grounds. Old men dominate the crowds, but there are also young families with children, who spread their food out on blankets for a picnic under the trees after paying respect at the shrine entrance. An impressive number of international and Japanese reporters are eager to get a good shot of what later on television will look like a massive resurgence of militarism in Japan. Dozens of uniformed young men, who belong to one of several hundred right-wing organizations, march up and down the main path and later hold forth in the rest area where soft drink machines, tables, and benches invite visitors to rest, watch, and participate in the spectacle. One group of young men sports crew cuts, camouflage uniforms, and military boots. Another group appears waving large national flags. Some wear black pants, white shirts, and headbands reminiscent of the Special Attack Force of the last few months of the Asia-Pacific War. Yet another group's uniforms are modeled on the German Wehrmacht, and its members wave a huge flag that features a slightly modified *Schutzstaffel* (SS) symbol.[4] A handful of young male Italian neo-fascists in their uniforms of light gray suits and berets look on. Here and there individual men of a younger generation carry reactionary banners and scream militarist slogans at the top of their lungs. Small groups of Yakuza, members of the Japanese mafia, in double-breasted suits, flanked by heavyweight bodyguards, make their carefully choreographed entrance. Dozens of old men in Imperial Navy uniforms carry bayonets, brass instruments, and rifles from the Asia-Pacific War. Brought to Yasukuni on tour buses, these veterans enjoy the midsummer outing, catching up with former comrades, and paying respect to comrades and friends who have died. Old men in Imperial Army uniforms, by contrast, appear only individually and seem somewhat forlorn among the crowd, as here too the IJA legacy lingers. None of these groups have female participants. And none of these groups make contact with one another; too immersed are they in the intricacies of their self-presentation.

On a smaller scale, Self-Defense Forces officer veterans and active officers, some of whom are members of the Association to Honor the Spirits of the Fallen Heroes (Eirei ni kotaeru kai), attend the Festival to Comfort the Spirits of the Fallen Heroes, also held annually on August 15 at Yasukuni Shrine. This occurs largely out of public view and away from the show of militarisms on this day. This "secrecy" is no coincidence. Critical voices within and outside the Self-Defense Forces argue that because the shrine officials praise Japan's imperialist efforts as a "holy war," service members should not be allowed to visit it in their uniforms (*Shūkan Kinyōbi* September 7, 2001:26–27). The question of whether a visit to Yasukuni Shrine in uniform is a breach of the separation of the state and religion remains a contested issue. According to the Self-Defense Forces Law, service members are allowed to wear their uniforms in their free time; they are also allowed to pursue religious activities during their free time. According to a spokesperson for the Kaikōsha, the veteran officers' organization of the IJA, GSDF, and ASDF, troops do not formally visit the shrine en masse because that would be considered a religious activity and thus a breach of the separation of religion and state.[5]

Very few NDA cadets or service members choose individually to visit the shrine and the adjacent museum during their days off. In the case of one regiment in Tokyo in 2001, for example, only 10 of 9,000 men requested a vacation on August 15 in order to be able to visit the shrine (*Shūkan Kinyōbi* 2001:26–27).[6] Organized IJA veterans are disap-

pointed by this absense of Self-Defense Forces service members. These
veterans claim that a small number of lower-ranking service members are
eager to connect to the IJA but officers have kept their distance, and not
one of the Self-Defense Forces top brass, whom the Imperial Army Veterans' Association invites to the commemoration activities at the shrine,
has ever shown up (*Shūkan Kinyōbi* 2001:26–27).[7] Although some concerned observers predicted that Prime Minister Koizumi's visits to the
shrine would eventually normalize such visits by Self-Defense Forces service members, that has not happened (*Shūkan Kinyōbi* 2001:26–27).

Their lack of visits to Yasukuni Shrine does not mean that service
members have no interest in the history of their predecessors. Rather, for
service members of the Self-Defense Forces, neither Yasukuni Shrine nor
the War Memorial Hall (Yūshūkan), which sits on its grounds, is the primary site to commemorate Japan's military tradition. Rather, the Self-
Defense Forces have created base museums where they produce "ersatz
histories" primarily for service members; these museums function
against the overbearing backdrop of Yasukuni Shrine and the War
Memorial Hall, with their uncritical valorization of the Japanese military. Hence, I use the term "ersatz history" to imply the conscious effort
to create a history that is partial to the military. Beginning with an analysis of these museums, this chapter untangles the various strategies the
Self-Defense Forces have employed in order to both break with the past
(the discontinuity required for public consumption) and build a military
tradition (the continuity required for unit cohesion). Among these strategies are the localizing of specific ersatz history narratives told within and
beyond base museums, the use of oil painting and reproductions of these
events to authenticate past military experiences, and the redressing of
symbols much older than the Self-Defense Forces.

The making of military memory is problematic everywhere.[8] In Japan,
however, the Self-Defense Forces are attempting—with perhaps a greater
and more willful intensity than in the period of empire building more
than a century ago—to both shed the legacy of the IJA and build a military tradition that will raise troop morale. In the base museums, the Self-
Defense Forces try to construct their own version of military history.
This history emerges from a field of radically different histories of both
military establishments, of the Asia-Pacific War and modern Japanese
history more generally, which are prominently represented in iconic sites
ranging from the War Memorial Hall at Yasukuni Shrine to the Hiroshima Peace Museum (Hiroshima Heiwa Kinen Shiryōkan, 1955–).[9]
The Self-Defense Forces base museums, by contrast, constitute the core

site for fabricating a "communal military memory" *of* the military and *by* the military in post–World War II Japan.[10] Communal memory, writes Ian Hacking (1995:210), has always played a major role for group identities; almost any identifiable group of people has tales of origin. Each group of people has its own communal memory, its own chronicles, and its own heroic odes, which all help to define the group. The past is needed because it conveys community, and the community reassures itself of itself through the reconstruction of the past. Memories that are embattled outside the walls of base museums—in debates about history textbooks, officials' visits to Shintō shrines, and the constitution—are carefully moderated as communal military memory in Japanese base museums. The production of this communal memory is directed both inward, to the group whose memory demands continuity, and outward, to civilians, who must believe that that continuity has been effectively disrupted precisely because of the conditions under which the Self-Defense Forces were founded and the association of the IJA with suppression, war, and defeat.

Base museums represent a complex and specific take on Japan's militarisms past and present. They do not simply replicate in a miniature, amateurish format the grand-scale, scandalously reactionary representations of Japan's militarist past on display in the War Memorial Hall or the Showa Hall. Rather, they also look to the national representation of military history at such sites as the Hiroshima Peace Memorial Museum, the Nagasaki Atomic Bomb Museum, the Okinawa Prefecture Peace Memorial Museum, and the Chiran Special Attack Forces Peace Exhibition Hall, with their different perspectives on the Asia-Pacific War and the role of the military.

Base museums indeed are a place where memory is redressed, reinterpreted, reorganized, and repopulated. The processes of military memory production seem crucial here precisely because memory is valorized where identity is problematized. I do not use the notion "communal memory" in the belief that any one person could share the exact same memories with even one other person.[11] Rather, the term "communal military memory" signifies its very fictionality. The museum administrations across dozens of military bases all over Japan continuously work to create and maintain this fiction. "Communal memory" also implies the attempt to create a shared identity that unites the military as a social group, despite its members' different motivations, backgrounds, and personal connections to Japan's imperial history. Base museums mull over questions such as why some images of Japan's militarist past triumph while others remain invisible, or which memories the Self-Defense Forces should construct of themselves and the IJA; and they negotiate how their constructions conflict with other, competing memories. In this way, base museums must keep a multiplicity of connections and views in mind as they create a communal memory as ersatz history molded to satisfy a specific community's interests rather than being bound by some sort of objective or academic historiography. Rather than contrasting these ersatz histories with academic historiography, my interest is in pointing out the base museums' active, conscious efforts to provide a locally useful view of Japan's military history. Their interventions into this history are, of course, highly political ones and are driven by a specific vision of how that history should be organized in order to shed a specific light on Japan's military present that can be appropriated for the Self-Defense Forces' future.

LOCALIZING ERSATZ HISTORIES

Typically, an IJA camp was founded in the late nineteenth century and then a local headquarters for the base command was built. One camp, for example, was founded in 1896 for the tenth cavalry regiment of the IJA. Another camp was founded in 1898, and an IJA infantry regiment was established. After the dissolution of the IJA in 1945, and during the postwar occupation of Japan from 1945 to 1952, the original IJA headquarters buildings served as the headquarters for the Allied occupation forces. The headquarters buildings remained intact after the Allied forces left in 1952 and the Self-Defense Forces were established. Later, these buildings were transformed into base museums. Most base museums were founded during the 1960s. With the renewal of the U.S.-Japan Security Treaty in 1960, it had become clear that the Self-Defense Forces were there to stay, that the ties with the United States had turned into a long-term arrangement, and that the majority of the population had resigned themselves to both ideas.

Besides being smaller and less grandiose, base museums differ in other significant ways from the national icons among military and war museums. In contrast to museums that are administered by civilians, the Self-Defense Forces must cover the cost of establishing and maintaining the museums from their local budgets. The local administrative units of each museum cannot purchase exhibits but must rely on donations. Veterans or their families typically donate exhibit items. In some cases, the local branches of the Japan Association of Bereaved Families (Nihon Izokukai)—the main driving force behind the establishment of the War

Memorial Museum at Yasukuni Shrine and the building of the Showa Hall—have also been active in creating base museums. Museum directors tell nearly identical stories about the acquisition of exhibits as a result of a chain of personal relations and contacts. For the establishment of one museum, the local population was asked to donate exhibits when the museum was created. At other base museums, family members who found military memorabilia among the belongings of a veteran contacted the base administration. Some family members emphasized that they had no use for these objects now that their owners were deceased. Others expressed embarrassment at having kept such things in their homes in the first place and were happy to rid themselves of objects that physically connected them to the IJA and wartime Japan. The name for a base museum, *shiryōkan* ("Building of Specimen," or "Building for Historical Resources") suggests its role as one of collecting, maintaining, and displaying exhibits as if there were an innate truth in the objects themselves. As sites of enlightenment and documentation, they are geared toward transforming the identity of recruits, and they set the foundation stone of a communal military memory that is selective and presentist. They introduce ruptures in some places and establish continuities in others, in the language of the personal, of experience, truth, tragedy, and sacrifice. The simple arrangement of objects speaks of their role in fabricating a military memory for purposes internal to the military. Considering that the audience consists mostly of new recruits, museum administrators generally assume that the service members who act as docents can fill in the blanks.

The two-room layout of the base museum I briefly described in chapter 1 is rather common. One room is designated for the IJA. The second is filled with exhibits that represent the trajectory of the Self-Defense Forces. Typically, the rooms reserved for the Self-Defense Forces seem like closets filled with unclear achievements, and a similarly unclear future. There, the uniforms look clean and well ironed. The stripes that signify rank and participation in certain exercises are new and shiny. Nothing exudes an aura of physical strain or even just plain use. The rooms dedicated to the IJA, by contrast, seem to breathe—in even the smallest objects once used by men now dead—the history of the authentic, the local, the real, and the significant. The uniform and boots have been visibly worn. The red color of the draft notices has long since paled. The style of the handwritten letters is clearly of a different era. The variety of documents ranges from declarations of war and copies of the Imperial Rescript to Soldiers and Sailors, introduced in 1882 in order to "instill virtues of loyalty to the emperor and love of the country" (Kurushima 1899: inside front cover), to newspaper articles reporting on troop movements during the Asia-Pacific War.[12] Various objects representing the everyday life of imperial soldiers are arranged in glass display cases. Among these are draft notices addressed to men who lived near the camp, soldiers' letters from the battlefront to their families, and cigarette cases and similar objects that individualize the experience of war.

Base museums constitute a dichotomous order of ersatz histories that are established as authentic, tied to the IJA veterans' exhibits, and contrasted with the memory off base, which the museum management perceives as a product of elite manipulation and contested discourse that ignores individual soldiers' perspectives and experiences. The memory represented in base museums—or so the underlying message implies—has been derived from the shared, lived experiences of small groups of IJA members. The display of the belongings of now mostly dead IJA soldiers next to the very same artifacts of living Self-Defense Forces soldiers underscores the attempt to symbolically transform war heroes into peacetime saviors. Unlike official, off-base culture, which continues to blame the Asia-Pacific War and its aftermath almost exclusively on the IJA and—by affiliation—the Self-Defense Forces, base museums strive to harmonize the myth of the tragic IJA hero with their portrait of the Self-Defense Forces savior. Base museums work to transform the former readiness of soldiers to die for the emperor into the present-day willingness of service members to devote their lives to the welfare of the national (and, possibly, international) population. They employ several subtle but simple techniques to produce a sense of authenticity. One such technique is the strategic localization of Japan's military history, which limits the histories of the IJA and of the Self-Defense Forces to the specific locales of each base through the presentation of intimate military artifacts from that area. At the entrance to one such museum on a GSDF base several woodblock prints represent a famous battle fought several hundred years ago on the hills nearby. Here, the battle appears as a better, simpler past, which helps to establish an unproblematic local military history. The battle was successfully fought, the prints suggest; thus national unity was accomplished, and its leaders can safely be celebrated as politico-military heroes of feudal Japan. In another base museum, numerous images of Mount Fuji, which is visible from the camp, add to localization efforts. Here, these recurring representations of the immediate environment suggest a (topographic) continuity—across historical periods, military regimes, victory, and defeat—that appears as a surrogate for the ostensibly once warm relations with the local population, relations that today must be cultivated with great effort, as I have shown in chapter 4.[13] Other museums display additional attempts to intertwine the regiment's history with the town's or city's history, as well as with local gods and customs, through careful and subtle attempts at militarizing the everyday.

The history of the local regiment is carefully cut out from the larger history of the IJA. Both strategies work to isolate the base's military history from the historical legacies that the Self-Defense Forces feel haunt them to this day. Despite these attempts at isolating the local regiment, the history of the IJA and its relationship to the Self-Defense Forces are not forgotten but rather re-created, managed, and appropriated. The strategies of localization aim to intertwine a narrow slice of Japan's military history with the history and culture of the immediate environment of the base. The pride in the local regiment, museum directors note, also rests on the long history of the base—even though some local military personnel subscribe to the split between the Self-Defense Forces and the IJA that is promoted by the various public relations divisions. In the base museums, military-societal relations of the past are wrapped in a fog of nostalgia.

Certainly, civilian-military relations during the first half of the twentieth century were organized by different rules, but militarist propaganda then also entailed localization efforts that aimed at representing these relations as intimate.[14] How did this come about? After the IJA was founded in 1872, young men found a number of reasons to pursue a military career. Military academies offered a good education and graduated an impressive number of prime ministers and other members of the political elite, up to the 1950s, when military expertise and status ceased to be advantageous for a political career. For the less privileged classes, the drafting of one or more sons signified fewer mouths to feed but also the loss of an important labor force. The IJA played an important role as a modernizing and democratizing force that facilitated the spread of modern culture from the urban centers into the provinces. The military became a force for the establishment of a new social order and a pioneer for social, cultural, and technological developments ranging from brass music to electric lighting (Takazawa, Abe, and Tōya 2001). A military career became the basis for a career in civilian life. Out of sheer necessity the military strove to homogenize language. In turn, military terms were gradually integrated into regular Japanese. Beer, pork, beef, and bread were first consumed on a large scale in the military, and many men boarded a train for the first time as soldiers. Conscripts and soldiers were the object of the first large-scale studies of hygiene, health, and literacy

(Abe Kanichi et. al. 2001; Yoshida 2002:12, 27, 29, 38, 44; Frühstück 2003:17–55; Cwiertka 1998, 2002). During the late nineteenth century, IJA reserves and veterans fondly remembered the military as the place where one could go to sleep when it got dark, sleep until dawn, and receive meals with rice rather than barley and other cheaper alternatives (Yoshida 2002:58).

During the late nineteenth century, relations between the military and regional communities were relatively tight, and only small segments of the intelligentsia were critical of the military. The majority of the population believed that group activities and training in the military would improve men's health (Arakawa Shōji 2001:291; Yoshida 2002:6). The appreciation and respect for the military, however, had not only been grounded in the possibility of upward social mobility but had also been the result of decades of propaganda, which all areas of popular culture began to reproduce by the beginning of the twentieth century. After the Sino-Japanese War (1894–1895), texts and pictures began to be used to introduce the military to boys. In stark contrast to current-day Self-Defense Forces images (see chapter 4), the IJA was represented as an organization that would turn boys into men capable of defending Japan against enemy forces and willing to sacrifice their lives on the battlefield. Specialized military magazines, as well as special issues and reports in other magazines, brought war, battle, and the soldiers' everyday concerns home (Harada 2001:8–11). Although they did not do so in the pacifying and trivializing manner of Self-Defense Forces imagery today, they used heavily aestheticized imagery nonetheless. At the time of the Sino-Japanese War, for instance, Japan's first illustrated magazine, *Pictures of Everyday Life (Fūzoku Gahō)* featured an IJA maneuver depicted in dozens of elegant drawings in black, white, and red; the issue also detailed information on the maneuver, as well as the condition of the army and its ranking system.[15]

Commemoration postcards with military themes became a popular medium for instigating good relations between the military and society (O'Connor and Cohen 2001). In 1906, for example, at the occasion of Japan's victory over Russia in the Russo-Japanese War (1904–5), the Bureau of Communication printed two multicolored, gold-framed postcards as souvenirs to be sold at the army parade in Tokyo (see figure 15). Both postcards depict military successes. One carries the title "The Triumphal Celebration in the Middle Ages" (in English) and represents Oda Nobunaga, Toyotomi Hideyoshi, and Tokugawa Ieyasu (the three unifiers of Japan). The other features Yamagata Aritomo (one of the founders of the IJA), Nogi Maresuke (a key figure in the Russo-Japanese

FIGURE 15. These two gold-framed postcards were sold as souvenirs at the army parade in 1906.

War who committed suicide upon the death of the Meiji emperor in 1912), and other prominent military figures in the general headquarters of the Manchurian Army at Mukden. The first postcard marks the unification of Japan under the feudal order of the Shogun. The second represents the last victorious war in Japan's history. Both point to a positive attitude toward the military and wars that had been victoriously fought.

After the Russo-Japanese War, militarism began to permeate the emerging children's print and visual culture, where it worked to transgress new claims about children and childhood, such as the idea that children were and should remain removed from danger, violence, and war. The notions that childhood was a realm separate from adulthood, and that children were particularly vulnerable and worthy of special care and protection had been scientifically sanctioned since around 1900, when the field of pediatric medicine was established, welfare institutions for children developed, and child protection laws were implemented (Frühstück 2003, 2007a). Nevertheless, during the first half of the twentieth century, Kōdansha and other large publishers produced hundreds of books and magazines for children and youth with military themes. Among these were the *Picture Book for Children: The Imperial Japanese Army* (*Kodomo no ehon: Nippon no rikugun,* 1940), *Youth of Greater Japan* (*Dai Nippon Seinen*), and *Japan's Children* (*Nippon no Kodomo,* 1941; see figure 16).[16] Idealizing soldiers and the military, publications for youth first condoned and then promoted war games. During the first three decades of the twentieth century, on the flip side of the military's increasing alienation from society, the embrace of popular culture and the military became even more intimate. The November 1933 issue of the leading boys' magazine, *Boys' Club (Shōnen Kurabu),* contained a *Photo Album of the Imperial Army (Teikoku rikugun dai shashin ten),* which had been produced with major support from the IJA administration. Among those who provided black-and-white photographs and information were the press club of the IJA, the Bureau of Land Surveying, the military research institute, several regiments from Chiba and Nagano prefectures, and numerous officers, all listed with their full names and ranks. The book is primarily a collection of photographs of Emperor Hirohito at troop inspections, maneuvers, and parades, but it ends with a one-page cartoon that crystallizes the purpose of the publication: the boy hero confidently claims that "all pupils [in my class] pursue three stars" (Dai Nippon Obenkai Kōdansha 1933: last page).[17]

The militarization of mass culture for girls hardly lagged behind that for boys. Girls were given the role of writing "comfort letters," sewing "comfort bags," and acting as productive and responsible mothers

FIGURE 16. The April 1941 issue of the magazine *Japan's Children (Nippon no Kodomo)* was one of many children's books and magazines that playfully familiarized children with war and the military.

(Imada E. 2003). In 1922 and again in 1939, for example, the girls' magazine *Girls' Club (Shojo Kurabu)* presented its readers with a colored paper board game *(suguroku)* that had been officially approved by the army and navy ministries. The various squares include depictions of military personnel at work. In the last square a smiling IJA soldier holds a child, with whom the lucky winner was expected to identify (Rikugun-shō jōhō-bu and Kaigunshō jōhō-bu 1939 [1922]).

It is the spirit and power of these kinds of representations of the IJA in wartime propaganda, rather than memories of actual wartime life, that linger on in base museums, where a sense of loss for the ostensibly once warm relations between the military and the civilian population becomes visible in the stark contrast between the sections for the IJA and those for the Self-Defense Forces. The collections seem to suggest that this military-societal unity rested on an unspoken willingness to suffer and sacrifice one's life for a greater good as the one and only (noteworthy) way of life and death. The grandiosity of this era is not expressed through Japanese victories in wars before the defeat in 1945, through territorial gains, or through representations of the ideological vision of a Greater East Asia Co-Prosperity Sphere, as is the case in the collection of the War Memorial Hall at Yasukuni Shrine, with its large triptychs showing battle scenes, the emperor on his legendary white horse, and the army advancing. Nor is attention drawn to the suffering of the Japanese population during wartime and immediately thereafter, themes on which the Showa Hall focuses without any mention of Japan's imperialist war and the suffering caused by the IJA and the Japanese colonial regime in the colonies. Rather, base museums are driven by a sentimental nostalgia for an era when—at least in the imagination of the museums' creators—the military was still an unquestionable pillar of the nation state and an entity organically interwoven with civilian society.

Picking up on the immediate postwar sense of loss (of the war, of lives, of good civil-military relations), soldiers of the IJA are not presented as rigid, militarist young men but as sentimental, vulnerable ones. According to the pictures displayed in these museums, it was not just their courage, discipline, fighting spirit, or the capability to do their job well that made them noteworthy. The lost look on one young man's face mirrors the sense of resignation to fate in another's. The memory of the IJA generated in base museums is easily embraced precisely because it evokes a sentimental humanism. It is this sentimental humanism that allows service members today to translate the IJA's aggressive characteristics into the protective ones with which active service members like to associate themselves and the Self-Defense Forces. In this way a sense of continuity is established between the IJA and the Self-Defense Forces, between a military that primarily was supposed to be able to fight, to kill, and to die honorably and one that is able to take care, to help, and to save others from suffering.

Base museums typify IJA soldiers as good and friendly men who are, by implication, cleansed of any association with the IJA as an aggressor in imperialist wars and a perpetrator of massacres and other war crimes. They reinforce the dominant discourse of mourning, which serves to legitimate sacrifice for an allegedly higher cause (Jay 2003:4), and leave unmentioned the IJA's strenuous basic training, brutal treatment of recruits by superiors, severe punishments for infractions of military law, psychiatric illnesses caused partly by soldiers' increasing isolation from civilian society, and cautiousness in dispatching troops late at night so as to not upset the civilian population (Harada 2001:8–11, Yoshida 2002:24, 223). This ersatz history of a much more complicated and conflicted time attempts a symbolic recuperation of the dead through communal efforts to justify their alleged sacrifice and ignore their unassuaged pain—a move Walter Benjamin once viewed as the most fraught of all attempts at institutionalized remembering (Jay 2003:24).

The "digestive remembering" (Jay 2003:19) that a base museum engages in and offers to the visitor can be premised only on a certain forgetting, the forgetting of everything that resists incorporation into its system, such as the atrocities, sexual slavery, and other forced labor. In one base museum, a banner that apparently had been given to the Japanese regiment by a Chinese commander indicates the gratitude toward the Japanese soldiers for their good treatment of the Chinese population. "Something certainly happened at Nanking," Major Yonemoto Akio* explained, "but this banner makes clear that the IJA has not been all bad."

Ersatz histories in base museums also reestablish the gender order of wartime propaganda. Only occasionally are photographs included in the collection of former female activists in local branches of wartime organizations, such as the Japanese Association for Patriotic Women or the Greater Japan Women's Association for Defense (and their respective banners). Most of the imagery, however, casts the IJA as exclusively populated by male combatants and women as fertile mothers, hard-working factory employees, self-sacrificing nurses, frugal wives—or in some other home-front role meant to support and comfort men. Yet this separation was transgressed by both men and women, including men who were too old or unfit for service and women who worked as nurses, entertainers, "comfort women," and sex slaves (Frühstück 2007a).

In a similar vein, hardly any base museum even so much as suggests that women now serve in the Self-Defense Forces. I have already discussed the limited integration of women into the Self-Defense Forces and their exploitation as symbols of gender equality in chapter 3. Here I would like to note that in contrast to the aggressive advertising of the Self-Defense Forces as an organization with built-in gender equality, base museums do not even take note of women's accomplishments. Here, the attempt to create a military genealogy retreats to a notion of the military as male and masculine despite both historical and contemporary evidence to the contrary.

AUTHENTICATING EMBATTLED MEMORIES

The communal military memory that is fabricated in base museums does not come easily. It is calibrated and employs the strategies of historicity and iconicity. One of the more powerful ways of interweaving the necro-heroism of the IJA with the service heroism of the Self-Defense Forces is the representation of the latter with the means of the former, namely oil painting, the primary medium for depictions of the military in battle during the Asia-Pacific War. At times of war these paintings took on important roles as instruments of propaganda in the homeland in such exhibition halls as the Navy Hall (Kaigunkan) and the Art Gallery for the Commemoration of Imperial Virtues at Meiji Shrine (Meiji Jingu Seitoku Kinen Egakan), as well as in similar places in Japan's colonies (Wang Hsui-hsiung 2001). They were exhibited with the explicit intention to display "paintings that represent important events one must not forget as a Japanese based on the history of the Imperial Navy" and "paintings made by contemporary first-class western-style painters who were driven by the passion of patriotism," as well as to "appeal to ordinary citizens in an effort to foster the cultivation of the noble spirit to die as a martyr for the fatherland" and "as patriotic teaching material appropriate for youth" (quoted in Tan'o and Kawada 1996:30).

War art had also been produced as *nihonga,* printmaking, and photography, but none of these offered the particular combination of features associated with oil paintings—the possibility of a strong sense of realism combined with the grandeur of historical drama. In Japan, the historical connection between oil painting and war is particularly intimate. At the end of the nineteenth century, oil painting by Japanese artists was generally referred to as *yōga*, literally "western painting," a term calling attention to the European sources of its materials, techniques, and often iconographies and styles. *Yōga* developed in dialectic opposition to *nihonga*, literally meaning "Japanese painting," which typically was regarded as a venue for indigenous or "traditional" expression. Before military photography began to complement painting on the battlefields of Asia at the time of the Sino-Japanese War, it was the exclusive role of painters to capture, in oil, scenes from the battlefront for documentary and propaganda uses. Even though *yōga* was stamped with foreignness, it emerged as the primary medium for war painting, in the early 1940s when the art world was reorganized in order to unify and direct all creative energies to the war effort (Kaneko Ryūichi 2003b; Winther-Tamaki 2003:348).

The IJA commissioned some of Japan's most respected *yōga* painters to don uniforms, travel to distant battle sites, and create dramatic tableaus of the Asia-Pacific War. Painters who had been identified with the European Bohemian milieus of *yōga* innovation in the 1920s so deeply as to become marginal figures in Japanese society thus eventually came to redirect their art into complicity with militarism (Winther-Tamaki 2003:349; Sandler 2001). After the end of the Asia-Pacific War, *yōga* emerged as a more vigorous form than *nihonga*, which was seen as stagnating and fell to the status of a secondary art. It is not surprising, then, that base museums display reproductions of the original oil paintings from the grandiose halls of war, even if only in small versions, typically one square foot in size, when the originals measure several feet in length and breadth. These paintings of battle scenes were meant to instantly transform the Japanese war experience into a glorious one. As Paul Virilio (2000 [1984]:10) notes, it is hoped these paintings will repeat their wartime task of imbuing audiences with fresh energy, that they will pull people out of apathy and overcome that broad demoralization so feared by generals and statesmen alike. Yet the effect of these much smaller reproductions of wartime oil paintings is more documentary, given their modest size, as well as a kind of sterility that comes from displaying them behind glass.

The iconic potentiality of oil painting is further exploited in visual documents of the Self-Defense Forces' activities, the most prominent elements in the history room within the GSDF Public Relations Center (Securitarian 2002c), which opened its doors to the public in April 2002 and is located in Tokyo's Nerima ward, close to the Asaka GSDF Base. This room documents the history of the Self-Defense Forces without any mention of the IJA. Oil paintings are used for this purpose despite the fact that photographers capture the Self-Defense Forces' missions for glossy public relations materials and other publications of the Self-Defense Forces and the JDA. Featuring Self-Defense Forces missions in the format of oil paintings allows for the recouping of wartime heroism evident in representations of the IJA.

To this day, countries at war employ not only reporters and photographers but also painters, who continue to capture scenes from the front lines in oil. In the United Kingdom, the artist John Keane covered Operations Desert Shield and Desert Storm in 1991 as the official war artist sponsored by the Imperial War Museum in London; while in the United States, the Staff Artist Program has been established to create heroic oil paintings of the U.S. troops in Iraq. For the GSDF Public Relations Center, the painter Ono Hisako, internationally known for her portraits of leaders in government and business, created paintings based on photographs of major missions to mark the history of the GSDF's achievements.[18] Hung in heavy golden frames, the paintings capture the beginning of the Police Reserve Force in 1950, a support mission at the 1964 Tokyo Olympics, the first combined exercises with the U.S. armed forces in 1981, the first peacekeeping mission to Cambodia in 1992, and the Kōbe-Awaji earthquake disaster relief mission in 1995, among other events (see figures 17 and 18 on pp. 168–69). Susan Sontag (1990 [1973]:23) has observed that "event" means "something worth photographing"; the GSDF Public Relations Center has turned that notion on its head: In base museums and in the Public Relations Center a military event means something worth capturing in oil, with all its weight, grandeur, and militarist baggage. The difference between the aura of a photograph and that of a painting lies in the different relation to time, writes Sontag (142). It is that quality of time that elevates the event captured on these oil paintings to one of historical significance, be it an IJA battle during war or the Self-Defense Forces' involvement in securing the safety of the Tokyo Olympics during peacetime. In contrast to photography, oil painting increases the importance of the historical moment and fixes it. "If photographs demean, paintings distort in the opposite way: they make grandiose" (Sontag 1990 [1973]:166). In contrast to war art, the oil paintings displayed in the history room of the GSDF Public Relations Center speak, somewhat undramatically, primarily to service members, their families and acquaintances, and those sympathetic to the military, not to a wider audience of civilians who might visit a general museum. They assure service members that what they do is worthy of being captured in a medium of historical significance, whatever their frustrations over the lack of public recognition. At the same time, the fact that the Self-Defense Forces' achievements are captured in the same medium as those of the IJA symbolically reassures service members, their families, and other visitors that the Self-Defense Forces are important and thus worth immortalizing in military memory.

These intentions are reinforced by the enormously detailed chronologies of activities and achievements listed on white boards in an adjacent section of the history room. Here, the GSDF Public Relations Center has appropriated the timeline format, which permeates most efforts of historical documentation, ranging from textbooks to museums and white papers. As Yamaguchi Tomomi (2005) has shown, adopting a linear depiction of history is far from an innocuous act. Rather, these overwhelming chronologies in chartlike form, with multiple columns, help claim the Self-Defense Forces' place within Japanese society and internationally, and attempt to assert their position in the past, present, and future. Their very format makes these chronologies look objective and fact-based, much more so than with other written forms of history. Museum curators consider making these chronologies a straightforward process that does not involve any subjective evaluation of historical events or their contexts. Yet, in the War Memorial Hall such detailed timelines work to minimize the significance of the defeat in the Asia-Pacific War, by presenting this war as one of an endless string of military conflicts ostensibly in defense of Japan so that it appears as just one of any number of moments in Japanese history. In the history room of the Public Relations Center, timelines list important and not-so-important activities in a show of the Self-Defense Forces' usefulness, versatility, busy-ness, and, perhaps most important, political relevance. In separate columns, the history of the Self-Defense Forces (beginning with its foundation) is presented as one interconnected with other national events and with international events. In 1960, for instance, a crucial year for the Self-Defense Forces as the U.S.-Japan Security Treaty was renewed against fierce resistance of the Japanese left, the move of the JDA to Roppongi in Tokyo is documented next to the demonstrations in front of the parliament, the first French atomic test, and a U.S. U-2 plane incident over Soviet airspace. Similarly, in 1966, the opening to the general public of the Mount Fuji live-firing demonstration, examined in the previous chapter, is lined up next to a disaster relief effort in Aomori prefecture after a fire, a dispatch of GSDF service members to help with the planting of rice in Yamagata prefecture, and the beginning of the bombing of

FIGURE 17. This oil painting represents the first international disaster relief mission to Honduras. It is one of many that represent the present-day missions of the Self-Defense Forces. Painted by Ono Hisako, it is displayed in the history room of the GSDF Public Relations Center in Tokyo (Rikujō Jieitai Kōhō Sentā).

North Vietnam by the U.S. military. Similarly, in the 2005 defense white paper's section on "defense chronology," the "order for the 5th contingent for the Iraqi humanitarian and reconstruction support activities to take over from the 4th contingent" parallels in the domestic rubric a "ruling made for the 4th lawsuit on the noise of Kadena Base by the Okinawa Branch of Naha District Court" and, in the international rubric, "North Korean Foreign Ministry claims that the country has already manufactured nukes" (Japan Defense Agency 2005:603).

A closer look at timelines that accompany exhibitions in base museums, military museums beyond the confines of bases, and Self-Defense Forces publications reveals, then, that they effectively mask the political and ideological biases informing their making and take advantage of their power to present a specific history as truthful, material evidence. By beginning Japan's military history in the 1950s, deciding how to divide the history of the Self-Defense Forces into different categories, and de-

FIGURE 18. This oil painting represents an instance of combined exercises of the Self-Defense Forces with the U.S. Forces, Japan. Painted by Ono Hisako, it is displayed in the history room of the GSDF Public Relations Center in Tokyo (Rikujō Jieitai Kōhō Sentā).

termining what qualifies as an event worth noting, the makers of chronologies cannot but construct their own versions of history, even as they claim to merely document such history.

SYMBOLIZING WAR AND PEACE

In addition to the localization and historization efforts, the strategic uses of once unambiguously militarist symbols further reinforce the manipulative quality of the ersatz history making within the Self-Defense Forces. Base museums mobilize and reclaim various contradictory versions of these symbols in a concerted effort to create a new, positive, and uncompromised communal military memory. These symbols appear on the uniforms, weaponry, flags, banners, badges and insignia of various Self-Defense Forces units that are carefully arranged in glass display cases, and this use reveals, rather literally, a loss of memory dating back to the first generation of Self-Defense Forces service members. Perhaps the most obvious and, at the same time, ambiguous appropriation of militarized symbols involves signs of rank and markers of performance introduced to break with the militarized aesthetic of the IJA. Each of the twelve GSDF divisions, for example, carries its own multicolored insignia. Most are simple in design, with the prominent feature typically being the number of the division.

In stark contrast to the break with the use of rank and equipment names that I described in chapter 2, the Self-Defense Forces reward outstanding performance with colored cloth stripes attached to the uniform where the left chest pocket would be. An officer's rank is not symbolized by metal stars but by metal cherry blossoms. The choice of the cherry blossom for all three service branches was made when the Self-Defense Forces were first founded and the military administration was keen to emphasize that the Self-Defense Forces were not a conventional military establishment. Even then, however, the choice must have seemed odd given that the Imperial Japanese Navy had already used the cherry blossom symbol. The "flower of the aristocracy" during the Middle Ages, cherry blossoms became associated with warriors when cherry trees were planted around castles during the modern period. As a national symbol, cherry blossoms emerged after the Sino-Japanese War when a cherry blossom tree was planted at a celebration in 1900 in honor of the prince (and later the Taishō emperor). Since then, cherry blossoms have become a symbol of pride in Japan and in turn a major source of nationalism (Takagi 1999:149–150). In 1934 the Japanese railway ministry published a brochure for foreign tourists in which cherry blossoms are presented as essential to Japanese culture. A propaganda poster of the Japanese Association of Defense carried the slogan, "The country where cherry blossoms bloom shall be the leader of East Asia" (Tan'o 2004:112). During the Asia-Pacific War, cherry blossoms became a metaphor for fallen soldiers generally, and for the members of the Special Attack Force or kamikaze more particularly; they thus served as a central element of a highly militarized wartime aesthetics (Takagi 1999; Ohnuki-Tierney 2002).[19]

Today, the cherry blossoms' symbolic currency has long superceded its former militarist uses. Decorating advertisements for anything Japanese outside Japan and anything "traditional" within the country, the blossoms have become the occasion for mass picnics and collective "cherry blossom viewings" (Ohnuki-Tierney 1998). One IJA veteran who had been proud of the wartime symbolism of the cherry blossom angrily commented, "One can't tell whether the rank symbols on one's shoulders really are cherry blossoms" (Sase 1980:98). But the irony of their use for officers' ranks on Self-Defense Forces uniforms seems to escape those active service members who direct base museums today. Asked about the Self-Defense Forces' choice of cherry blossoms over the common stars as markers of military rank, one base museum director wanted to move on, seemingly embarrassed by the cherry blossoms, which perhaps in his eyes emphasized not a specific Japanese aesthetic and symbolic tradition, or pride in Japan's culture or military tradition, but rather the somewhat lesser status of the Self-Defense Forces in the international arena. Upon their return, the commander of the first unit that had been dispatched to Iraq, by contrast, proudly presented the unit banner, featuring a huge yellow cherry blossom on white background and three red horizontal stripes, to the director of the JDA (Bōeichō 2004a:illustrations).

Even more complex, if less well known, is the trajectory of dove/pigeon symbols that used to decorate the banner of the independent communication battalion of the National Police Reserve. Displayed in one base museum, the banner featured a white dove with its wings spread, and a red and yellow sun behind its head (see figure 19).[20] The same bird on differently colored backgrounds (occasionally accompanied by cherry blossoms) was also used for most other units and banners of the National Police Reserve and the early Self-Defense Forces. To this day, the emblem of the NDA features the same kind of white dove on a blossoming cherry tree. To the public relations representative at the NDA, as well as to base museum directors across the nation, the dove simply symbolizes peace, and the blossoming cherry tree stands for strength.[21] However, the historical connections of doves and their representations to war in Japan run deep, a fact of which service members are commonly not aware. Associated with Hachiman, popularly referred to as the god of war, the origin of the name *hato* for dove (or pigeon) is *hachi*, from Hachiman. During the Edo period, traders used pigeons as messenger birds and feudal lords raised them to feed them to their hawks and falcons. After their use was prohibited by the Shogunat, it was the IJA that reintroduced the use of pigeons as messenger birds from the 1880s onward.

The Imperial Army Ministry reimported the practice from Europe around the time of the German-French War of 1870–1871, and it trained pigeons as messenger birds based on extensive research by the armed forces of Germany, France, and Belgium (Okada A. 1979:44–45). The IJA imported and began to train 300 pigeons *(denshohato* or *gunyōhato)*

FIGURE 19. Many symbols on the banner of individual regiments and of smaller units are created by members of these units.
This one represents a dove (or pigeon), today a symbol of peace,
as the director of a GSDF base museum explained to me.

from China in 1901, another 300 from Belgium during the same year,
and 50 from Germany a year later—all countries which had used carrier
pigeons in their postal system. The IJA first used them in the Russo-
Japanese War (Jidō Hyakka Daijiten Kankōkai 1937). In his article "Animals as Comrades" for the military magazine *Comrade (Senyū),* Sakurai Tadayoshi (1911:29–34), an infantryman in the IJA, laconically
writes, "During wars, animals have to work. In that sense, they are not
much different from soldiers."

The development of new communication technologies created doubts
about the use of pigeons during war. However, after World War I in Europe again proved the military usefulness of the pigeon, the IJA founded
a research institute for the study and training of pigeons, and in the Asia-
Pacific War pigeons were again used. For their contributions in the so-
called China Incident and the Shanghai Incident, awards for well-
performing pigeons were introduced (Jidō Hyakka Daijiten Kankōkai,
1937:197–199). Pigeons were used for long-distance communication because they are capable of flying at speeds of 60 to 90 kilometers per hour
(*Gunji Nenkan* 1943a:414). Only when other forms of long-distance

communication developed did the pigeon lose its status for military purposes, and since then it has been raised and used primarily for pigeon
races (Kaneko et al. 1992:118–119).

The preface to the early post–Asia-Pacific War children's book *Animal
Book of Paintings (Dōbutsu Gashū)* provides clues for the sudden, ostensibly smooth transformation of certain animals, including horses and
dogs, once praised in military propaganda as "loyal warriors," into symbols of peace. The authors, Oka Yoshi and Koga Tadamichi (1950:1),
announce that raising children as pacifists starts with teaching them a
love for animals, because a true love of animals is directly connected to
humanity. The best way to instill in children the love of animals is to
teach them as much as possible about animals, because "knowing is the
beginning of loving." For Oka and Koga, if parents introduce rabbits,
dogs, and birds to their children, the children will discover how lovely
animals are, and this is the way to become "a truly pacifist nation."
Twenty-some years later, in the short story "Te" ("The Hand"), Abe
Kōbo (1972:153–159) portrays the fate of a dove that is transformed
through a sleight of hand from an army carrier pigeon *(denshobato)* into
a peace symbol *(heiwa no shinboru)*. Set in the postwar era, the story addresses the pigeon's ambiguity throughout modern and contemporary
history and captures the ambivalence and ambiguity that has accompanied its flight. Within the Self-Defense Forces, what was once the "pigeon
for military use" *(gunyōhato)* was also transformed into a peace symbol
and appropriated for the new agenda of the Self-Defense Forces, as documented in base museums throughout Japan.

In defense of base museum directors, it is important to note that in
Japan a great deal of ambiguity surrounds the differentiation of the carrier pigeon and the dove. Ornithologically, a dove is a small pigeon. The
rock pigeon is the ordinary-looking pigeon that populates today's cities
and has been used as a carrier pigeon all over the world. There are dozens
of different kinds of pigeons in Japan that are usually subsumed under
the designations Kawarabato (rock pigeon), Kijibato (rufous turtledove),
and Shirakobato (Eurasian collared-dove) (Okada A. 1979:44–45).
Kawarabato include not only the messenger birds used by the military
but also the pigeons one encounters today in Japanese parks and train
stations. According to the Japanese Association for Carrier Pigeons,
they also are the kind of pigeon that most Japanese think of as doves
and thus as peace symbols.[22]

While images of dove/pigeons and cherry blossoms together with
Mount Fuji underwent an intense militarization during the modern era,

specifically during the Asia-Pacific War, it is important to note that none of the IJA flags and insignia from that time period depicted any of those images. Hence, the postwar move to employ them for military symbols has created an odd quandary: once highly militarized symbols are being used for a new military, one that is committed to peace, in order to differentiate it from the older, fighting military establishment. Base museum directors, however, seem oblivious to that irony. At the age of seventy-five, an IJA veteran and former GSDF chief of staff nostalgically remembered the IJA banners as "artistically beautiful." In his view, hawks and eagles should have appeared on Self-Defense Forces banners as well. In the late 1970s, this veteran expressed the following view on the less-than-conventional Self-Defense Forces unit symbols:

> . . . if this is a military shouldn't there be eagles and hawks instead of the pigeons/doves on the Self-Defense Forces banners!? . . . This weird camouflage has been carried on to this day. The camouflaged state emerged because we, the Self-Defense Forces, have not started as a 'military' ('*gun*') (Sase Minoru 1980:98).

Perhaps this veteran spoke for a considerable portion of IJA veterans who also served in the Self-Defense Forces during its early years. Active service members today, however, embrace rather than object to the more modern, if less militaristically informed, symbols of the Self-Defense Forces. The very confusion over whether the white bird featured on Self-Defense Forces banners and emblems today is a militarist reference to messenger birds in the service of the IJA or a pacifist reference to the white dove as peace symbol serves the builders of a communal military memory within the Self-Defense Forces well, as they embrace this very ambiguity.[23]

It is not only the Self-Defense Forces that have appropriated the symbolism of pigeons/doves for their own purposes. That other politically diverse organizations have employed pigeons/doves—sometimes for contradictory purposes—further complicates the matter: They are, for example, released to atone for the deaths in the name of the emperor to appease the souls who rest there at Yasukuni Shrine and at the annual commemoration of the atomic bombings at the Hiroshima Peace Park. They also appear on a variety of emblems—for instance, as a mother dove and a baby dove on the emblem of the New Japan Women's Association (Shin Nihon Fujin no Kai), an NGO recognized by the United Nations.

The latest unit banners designed by the members of the Self-Defense

保管部

第1保管課 →

FIGURE 20. Although unit emblems today may feature a hawk rather than a dove, as pictured here on a sign on an ASDF base that points to the storage department, their edge is softened by the comic figure style (ASDF base, 1998). (Photograph by the author)

Forces—ones that have not yet made it into the base museums—no longer feature doves; instead, they range from cartoon-like animal characters to skulls in aggressive colors and designs. Different units on an ASDF base outside of Tokyo, for example, are represented by a yellow eagle on a bluish-green background; a funny-looking gray and black dog-like figure with a bright red tongue hanging out of its mouth, holding a plate with an airplane in its front paw; and a friendly-looking orange-colored eagle that balances a missile on one wing and with the other points in the direction of the building that houses its unit (see figure 20). Elsewhere, the GSDF rangers who undergo exceptionally brutal training in order to achieve their Special Forces status carry a banner that features a white skull on a bright red background (Kurita 2001; Matsuzawa 2001).

By and large, then, base museums do not blatantly attempt to whitewash the IJA and glorify an aggressive militarist past. Rather, they put a complex web of contradictory strategies—localization, historization, and symbolization—to work in creating a communal military memory for use primarily within the Self-Defense Forces. The willful suppression of the more gruesome sides of the IJA in base museums has been deemed necessary in order to forge a connection to the IJA and a military tradition into which the Self-Defense Forces can be incorporated. Packaged in sentimentality and humanism, the old idea of "sacrifice" (for the emperor) is appropriated as "service" (to the entire population) and used by base museums to synthesize the very continuities and connections so vehemently denied by the JDA's public relations division. If "any type of amnesia results in something's being stolen from oneself how much worse if it is replaced by deceptive-memories," writes Ian Hacking (1995:264). It is such deceptive memories that come together in base museums to (re)educate recruits about the trajectory of the organization for which they have volunteered.

Of course, no one museum on or off base, or any one point of view, has a monopoly on how the war years are remembered. After all, different museums exhibit different perspectives on the relationship between the IJA and the Self-Defense Forces, ranging from the links being clearly severed, with the IJA rendered invisible, to an unspoken alignment, indicated by displays placed next to each other. But base museums intimate the possibility of such a monopolization when they create ersatz histories especially and almost exclusively for service members.[24] These collections produce certain kinds of knowledge, and in some camps, new recruits must participate in a guided tour of the local base museum in order to develop an understanding of Japanese military history. Sergeant Kono Hiromasa*, who served as an amateur docent on these tours, was convinced of the necessity and significance of the base museum as a site of enlightenment and identity formation. The friendly, quiet man, now at the end of his military career, admitted that he was frequently shocked at the young recruits' lack of respect for the history housed in the museum he guards. "Most of them know nothing," he claimed, "either about the role of the emperor, for whom so many soldiers fought and died, or about history more generally." Other senior service members agreed with that assessment, and pointed out that recruits and cadets were surprised when they learned how to pull up a flag and listen respectfully to the national anthem. They knew nothing about these rituals beforehand.[25] General Nerima Hikaru*, at one point commander of an ASDF base was convinced that "these young people have no sense of patriotism and don't even recognize the flag and anthem of their country. They don't learn to sing the national anthem in school or anywhere else. They don't even know why they don't sing it. When recruits hear the national anthem for the first time on base, they call it 'the

Sumo song.' " (In contrast to festivities at school, the national anthem was then played at Sumo competitions.) In Nerima's eyes, the root of the lack of patriotism among Japan's youth lies in the fact that "these young people don't know their history." Asked about the lack of historical knowledge among his subordinates, base commander Colonel Katō also suggested that the younger generation of enlisted service members did not receive any education on Japan's recent history and certainly not on the role of the IJA within this history: "Consequently, they know nothing about the IJA."

However, not all recruits are so naive and ignorant. Underlining what Wulf Kansteiner (2002) argues about the relationship between events and their memorialization, some young service members associated the base museums primarily with their grandfathers, who fought in the IJA or at least had lived during the Asia-Pacific War. Kansteiner reminds us of the plausibility of such connections by pointing out that the physical and social proximity to past events and their subsequent rationalization and memorialization do not have to coincide. There is no natural, direct connection between the real and the remembered. On the one hand, collective memories may exclude events that played an important role in the lives of members of the community. On the other hand, socially and geographically distant events may be adopted for identity purposes by groups with no involvement in their unfolding (Kansteiner 2002:190). Besides those fathers who also have been or still are members of the Self-Defense Forces, grandfathers are in many cases the only family members who welcome their grandsons' entry into the Self-Defense Forces. Hence, some recruits saw the base museums as a representation of their own grandfathers' experience and support of their own decision to join the military.

Returning to Sergeant Kono's assessment of the base museums' role in historically educating young men and women whose history education has never touched upon the twentieth century, let alone the time of Japan's aggression in Asia, it remains questionable whether the museums indeed establish some understanding of modern Japanese (military) history. "Despite the fact that the memory of every people has its own character," Hacking (1995:211) warns, one should not be misled to believe that group memories cement group identity and difference. What they successfully reinforce in recruits, however, is a sense that that history is deeply problematic and not an easy source of pride. Graduates of the NDA and others who have joined the Self-Defense Forces long-term report that they developed an understanding of national security only dur-

ing their tenure in the military. Some claim that they have become proud
of Japan, even though—according to their own accounts—before their
contact with and their socialization into the Self-Defense Forces they had
no pride in their country. Others are sure that NDA graduates are particularly aware and wary of Japan's wartime past. Claiming that Japan
has remained under the mind control of the United States, yet other officers join the Association to Honor the Spirits of the Fallen Heroes. By
and large, however, potential recruits and service members, much like
men in other organizations, are concerned with their careers—in this
case, in the Self-Defense Forces. As the votive plaques quoted at the beginning of this chapter indicate, they pray for promotion. They hope for
professional success. Even in the semi-anonymous realm of the wishes
expressed on votive plaques, they do not voice any desire to join in the
tradition of Japan's ancestral warriors honored at Yasukuni Shrine or to
some day join those men's spirits in service of the nation.

Epilogue

We base our planning on "worst-case scenarios" and then
come to believe that we live in a world where vast resources
must be committed to "prevent" them from happening.

Carol Cohn 1987:707

War is only an invention, not a biological necessity.

Margaret Mead, *Asia* 40, 1940

In 1899, Japan was invited to join an international gathering of the great
powers for the first time. The irony of this invitation to the Hague Peace
Conference was that Japan's place at the council table had been earned
by the success of the Imperial Japanese Army (1872–1945) in China—
just as its status as a great power would be confirmed by its victory over
Russia in 1905. Roughly one hundred years later, on January 26, 2006,
Japanese papers reported that all GSDF troops had "safely [returned]
home from [their] historic mission to Iraq," putting an end to two and a
half years of the first deployment of the Self-Defense Forces to a war zone
since their foundation in 1954, albeit for a noncombat, humanitarian operation (*Japan Times,* January 26, 2006). For months, lawmakers had
been grappling with the difficult question of setting a date for the return
of the troops because—similar to all international missions of the Self-
Defense Forces—their security revolved around the presence of other allied nations' troops. In Iraq, the British Army especially was of vital importance to the GSDF, as it was in charge of maintaining security in
southern Iraq, including the Samawa region where the GSDF units had
been deployed. As one JDA official put it, "We want to avoid at all costs
being the first country to announce its withdrawal" (*The International
Herald Tribune,* May 20, 2006). In an eerie resemblance to the invitation to the Hague Peace Conference, the mission in Iraq increased
Japan's international profile and strengthened the ties with Japan's
biggest ally, the U.S. Significantly, the international press claimed that it

marked no less than Japan's transformation into a "grown-up nation" or even a "normal state" and that of its armed forces into a "true military."[1]

In this book, I have examined the immediate repercussions of the concern with the normality of the Japanese state and its military for individual soldiers, for their sense of what constitutes a "normal" or "real" soldier. For much of the era after World War II, an existential question for those Japanese men whose lives are permeated by military rules, values, and interests was how they were to negotiate their soldierhood in conjunction with the military organization that trains them for war, on the one hand, and their exclusive experience of noncombat operations that prohibit the exercise of violence, on the other. Perhaps more than service members anywhere else in the world, Japanese service members are conscious of an anxiety about how to properly perform their soldierhood and often appear hyperaware of their camouflaged identity as (trained) warriors and (practicing) humanitarians, saviors, engineers, construction workers, and handymen.[2] As I have emphasized throughout the book, the effects of the concern with and anxiety about the "normality" and "maturity" of the Japanese state and its military on individual soldiers are constantly reinforced through soldiers' everyday experiences. These concerns create an uneasiness and ambivalence about their sense of what it means to be a "normal" and "true" soldier and to do one's duty. Here, both "normal" and the "real" emerge from experience and repetition as well as from Japanese soldiers' perceptions of what they themselves and soldiers of other military establishments do and how they do it. Thus, it is important to keep in mind that the meaning and significance of normal military conduct are historical in two ways: they are affected by grander historical changes such as the rupture between the dissolution of the war-making imperial armed forces in 1945 and the foundation of the Self-Defense Forces in 1954 under the so-called peace constitution *(heiwa kenpō)*. But it is also molded by the smaller histories of individuals such as the service members of the Self-Defense Forces whom I have introduced in the previous pages.

The mass media's notion of Japan as a grown-up state suggests that Japan has overcome the childlike state General MacArthur once attributed to it and turned into a "normal state," thus inadvertently referencing not a commonsensical concept but a debate with the power of dividing the social sciences and the humanities. In this debate about the normal state, John W. Meyer and other sociologists essentially argue that normal states are willing and able to exercise their monopoly on the legitimate use of violence. Thus, normal military establishments are those that are willing and able to take full part in war making (Meyer, Boli, Thomas, and Ramirez 1997). It seems that a growing number of politicians in Japan have been subscribing to this logic as well. At least since the early 1990s, which were marked by the end of the cold war and Japan's contribution to the Persian Gulf War, political figures—including the leader of the Democratic Party of Japan, Ozawa Ichirō, Tokyo Mayor Ishihara Shintarō, and Koizumi Junichirō's successor as prime minister, Abe Shinzō—have demanded that Japan become a normal state and the Japanese Self-Defense Forces a normal military (Ozawa 1994).[3]

Scholars on the other side of the debate insist that the meaning of the "normal state" has changed. Most forcefully, James Sheehan (2003) reminds us that states are defined not simply by their monopoly on violence, but by the nature of those violent means and the ways in which they are legitimized. European states, for instance, have changed particularly radically between the beginning and the end of the twentieth century so that they now both guarantee and require the preservation of peace. Subsequently, Ute Frevert (2001:356) notes, the German military in particular has become obsolete as a place for the creation of national cohesion and education. In Germany, national pride no longer attaches itself to the military but—if at all—to a car brand or a soccer team, and patriotic values have lost their place in official and popular European culture. Clearly, World War II and its consequences influenced Germans' attitudes toward state violence and the military in ways radically different from those in the allied nations. At least in West Germany, the break with a military past resulted in an immense loss of prestige for officers, who then had to justify why their costly activities were necessary at all and who generally faced a public that viewed the military with a mixture of distrust and a lack of interest. A military continued to seem necessary but Germans expected it to follow the rules of democracy. When it failed to do so, scandals emerged that further ingrained in the German population a latent distrust in the military's commitment to democracy (Frevert 2001:350–351).

Hence, European states have retained the capacity to kill, but it is of diminishing importance for the practical life of the state and its citizens. The salience of this capacity has declined as intrastate violence has been displaced from the European scene. Violence is no longer thought to be a regrettable but inevitable part of the international order, but rather has come to be regarded as something pathological, a form of disease or disorder that might eventually be removed from the body politic. Hence,

Sheehan concludes, today European men are no longer willing to fight (Sheehan 2003:19).[4]

The debate about the normal state (and the real military), however, has failed to address how the different and changing conceptions of a normal military affect the concept of the "normal" or "real" soldier among the troops themselves. In sharp contrast to Germany and other European states, Japan formally renounced its monopoly over legitimate state violence in a constitution that prohibits Japan from possessing a standing army. Japan's postwar economic miracle has been built on its reliance on the U.S. military for security matters, and the fact that the Self-Defense Forces have never been directly engaged in combat. At the same time, Japan has built a military with the most advanced technology and one of the largest budgets in the world. But similar to Germany and other European states, in Japan the warrior ethos has long faded and the will to kill and die for the emperor has lost its wartime force. While European states no longer feel the need to create citizens willing to fight and die for them, the Japanese state is certainly ambivalent about and unsuccessful at doing so as well. Japan's military has succumbed to a style of self-presentation that attempts to diffuse the very core of what a "normal" or "real" soldier used to signify in the IJA: the absolute subordination to one's superiors, the readiness to die for emperor and nation, the exercise of the heroic morale par excellence through sacrifice, distinction, discipline, dignity, self-denial, self-restraint, and commitment to the cause (Braudy 2003; Ohnuki-Tierney 2002).

Proportional to the increase of international missions and the proximity to combat-type engagements, the violent potential of the Self-Defense Forces is increasingly obscured in the public eye. When Prime Minister Koizumi Junichirō announced the deployment to Iraq in the face of domestic criticism and unfavorable public opinion, for instance, he felt it necessary to say categorically that "no service member would kill or would be killed." Once in Iraq, despite reconnaissance reports that described the situation as far less secure and safe than Koizumi had let on, troops stayed inside the camp for months to ensure that indeed troops would not get in a situation where they might kill or be killed (Konishi 2006).[5]

Despite the symbolic significance of the first deployment to a war zone since the Self-Defense Forces' foundation in 1954, and the media hype about the potential impact on the service members who returned from Iraq, the experience in Samawa was a familiar one to individual service members (Bessatsu Takarajima 2004). From deployments to other missions in Japan and abroad, they had repeatedly encountered local resentment for not getting things right or not doing things fast enough or not doing the right things. They were accustomed to their position at the very margins of an international operation—in the case of Samawa, a place that was considered by observers to be virtually the safest place in Iraq to carry out such an operation. They were familiar with the arrangement of working under the protection of other military establishments because of the priority of the Self-Defense Forces' safety and the prohibition against engaging in combat of any kind. And they were well aware that public opinion at home depended on their every move: a single Japanese soldier's death in the line of duty might have resulted in the collapse of the entire operation and a major backlash against overseas engagements altogether.[6]

With the exit from Iraq, thousands of Japanese troops have returned to one of those missions with which they have been associated for decades in the minds of Japanese citizens; that have marked their identities as soldiers, as men and women; and that have provided them with the basis of their professionalism, their sense of purpose, and their esprit de corps. Among other such operations, 1,400 Self-Defense Forces troops were dispatched to Sumatra in order to provide medical care and help in suppressing epidemics in the aftermath of the tsunami there. Hundreds of others spent a month on a disaster relief mission after an offshore earthquake in Fukuoka, Kyūshū, and yet others provided assistance after a train accident of the Fukuchiyama Line in the larger Kyōto area (Yoshioka 2006). As I hope this book has illuminated, the lives of Japanese soldiers are permeated by an uneasiness, ambivalence, and discomfort, a nostalgia for times imagined to have been simpler, as well as a subdued pride in their work. Their heroism continues to be narrated and re-narrated, but it is a heroism that borrows nothing but its rhetorical shell from the times of the IJA soldier. As a narrative construct, (military) heroism has lived on in the Self-Defense Forces in the absence of war, while the meaning of (military) heroism has radically changed from the dictum of dying for the emperor and nation to the new mantra of risking one's life for the public.

Like most Europeans, the Japanese citizenry now live in what Edward Luttwak has called a "post-heroic" culture (Sheehan 2003:20), constituting a citizenry that is no longer willing to buy into the once-valid equation between military violence and proper masculinity (Frevert 2001:348). Most Japanese, including Japanese service members, also have rejected that equation for most of the postwar era, and the Iraq experience suggests that that perception is unlikely to suddenly change, precisely because the soldier mobilized for international peacekeeping missions has more in common with the (military) hero of a forest fire than with the soldier of conventional modern nation-to-nation warfare. Neither aspires to kill or die for the nation even though both might risk their lives. Even this new kind of (military) heroism, however, remains largely encoded as male despite the—admittedly, small-scale—integration of women, who have made their own sense of their military careers while at the same time being exploited for image-building purposes.

Image-building and other public relations efforts of the Self-Defense Forces play up their violent and their caring, their destructive and their constructive capacities, strategies that can be looked at as multiple layers of a concerted effort or as contradictory, mutually exclusive attempts to get the attention of a public that does not care much for the military. Today, a large majority of the Japanese population has a "good" or at least "not a bad" impression of the Self-Defense Forces, even though only about 30 percent would view it positively if a person from their social environment joined the military (Naikakufu daijin kanbō seifu kō-hōshitsu 2003: 14 and 44). Opinion poll data do not simply reflect public opinion on military matters, but should also be examined as vehicles for the manufacture of a pro-military attitude among younger generations of Japanese who do not share wartime experiences with their grandparents and great-grandparents or the apprehension toward the military of most of the postwar era. Nor do these younger Japanese necessarily associate the civilian control of the present-day armed forces and the restrictions within which they operate with the legacy of Japan's imperialist past. Rather, they consider the strict civilian control of the Self-Defense Forces an abnormality in relation to the U.S. armed forces, which are widely viewed as the international norm, even though they are probably better understood as an exception within the world of military establishments in the current-day world.

The public relations division of the Self-Defense Forces claims that large portions of the Japanese population still suffer from the "allergic reaction" to the military of the immediate postwar period and need to be convinced of the legitimacy, utility, and good intentions of the armed forces. The military establishment uses these ambiguous and contradictory data in a variety of ways: to assure the troops that the armed forces' reputation is improving; to insist on the supposedly uniquely fraught military-societal relations; to convince the bureaucratic framework within which the armed forces operate that an enormous effort still must be put into the improvement of these relations; and to claim that the improved reputation and acceptance of the armed forces is a result of their performance (rather than of reasons outside the control of the armed forces, such as the recession that started in the early 1990s).

Just as the Self-Defense Forces work hard to secure their place in Japanese society in the future, they have taken the making of their history into their own hands. To be sure, such efforts remain entangled and tortured in terms of which story they want to tell of the Self-Defense Forces' relationship to the IJA and how they want to tell it. Aleida Assmann (1999:15) has suggested that at the beginning of the twenty-first century, the development of historical memory regarding World War II has entered the stage where the past experiences of contemporaries, if they are not to be lost, have to be translated into a cultural memory for posterity. Living memory has given way to a memory based on media with carriers such as monuments, memorials, archives, and museums. The Self-Defense Forces' base museums are one kind of place where communicative memory is translated into a permanent cultural memory involving—as with any other such site—distortions, reductions, and manipulations specific to the Self-Defense Forces' vision of their place in Japanese history.

As I have tried to show, negotiations of gender, memory, and popular culture are issues with which the Self-Defense Forces have wrestled throughout the postwar era. But gender, memory, and popular culture are also technologies of engagement with the larger debates that—once silently and only recently increasingly explicitly—have involved the military in Japan: debates about Article 9 of the constitution, the "militarization" of Japan, and the "normalization" of the armed forces. Even if these debates, which have been under way for more than a decade, were to be resolved in the near future and affect policy, sudden changes in the make-up of men and women who join the Self-Defense Forces, as well as in the self-perception of Japan's current service members, seem unlikely, precisely because the experience of the past sixty years has produced a military with its own logic of self-valorization that seems better equipped for the military missions of today than any more conventional, supposedly normal military is. In spite of this recent history, public discourse—some alarmed, some hopeful—has repeatedly resurfaced about the eventual "normalization" or the transformation of Japan into a military power commensurate with its economic might and the will to exercise violence in the name of the state. As discussed in chapter 2, some

Self-Defense Forces' service members share the desire to be associated with the more conventional military side of the Self-Defense Forces—its powerful technology, its associations with the U.S. military, and its potential for making war. Even service members who reproduce the rhetoric of normalization, however, are more likely to wish for an improvement of the Self-Defense Forces' image in wider Japanese society rather than a major reconfiguration of their roles.

The powerful concept of normalization also permeates some of the public relations efforts, which I analyzed in chapter 4. It has been promoted most prominently by Ozawa Ichirō in his *Blueprint for a New Japan: The Rethinking of a Nation (Nihon kaizō keikaku, 1994)* and in an extensive debate thereafter that focused on the question of whether the Self-Defense Forces should become a full-blown combat military or should be fully transformed into an organization specialized for disaster relief missions (Mizushima 1994:21, Fujii 1995).[7] The 2005 defense white paper carried the title "Towards Self-Defense Forces that are stronger in the face of crises" (*Yori kiki ni tsuyoi jieitai o mezashite*), but the Self-Defense Forces continue to fail at filling their ranks and the number of suicides among the troops has soared (Konishi, Watanabe, and Yabuki 2004:162–163).

In wider society, the notion of normalization, and thus the implicit understanding that Japan is not a "normal" country, has remained persuasive as well. It frequently reappears recast as the sense of subordination in relation to the United States, which according to some contemporary critics, "has given life and nurtured postwar Japan." The visual artist Murakami Takashi (2005:152), for instance, claims that Japan's postwar generations were "forced into a system that does not produce 'adults.' As Murakami elaborates, "The collapse of the bubble economy was the predetermined outcome of a poker game that only America could win. Father America is now beginning to withdraw, and its child, Japan, is beginning to develop on its own. The growing Japan is burdened with a childish, irresponsible society; a system guaranteed to thwart the formation of super wealth; and a pervasive anti-professionalism." Reiterating a point Chalmers Johnson has made, Harry Harootunian (2004:75) claims that Japan has become an "American colony and client state, complete with a permanent army of occupation. . . . Japan, a former foe, was transmuted into a friend but not full-fledged partner, an autonomous nation into a dependent client of a newly emerging, postwar imperium" (78–79). These sentiments of a state that is somewhat less than normal also drives recent war films, whose most central undercurrent is that a warped postwar history has robbed Japan of its standing as a "true nation" (Gerow 2006). So it might seem that an increasing majority of people who have grown up under the American nuclear umbrella appear uninterested in resisting the normalization of the Self-Defense Forces. However, critics have pointed out that such a development would not correspond with Japan's constitution. Even more pressingly, they say, as recent examples such as Operation Restore Hope in Somalia have shown, most conflicts are much better handled by nonmilitary means, and that with an increasing number of large-scale natural disasters, a nonmilitary response may be more effective than a military one (Mizushima 1994:16–17).[8]

While violence is no longer at the center of statehood, and while what it means to be a Japanese state has been fundamentally transformed, among the most pressing questions facing contemporary Japanese is how they will deal with the violent world beyond their borders. Thomas U. Berger (1996:323) has long seen evidence that Japan's (and Germany's) current military-societal configuration may not be an aberration of an international norm but rather a harbinger of attitudes to come. For now, however, Japan seems to be taking a different route, as indicated on October 29, 2005, when the heads of foreign affairs and defense departments of Japan and the United States signed the "Interim Agreement of the Realignment of U.S. Forces in Japan." In the absence of public or parliamentary debate, the agreement amounted to a major new step in the transformation of the cold war security relationship, from one in which, at least nominally, the defense of Japan had been the major orientation, to a military alliance of partners in support of U.S. regional and global objectives. It amounted to the forging of a true military alliance, formally transforming the limited cooperation of the 1951 and 1960 versions of the security alliance, with "interoperability" being one key word of the new agreement (McCormack 2005).

Subsequently, more Japanese than ever since the Asia-Pacific War believe that it has become more likely that Japan may be unwittingly drawn into a war, especially now that Japan's quest for a seat in the Security Council may only be successful if it is willing to shed the blood of its soldiers. However, as most Japanese citizens, including service members, share with Germans and other Europeans, an unwillingness to buy into the once valid equation between the exercise of military violence and normal statehood, it remains to be seen whether the Vietnam veteran Tim O'Brien's insight will continue to prove its validity in East Asia. O'Brien (1999:68–69) wrote:

A true war story is never moral. It does not instruct, nor encourage virtue, nor suggest models of proper human behavior. . . . If a war story seems moral, do not believe it. If at the end of a war story you feel uplifted, or if you feel that some small bit of rectitude has been salvaged from the larger waste, then you have been made the victim of a very old and terrible lie.

The "war stories" Japanese soldiers have been telling in this book and beyond have been in awe of the rhetorical intricacies of *war* stories, but they have wisely carried the awareness of O'Brien's warning within them.

Notes

1. By all accounts, the calculation of military budgets is difficult because the way figures are calculated often remains opaque and differs greatly depending on the agency that does the counting. As a report by the Stockholm International Peace Research Institute further cautions, the amount of information about arms is sparse, whether it is quantitative data on the value of arms production and arms sales, data by company, or data in terms of national totals. There are two basic reasons for this lack of information: first, the secrecy surrounding arms production, because of the military and political sensitivity of military products; and second, the difficulties involved in defining arms production and drawing the distinction between military and civil products (SIPRI 2006). Hence, available data on total national arms production/arms sales are estimates, based either on special efforts in which companies are asked to provide estimates of their arms sales or on data on total national arms procurement expenditure, excluding arms imports but adding arms exports. In countries like Japan, such estimates are made by ministries and by defense industry associations. Thus, for example, in the most recent defense white paper the JDA lists Japan's defense budget of $35 billion (0.98 percent of GDP) as third behind those of the United States and the United Kingdom, followed by France and Germany, but it does not mention other major military powers in its international comparative data on military expenditure (Bōeichō 2005:122). The figure presented by SIPRI, however, is considerably higher at $42 billion, and that does not even include military pensions and the expenses for the Special Action Committee on Okinawa (SIPRI 2006).

2. The number of U.N. peacekeeping missions has increased tremendously over the years, specifically since the end of the cold war. There were thirteen such

missions between 1956 and 1989, and thirty-nine since then, fourteen of which are ongoing (Bōeichō 2005:357–358).

3. As of May 31, 2005, roughly 3,000 Self-Defense Forces troops had participated in peacekeeping operations in addition to the activities based on the Special Measures Law for Humanitarian and Reconstruction Assistance in Iraq. About 2,300 troops had engaged in international disaster relief operations since the first such mission to Honduras in 1998 (Bōeichō 2005:535–537).

4. In concrete terms, the law prescribes the engagement of the Self-Defense Forces as follows: The MSDF provides not more than two transport ships and not more than two escort ships; the ASDF provides not more than eight transport planes and airport planes as well as enough handguns necessary to protect their safety; the GSDF provides not more than 600 service members and not more than 200 transport vehicles, handguns, rifles, and machine guns, as well as recoilless rifles and mobile anti-tank shells that are necessary for their safety (Zaidan Hōjin Bōei Kōsaikai/Securitarian 2004a:14–15).

5. According to recent opinion polls, the armed forces are the most prominent concern related to the constitution, second only to environmental issues. The "renunciation of war" clause concerns 33.9 percent, compared to 45.2 percent who consider the environment the most important constitutional problem. These data are from a public opinion poll (question 11) carried out by the *Yomiuri Shinbun* in March 2001 of 3,000 voters over the age of twenty, from throughout Japan. The number that responded in individual interviews totaled 1,946, or 64.9 percent (Naikaku Sōri Daijin Kanbō Kōhō-shitsu 2001:510).

6. As if proving Zinni's point, and as a result of the military's study of shortcomings in the relief effort after Hurricane Katrina in 2005, the U.S. armed forces are currently debating the creation of a specially trained and equipped active-duty force that could respond quickly to assist relief efforts in the event of natural disasters, such as major hurricanes, floods, or earthquakes (Eric Schmitt and Thom Shankar, "Military may propose an active-duty force for relief efforts," *New York Times*, October 11, 2005).

7. For overviews of the Self-Defense Forces trajectory since their foundation, see James H. Buck (1975) and R. K. Chamban (1997).

8. The ASDF receives 23.1 percent, and 22.6 percent is allocated to the MSDF, followed by 11.1 percent for the maintenance of defense facilities and 5.4 percent for "other." (Bōeichō 2005:121). The ranks are filled to the extent of 90 percent (GSDF), 96.9 percent (MSDF), and 96.4 percent (ASDF) (Bōeichō 2002:354). The GSDF consists of twelve divisions, the twelfth and thirteenth brigades, and the first and second mixed groups, all of which are distributed across the Northern Army located on Hokkaido; the Northeastern Army and the Eastern Army, both located on Honshu; the Middle Army, which is spread out on Honshu and Shikoku; and the Western Army in Kyushu.

9. Born in 1922, Sugita had attended the Imperial Army Academy and had been posted to Malay. After World War II, he held a series of high-ranking posts in the GSDF and eventually retired in 1962. In a conversation regarding the possible deletion of the clause "mobilization for the maintenance of order" within Japan's borders in the late 1970s, he insisted that the clause should be maintained. In his eyes, those people who "criticized the Self-Defense Forces for their

power to turn their weapons against Japanese people fight a psychological war to weaken the country, just like the communists had done." Sugita was referring to an earlier deployment of the Special Police Reserve Forces that had helped the police on the bloody May Day of 1952 to suppress the demonstrations then (Sase 1980:98–99).

10. The law that regulates Japan's participation in peacekeeping missions (Kokusai heiwa kyōryokuhō) passed the Diet on June 15, 1992, and was implemented on August 10 of the same year. It consists of five principles regarding the conditions and circumstances that allow Japan to participate in a peacekeeping mission: (1) The parties under conflict must have reached an agreement on a cease-fire. (2) The parties under conflict, including their territorial state(s), must have given their consent to deployment of the peacekeeping force and Japan's participation in the force. (3) The peacekeeping force must maintain impartiality, not favoring any of the parties. (4) If any of these requirements cease to be satisfied, Japan's unit must withdraw from the operation. (5) In addition, the use of weapons shall be limited to the minimum necessary to protect personnel's lives. According to an amendment introduced in June 1998, the use of weapons is allowed only under the orders of the senior officers present at the scene, except in cases where the imminent threat to lives makes it unfeasible to await such orders. The purpose of this revision was "to prevent danger to lives or a state of confusion arising from the unregulated use of weapons, and to ensure a more proper response" (Bōeichō 2001a:212–213).

11. The National Defense Academy (NDA) was built in 1952 as a subinstitution of the Defense Agency, which was then called Hoanchō. At first the National Defense Academy was called Hoan Daigaku; then it was renamed National Defense Academy or Bōei Daigakkō in 1954. Only in 1991 was it recognized as a formal academic institution by the Ministry of Education. Since then, cadets graduate with a B.A., and M.A. programs have been established. To this day the NDA has trained 19,174 undergraduates (127 foreign cadets), and 2,155 as postgraduate students (13 foreign students). While the president is a civilian, there are two vice presidents: one civilian and one uniformed. The department heads are all civilians except for the director of the training department. On the teaching staff there are 350 civilians and 50 uniformed persons. Among the current cadets, 1,850 are male and 150 are female. Cadets receive about 1.6 million yen compensation in addition to provisions. The prime minister attends the graduation ceremony (see www.nda.ac.jp/cc/campus/history.html).

12. Public opinion on the armed forces differs widely from country to country and is difficult to compare because of the dramatic difference among military establishments and their roles within different societies. Japanese public opinion on the military could hardly be more different from that in the United States, where the military remains the highest-rated government institution (Leal 2005:123).

CHAPTER 1: ON BASE

1. In addition to the items I received, a new recruit receives more than thirty other items, including the uniform, boots, socks, gloves, and underwear, all of which are supposed to be used for two to four years (Bandō 1990:286).

2. The program that had been put together for me was loosely modeled on the Experience the Self-Defense Forces Tours *(Jieitai nyūtai taiken tsūa)*, which many bases offer to groups of ordinary Japanese citizens and corporate employees as one important strategy of image improvement, or—as the public relations division in the JDA put it—of "deepening the understanding of the Self-Defense Forces in the population." According to companies who require their new employees to participate in such tours, the Self-Defense Forces experience helps them "shape up," "straighten out their lives," and "prepare themselves for the challenges of a professional life in a company through the physical experience of following strict rules and discipline" (Ishikawa 1995a; *Securitarian* 1997, 1998f, 2000h, 2002d; Higa 2001).

3. The NDA is under the jurisdiction of the Defense Agency and has full university rights. Students are "special public servants" *(tokubetsu-shoku kokka kōmuin)* and students at the same time. All students live in campus dormitories and eat their meals on campus. They do not pay any fees but instead get a monthly stipend. The curriculum is the same as at other universities with the addition of military instruction and training. Students graduate with a bachelor of arts degree and receive instruction and training for a career as an officer. Instructors include both civilian academics and military personnel.

4. With the exception of interviews and conversations with foreign military experts, I conducted all interviews in Japanese. I taped most of my indoor interviews but found taking notes outdoors more efficient because of the background noise in the field. In most cases, I had to promise that not only would I refrain from using the names of my interviewees in my book and other publications, but I would also carefully avoid mentioning other information that might make a particular person identifiable to other service members.

5. In addition to one's name and address, a visitor has to note the office or person she has come to meet with and the time she checks in. The service member at the entrance then calls that office or person to verify the meeting and sends the visitor on her way. Any visitor must then have this form stamped by the office or person one meets with and bring it back to the entrance. There the service member fills in the time that the visitor checked out and files the form.

6. The term "spiritual training" has become problematic because of its wartime connotations. Older service members still use it, but in Self-Defense Forces publications today the newer term "mental preparation" is more common. It was first used by representatives of the Defense Research Institute in 1955. The original draft, *Mental Prospectus for Self-Defense Forces Personnel (Jieikan seishin yōkō)*, was completed in 1960 and distributed to instructors at the NDA and other experts of military training and education. In 1961 the final version was implemented as *Mental Preparation for Self-Defense Forces Personnel (Jieikan no kokorogamae)*.

7. In Japan, the blowing of a trumpet within the military was established with the foundation of the first brass band under the tenth British army command in September 1869. Then military music orchestras *(gungakitai)* were important windows into western culture in the military, churches, parks, and music schools (Tsukahara 2001:84).

8. When a new recruit does not return to base after a day off because he or

she wants to quit and is hiding out somewhere, the Self-Defense Forces' command goes after the recruit and then "discharges the person upon the person's request" (*igan taishoku*) (Ishikawa Mao 1995:105).

9. Once a graduate of the NDA, cadets are free to pursue civilian careers or continue their training as officer candidates and join the ranks of the Self-Defense Forces. Although data on the trajectory of officers' careers are hard to come by, it is clear that the NDA experiences a significant dropout rate; the numbers of NDA graduates who do not join the Self-Defense Forces have also varied considerably over the years. In 1980, for example, 552 of 8,949 applicants were accepted into the NDA. Of these, 451 graduated in 1984, but only 431 pursued military careers. In 1985 the dropout rate was 15.5 percent; in 1990 it was 23 percent; and in 1992 it was 16.5 percent (Bōei kenkyūkai 1996:229). Only 27, or 69 percent of the first 39 women who entered the NDA in 1992, graduated (Bōei Kenkyūkai 1996:228). In contrast to NDA graduates, graduates of the NMDA must serve as military doctors for six years before they can pursue civilian careers.

10. The Japanese word *shiryō* is alternatively written with the Chinese characters for "resources" and for "historical material."

11. Hayashi was the first GSDF chief of staff. Son of a lieutenant general in the Imperial Army, he became the chief of the National Police Reserve, and then after 1954 the GSDF chief of staff. He continued to serve in top positions in the Self-Defense Forces headquarters for fourteen years and had considerable influence during its formation in the 1950s and early 1960s. His affiliation, as well as that of his successors, with various institutions of the Imperial Army was occasionally cited as problematic throughout the postwar era. In 1984 Nakamura Morio served as the last GSDF chief of staff who had attended the Imperial Army Academy. With the exception of the chiefs of staff during 1986–90, when they were graduates of Rikkyō University and Tōhoku University, Nakamura's successors were all graduates of the NDA.

12. The Patriotic Women's Association was set up in 1901 by Okumura Ioko under the supervision of the Ministry of Internal Affairs and later under the Ministry of Health and Welfare. In 1932 the Greater Japan Women's National Defense Association (Dai Nippon Kokubō Fujinkai) was established under the supervision of the Army and the Navy ministries. In 1942 the three largest women's organizations, including the Greater Japan Women's National Defense Association, merged to form the Greater Japan Women's Association (Dai Nippon Fujinkai) in an effort to propagate the importance of national defense, the purification of family life, the disciplining of youth, and the encouragement and training of soldiers for national defense (Garon 1997).

13. The style of Taikō best known today is not more than fifty years old, but the instrument has been used and reappropriated by a variety of institutions for a variety of purposes. The first recorded use of Taikō drums was as a battlefield instrument; the drums were used to intimidate and scare the enemy, to issue commands such as an SOS signal, and to coordinate movements. The powerful sound of the Taikō drums could be heard across the entire battlefield. See Rolling Thunder: The Taikō Source, at www.taiko.com.

14. In contrast to Katō's assertion, in 2004 Japan cut its economic aid to

China to 100 billion Yen, a major decrease since the peak of 214.3 billion Yen in 2000 (see www.people.com.cn/english, December 13, 2006).

15. Chapter 2, Article 26, and Chapter 10 of the Grundgesetz (German constitution) regulate Germany's position on warfare and defense: Article 26: 1. Activities tending and undertaken with the intent to disturb peaceful relations between nations, especially to prepare for aggressive war, are unconstitutional. They shall be made a punishable offense. 2. Weapons designed for warfare may be manufactured, transported, or marketed only with the permission of the Federal Government. For the much longer Chapter 10, see www.iuscomp.org/gla/statutes/GG.htm.

16. Prime Minister Murayama Tomiichi gave a famous speech in 1995, in which he apologized by saying, "Through its colonial rule and aggression [Japan] caused tremendous damage and suffering to the people of many countries. I express here once again my feelings of deep remorse and state my heartfelt apology." Several state officials, including Prime Minister Koizumi Junichirō, however, have repeatedly watered down or even reversed that statement (McCormack 2005).

CHAPTER 2: POSTWAR POSTWARRIOR HEROISM

1. For insightful analyses of peacekeeping and other humanitarian missions involving the U.S. Forces and other military establishments, see International Peace Academy 1992; Harrison and Nishihara 1995; Miller and Moskos 1995; Morrison and Kiras 1996; and Dobson 2003.

2. Japanese examples of this new scholarship on men and masculinity include Inoue, Ueno, and Ehara 1995; Itō Kimio 1996; Yashima 1997; and Asai, Itō, and Murase 2001.

3. The mandatory retirement age of service members varies according to rank as follows (for GSDF): Sergeant and sergeant first class, 53 years of age; master sergeant, sergeant major, warrant officer, second lieutenant, first lieutenant, and captain, 54 years of age; major, lieutenant colonel, 55 years of age; colonel, 56 years of age; major general and lieutenant general, 60 years of age (Bōeichō 2003:144).

4. Anthropologists and historians of Japan have begun to scrutinize the salaryman as a dominant configuration of masculinity in Japan. Most notable are the books by Sengoku 1982; Nakamaki 1997; Asai, Itō, and Murase 2001; Nishikawa and Ogino 1999; and Roberson and Suzuki 2002.

5. In 2005, new recruits and NDA cadets had an annual income of roughly 1.63 million Yen (email information from JDA, November 29, 2005). A single life in the Self-Defense Forces also means that service members have hardly any costs for basic needs. Many have debts from gambling, but some who save their money can accumulate up to 500,000 Yen just during the first year. Some service members who leave the Self-Defense Forces around the age of forty are able to open their own businesses (Bandō 1990:288).

6. In Germany, the conscription system was introduced in 1956, and an alternative service was created in 1961 as part of the military service program. By the 1980s, civil service had become a mass phenomenon that was socially ac-

cepted. Whereas those who refused to do any kind of service were criticized as a potential danger to the conscription system, the civil servants were welcomed as "heroes of the everyday" (Bartjes 2000:132). Heinz Bartjes asserts that two-thirds of civil servants work in realms that once had been associated with women's work, and thus civil service offers opportunities to destabilize gender roles. Accordingly, most civil servants perceive civil service as the more modern form of service. Even representatives of the conservative Christian Democratic Party welcome the new trend toward civil service as a desirable indicator for a new "ecology of the social" and a "culture of helping" (Bartjes 2000:142).

7. More recently, however, observers of the German military have noticed a change that seems to lead away from the early transformation. I interpret the radically decreasing number of officers with a university degree since the mid-1980s as an indicator of the conservative, isolationist, anti-integrationist tendency in the Bundeswehr and a renewed emphasis on the appreciation of the "warrior" and the right attitude rather than academic qualification. Another indicator is the reduction of military-societal relations at the beginning of the 1990s (Bald 2000:122–123, 127).

8. A great variety of clubs are available, ranging from twelve different "culture clubs" to thirty-four sports clubs, the honor guard club, and fourteen clubs whose main purpose is the pursuit of a hobby. For a more detailed assessment, see NDA at www.nda.ac.jp.

9. I found that at first service members tended to use the more general terms, but in later interactions they switched to the more exclusively military language. This shift came with their growing familiarity with me and was probably influenced by my use of military language.

10. As opponents of World War II, communists were thoroughly repressed during the first half of the twentieth century. Emerging from the occupation era relatively unsoiled by the imperialist endeavor, communism was a strong intellectual force particularly in schools and universities during the 1950s and 1960s but had long ago lost its fervor by the time of this major's comment (Steinhoff 1989).

11. There is a considerable body of literature on how World War II is represented in Japanese history textbooks. The topic gained new momentum with the publication of a new history textbook by the revisionist movement for history textbook reform, which was approved by the Ministry of Education in 2001. For earlier analyses, see Inoue 1991; and *Gendai Shisō* 1997. For an examination of the more recent debate, see Kimijima 2000; Hein and Selden 2000; McCormack 2000b; and Nelson 2002b.

12. There are twenty-five provisions that regulate the use of weapons by Self-Defense Forces uniformed officials and units. Article 24 regulates the use of weapons during a peacekeeping operation as follows: "The Corps personnel (including those from the SDF) engaged in international peace cooperation assignments may use weapons to the extent considered proper and necessary in the light of the situation when there are reasonable grounds for the use of weapons to protect lives and bodies of themselves, other Corps personnel, and international peace cooperation personnel who are with them on the scene or those who have come under their control while conducting their duties. The use of weapons

shall not cause harm to persons, except for cases falling under Article 36 (self-defense) or Article 37 (act of necessity) of the Penal Code" (Bōeichō 2005:513).

13. The monetary incentive is also noteworthy for the deployment to Iraq, where Japanese soldiers have made roughly $100 per day, while Russian soldiers, for instance, only make that amount of pay in a month (http://nikkeibp.jp/sj2500/column/a/04/index.html?cd = column_adw).

14. Takazato Suzuyo is one of the prominent leaders of the movement for the removal of U.S. bases and a more general quest for peace in Japan. For the agenda of the organization, see Supēsu Yui at www.space-yui.com. In 1999 alone, Japan contributed $4.25 billion to maintain U.S. bases in Japan. During the same year, the cost to maintain U.S. bases in Germany was about 10 percent of that, whereas the English paid only about 2 percent of that for the same purpose on their land (Kiyotani 2002:78–79; Johnson 2003).

15. Because of the Kōbe-Awaji earthquake, for example, the Kansai region experienced the largest deployment of troops ever within Japan. Troops were involved in domestic relief activities ranging from the evacuation of citizens to medical care and the transport of water supplies. In 1999 alone, service members were called to 815 disaster sites within Japan (Bōeichō 2000a:159). On international disaster relief operations, from November 13 to December 9, 1998, 185 personnel (80 medical, 105 transport) were deployed to Honduras where Hurricane Mitch had resulted in a major disaster. From September 23 to November 22, 1999, about 427 maritime transport units were responsible for transporting materials for international disaster relief activities in the Republic of Turkey. And from February 5–11, 2001, 94 material support units and air transport units participated in international disaster relief activities in India. Both missions followed horrendous earthquakes (Bōeichō 2001a:338).

16. In addition to the military personnel, there are 52,000 dependents, 5,500 Department of Defense civilian employees and 23,500 Japanese workers associated with U.S. bases. Under Article V of the Treaty of Mutual Cooperation and Security, U.S. Forces, Japan's area of responsibility is the land areas of the Japanese archipelago and the adjoining sea areas out to twelve nautical miles. Under Article VI, the United States is given use of facilities in Japan for maintaining regional security (United States Forces, Japan at http://usfj.mil/fact_sheet/brochure.html).

17. America, Ueno Chizuko (1994:213) also argues, has been a dominant and ubiquitous presence in Japan in the postwar years and has been associated with the (hetero)sexual liberation of women, which allows them to "choose" American men, in contrast to the lack of such power on the part of defeated and frustrated Japanese men. The military journalist Kiyotani Shinichi (2002:78–79) makes a similar point in a rant about Japan being "a heaven for American GIs" and a "heaven for sex" for American soldiers. According to Kiyotani, American service members enjoy a certain status among women in Japan that is absent in other countries in which the American armed forces are stationed. In European and other first world countries, there is no such "America complex." Service members of the Self-Defense Forces, according to Kiyotani's account, are not considered desirable men by Japanese women. Apparently he asked women who were in relationships with American service members what

they thought about Self-Defense Forces service members and found that in their opinion service members were not considered "cool" and thus were viewed as undesirable.

18. This photograph has been reprinted in numerous books on wartime and immediate postwar Japan, including the cover of Inoue Kyoko's *MacArthur's Japanese Constitution* 1991. Interestingly, MacArthur himself was only 5 feet 10 inches tall.

19. Christopher Ames (2006) has shown that at least in Okinawa, the U.S. military faces the same insuperable public relations problems of finding ways to integrate into the community. They, too, must soften their masculine image there.

20. By October 1996, 1,657 service members had died "in the line of duty," all of them because of accidents. This woman refers, however, to Takada Haruyuki, who actually was not a Self-Defense Forces service member but a civilian policeman who died under attack in Cambodia on May 4, 1993 (Oka 1998:186).

21. U.S. troops are protected by the Status of Forces Agreement. For a critical discussion of that agreement see Ui 2003; my translation of Ui's article into English (Frühstück and Tokita-Tanabe 2003); and Johnson 2004.

CHAPTER 3: FEMINIST MILITARISTS

1. "Josei jieikan," the new name for "female service member," was introduced in April 2003 in order to reflect the equality of women regarding all aspects of their work and training. This move originated in the Office for the Promotion of Gender Equality within the JDA that had been established in May 2001, following the creation of the Japanese government's Basic Law for a Gender-Equal Society (Bōeichō 2004:272). In 1999 the Basic Law for a Gender-Equal Society was promulgated in order to promote measures, comprehensively and deliberately by the state, local governments, and citizens, for the realization of a gender-equal society. In accordance with this law, the Basic Plan for Gender Equality was formulated in 2000, taking into account the outcome of the twenty-third Special Session of the U.N. General Assembly, "Women 2000: Gender Equality, Development and Peace for the 21st Century."

2. Scholarly analyses of the training and recruitment of women to the front are rare, making this an important blind spot in modern Japanese war and gender history (Sasaki 2001).

3. Population projections suggest that the pool of male enlisted service members will further decrease in the future. In 1994 there were roughly 900,000 young men between the ages of eighteen and twenty-six, the regular recruitment age for enlisted service members. By 2004 the numbers had shrunk to 700,000 and 880,000 respectively. It is expected that they will further decrease by 2013 to roughly 600,000 (Bōeichō 2004:294).

4. The Italian army began to admit women only in 2000, when 23,000 women applied to military academies, making up 56 percent of the applicants. By 2002, however, female applicants represented only 21 percent of those seeking admission. Women seeking to enlist in the Italian military likewise dropped

from 40 percent to 25 percent within three years. A report in *L'Espresso* news magazine blamed sexual harassment by male soldiers for the decline in the number of women interested in a military career ("Female noncom a focus of probe: Faces charge of hitting recruit," *Washington Times*, December 23, 2004).

5. Nezu Shinji (1995:64–65) remembers from his career in the Self-Defense Forces that violence aimed at regular soldiers who stuck out because they did not have a complete education or performed badly was quite common even though prohibited. Each such instance bore the punishment of 50,000 Yen. As a result of that rule, Nezu recalls, service members simply tried to bully without causing a visible injury.

6. In 2000, for example, 3,182 out of a total of 16,833 applicants to the NDA were women. Of the 499 applicants who passed the entrance exam, 33 were women. At the NMDA, 1,749 out of a total of 6,528 applicants were women, while 7 of the 54 persons who were accepted were women. Among the enlisted, the situation is similar. Among the 39,341 applicants, 6,042 were women. Of 2,625 new recruits, 143 were women (Bōeichō 2000a:275).

7. Japanese labor unions began demanding menstruation leave in the 1920s. By the late 1930s, at least two companies provided menstruation leave for their female workers. The state followed suit in 1944. After Japan's defeat in World War II, menstruation leave was codified in the Japanese Labor Standards Law. Today, working women can request menstruation leave according to Article 68 of the Labor Standards Law, but—being afraid of possible discrimination if they take it—as few as 13 percent of women take it. Women feel that they must play by the business rules set by men or they may hit a glass ceiling (Taylor 1988).

8. The "light pill" was legalized only in 1999, but stronger, older versions of the contraceptive pill have been available to women with special needs (Frühstück 2003). At least Fujii never had a problem convincing her gynecologist that she fulfilled the "special needs" criteria because of the unusual demands of her job.

9. The first sexual harassment case was filed in Fukuoka in 1989. Subsequently, the Ministry of Labor reported the need to tighten the Equal Employment Opportunity Law of 1986, which was eventually amended in 1996. At the same time the Gender Equality Bureau in the Cabinet Office created the first draft of a Basic Law for a Gender-Equal Society.

10. The survey was carried out among 1,000 male and 1,000 female service members of all three service branches, the NDA, and several other JDA facilities. The results are based on 989 questionnaires returned by men and 975 returned by women. They were made available to interested parties by the personnel office in January 1999.

11. In terms of the perpetrators' rank there is a clear difference between the experience of female and male victims of sexual violence in the Self-Defense Forces. Whereas perpetrators of sexual violence against women are typically higher-ranking service members (37.7 percent), service members of the same rank (30.7 percent), and immediate superiors (28.8 percent), perpetrators of sexual violence against men are overwhelmingly of the same rank (31.5 percent) and to a far lesser degree superiors (23.4 percent) or immediate superiors (18.7 percent). Most victims of sexual violence do not report such cases. Of the assaulted

women, only 9 percent reported cases compared with 4 percent of the assaulted men. Men reported an even less satisfactory response to their sexual harassment complaints than women did.

12. Members of the United States Forces Japan (USFJ) stationed in Okinawa have repeatedly committed crimes against women, including rape, to which the Japanese national government has only paid attention when it seems politically useful. In 1995 the rape of a twelve-year-old girl by three USFJ service men, for example, prompted the national government to provide several billion yen of funds for major public works in Okinawa to silence the local anti-base movement and the newly enflamed considerations about the return of U.S. base land (Takazato 1996; Ui 2003; see also translation in Frühstück and Tokita-Tanabe 2003).

13. Hence female officers occasionally marry noncommissioned officers, who are transferred less often. Officially, married couples can be transferred to separate bases. Most of the couples on the same base or on bases close to one another did not belong to the officer class.

14. Representations of male service members of the Self-Defense Forces are not entirely free of sexualization. They either appear in gay porn or in weekly magazines of the scandalizing variety. Both examples are rare, however. Gay porn features U.S. soldiers more commonly than Self-Defense Forces members. I found only a few related stories including a homoerotic story of a male service member in the magazine *Badi (Buddy* and/or *Body)* and a magazine article about a stripper who used to be a service member in *Shūkan Shinchō* (1997).

15. In 1998 the right-wing newspaper *Sankei Shinbun* published a series of portraits of individual service members, which was later republished as a book titled *The Self-Defense Forces of the Heisei Era: Today's Swordsmen Are Immortal (Heisei no Jieitai: Gendai no kenkaku wa eien)*. Not a single one of these portraits features a female service member.

CHAPTER 4: MILITARY MANIPULATIONS OF POPULAR CULTURE

1. This episode was reported on the Kanegawa blog at http://cybar.cocolog-nifty.com/ginga/cat17394 on January 26, 2004.

2. It is true that new films—*Silent Service (Chinmoku no kantai)*, *Aegis (Bokoku no iijisu)*, and *Samurai Commando: Mission 1549 (Sengoku Jieitai 1549)*,) among others—give voice to many of the basic tenets of the Japanese right, the most central of which is that the warped history of the postwar has robbed Japan of its standing as a true nation (Gerow 2006). Yet these films also take great pains to create an inoffensive vision of war and the nation, especially by advocating life over death. They tread the delicate line between viewing war as unnecessarily ending young lives and construct certain battles as narratively acceptable. Rather than the nation, military protagonists in these films are protecting things closer at hand such as the family, loved ones, and hometowns. Furthermore, these films refrain from using direct symbols of the nation such as the flag or the emperor, thus following to a considerable degree the rules laid out in the Self-Defense Forces' public relations efforts.

3. This is not to say that popular culture overall is peaceful in Japan. In fact,

SeoTetsushi (2001) has found that toy companies in Japan aggressively advertise toy guns through television series, and Saitō Minako (2001) emphasizes that the world of boys in Japanese popular culture is dominated by "militarist empires," "future wars in the universe," and "wars simply to control 'the other.'" As Aaron Gerow (2006) has shown, newer films feature the Self-Defense Forces more frequently and have also been made with the support of the JDA. Most of them, however, feature the MSDF.

4. Aaron Skabelund (2006) has described Japan's efforts to become a "beloved Self-Defense Force" among the local communities in Hokkaido in the 1950s and 1960s.

5. The defense white paper in comic format *(Heisei 16 nenhan manga de yomu bōei hakusho)* is available in bookstores, but the videos can be ordered only by phone from the Public Relations Division within the JDA, or purchased at JDA events.

6. Usually, there are postcards attached to the posters, on which one finds information on the various ways and patterns of joining the military and the phone numbers of recruitment offices. Interested parties can either call a nearby recruitment office or fill in their name and address and send off the card in order to obtain written information.

7. Some of these older posters can be viewed at the Recruitment Poster Gallery on the JDA homepage at www.jda.go.jp.

8. For a reprint of the poster see the article, " 'Go! Go! Peace!' The SDF wants you," *Japan Times,* August 9, 2003.

9. Prince Pickles and Parsley are to the Self-Defense Forces what Flecki, Nelson, Tom, and Lawrence are to the German military. The German military's mascot is a teddy bear that has four different uniform outfits, corresponding to the four branches of service. (See the homepage of the LHdienstbekleidungsgesellschaft, accessed on August 11, 2004, at www.lhd-shop.de.) In a similar vein, the Austrian military has striven to emphasize its exclusively defensive character. During the 1970s, when Austria's declared defense strategy was still centered on the defense of the entire Austrian territory, a hedgehog mascot was employed explicitly to promote the Austrian military's defense and otherwise peaceful qualities. The accompanying slogan, which rhymes in German, ran: "The hedgehog wears stingers. I advise you not to touch it" (Der Igel ist ein stachlig Tier. Rühr ihn nicht an. Das rat' ich Dir). The animal's popularity lent itself to various uses in neologisms such as "tank-hog" (Tankigel), "infantry-hog" (Infanterigel), "artillery-hog" (Artillerigel), and so on (email communication with Norbert Schartner at the Austrian Ministry of Defense, August 18, 2004).

10. More recently, the public relations division has created another pair of "visual characters" *(bijuaru kyarakutā)* named Mr. Protect and Ms. Future. Their names are meant to convey the desire to "protect the country and build a prosperous future" (Rikujō bakuryō kanbu kōhōshitsu 2006:34).

11. I observed a clear example of the showcasing of soldiers' "humanity" in the personalization of soon-to-be service members at the NDA open house festival on November 14, 1998. In addition to the stages all over campus, four boards had been arranged in a central square. The boards were covered with one-page introductions of NDA cadets, including the cadet's name, cell phone num-

ber, sometimes an email address, hobbies, a brief self-description, and a photograph. All of these self-introductions explicitly expressed interest in finding a girlfriend. One cadet had posted a photograph of himself as a baby. Other photos included a cadet in uniform pants with his shirt off and a cigarette hanging from his lower lip; one could be seen together with friends on a sightseeing tour in France; one was hiking on his own; one cadet sat on another man's shoulders in the swimming pool; a nude cadet was photographed from the side with one leg up on a chair so as to cover his private parts; another posed during field exercise. Perhaps 10 percent of the photos showed the young men in uniform or at least uniform pants, while the majority of the photographs could have been representations of any young man. A group of female high school and university students—some of them in their school uniforms—gathered around the boards and giggled while reading the descriptions, occasionally crying out, "Cute!"

12. In addition, depending on where a person comes from, the live firing demonstration may involve a considerable financial investment that can include public transport, an overnight stay at a hotel, food and drink, and possibly the purchase of souvenirs.

13. In the last several years, the numbers of suicides within the Self-Defense Forces has increased but the last two or three years have particularly pointed at a larger crisis. In 2004, 94 service members killed themselves (GSDF 64, MSDF 16, ASDF14). In the ten years since 1995, 673 service members killed themselves (Konishi 2006:16–17). According to an internal poll, roughly 16 percent of all service members have thought about suicide. The majority of them are service members of the GSDF. Konishi Makoto, a veteran and prominent critic of the Self-Defense Forces who founded a telephone hotline for Japanese and American military personnel and their families, suggests that the increasing number of international missions and trainings has put additional stress and hardships on the troops (Konishi, Watanabe, and Yabuki 2004:162–163; Konishi 2006: 40).

CHAPTER 5: EMBATTLED MEMORIES, ERSATZ HISTORIES

1. Deceased Self-Defense Forces members are not apotheosized at the Yasukuni Shrine, but some are enshrined as deities in prefectural nation-protecting shrines, the prewar provincial branches of the Yasukuni Shrine (Hardacre 1989:153–159).

2. For a list of prime ministers' visits to the Yasukuni Shrine, see Sven Saaler (2005:195–196). While only four prime ministers before Nakasone made at least one visit to the shrine on August 15, Nakasone Yasuhiro visited in 1983, 1984, and 1985. In the 1990s, only Hashimoto Ryūtarō visited the shrine, doing so on July 29, 1996, but Koizumi made repeated visits: on August 13, 2001; April 21, 2002; January 15, 2003; January 1, 2004; October 17, 2005; and August 15, 2006 (see www.worldhistory.com/wiki/Y/Yasukuni-Shrine.htm). The rituals of support from the right and of protests from the left around the political significance of Yasukuni Shrine and the Yūshūkan reached a new peak in early 2003, when Prime Minister Koizumi first announced an official visit on August 15, but then rescheduled the visit for another time to curb protests within and outside Japan.

3. In a year, an estimated 5 to 6 million people, most of whom are veterans and relatives of deceased soldiers, visit the Yasukuni Shrine. The 200,000 who visited the shrine on August 15, 2005, set a new record. On August 15, 1998, when I first visited the shrine, only 12,000 visitors were reported. That was before the debate about the shrine had been reopened, mostly because of Koizumi's controversial visits.

4. The *Schutzstaffel* (defense squadron) was a large paramilitary organization that was a principal component of the Nazi party. Its most deadly branches included the Reichssicherheitshauptamt, the Sicherheitsdienst, the Einsatztruppen, the SS-Totenkopfverbände, and the Gestapo. Charged with war crimes and crimes against humanity, the entire SS was declared a criminal organization at the Nuremberg trials.

5. When they do visit, some appear in formal civilian clothes while others wear Self-Defense Forces uniforms. There is another, similar festival held at Chidorigafuchi, the alternative nonreligious memorial, on October 18. The chairman of the Joint Staff Council, the chiefs of staff of all three services, the Eastern Army's representative regiment, and a music formation participate in that formal ceremony in Self-Defense Forces uniforms. The defense attachés of various countries also attend (email exchange with a representative of the Kaikōsha, February 23, 2006). Nationwide, the association has 1.2 million members. Since members are registered on the prefecture, city, and town levels, it is unclear how many are service members or veterans of the Self-Defense Forces. Anyone can become a member for a one-time enrollment fee of 1,000 yen. The current head of the association is Horie Masao, a former member of the House of Councillors and a former GSDF officer. The head of the central steering committee is also a former GSDF officer named Kurabayashi Kazuo (email exchange with a representative of Kaikōsha, March 1, 2006). The association has no official English translation; the translation I am using here emerged from an exchange with M. G. Sheftall and Sven Saaler on February 26, 2006. In the official Japanese rendering of the group's name, *kotaeru* is written in hiragana, and this choice affords a lot more semantic range than with a Chinese character, and certainly more than English translations, such as "responding" or "acknowledging."

6. Since 1961, a 20-hour NDA night march covering 70 kilometers leads cadets to the shrine, where they pay their respects after changing uniforms, though not on August 15 (Yasukuni no inori henshū iinkai 1999:214).At the commemoration activities on August 15 at Yasukuni Shrine in 1998, 1999, 2001, and 2003, I only once saw a noncommissioned officer in a GSDF uniform visit the shrine together with his wife, who wore a summer dress with a flower pattern and seemed amused if not embarrassed by her husband's sudden ceremonial manner at the entrance to the shrine. She stayed away from the entrance herself and did not make any move to formally pay her respects.

7. This discussion is also based on my conversations with veterans visiting Yasukuni Shrine on August 15 in 1998, 2002, and 2003.

8. I note only several examples here that have dealt with the strategies of memory making in Japan: Figal 1997, 2001; Hein and Selden 2000; Nishikawa 1999; Yoneyama 1999; Yoshida Y. 1997; and Igarashi'2000.

9. Nowhere is the IJA so lavishly and stylishly commemorated as at the infamous War Memorial Museum or the Showa Hall nearby. A new building opened July 13, 2002, with a new collection of artifacts on display, but the museum has preserved and displayed articles associated with the war dead since 1882, making it one of the oldest museums of its kind in Japan (Smith 2002:35).

10. Since Theodor W. Adorno's (1986 [1959]) critique of German attempts to come to terms with the past and LeGoff's (1992 [1977]) examination of the conceptual divide between memory and history, the number of memory studies has exploded. Adorno asked what "coming to terms with the past" might mean. The more recent debate about this and related questions is carried out among scholars who claim that the emergence of memory in historical discourse is a healthy result of decolonization, others who attribute it to American identity politics, and those who warn of a "surfeit of memory" as a politics of victimization. For a critical overview, see Kerwin Lee Klein (2000).

11. Studies on the memory of Japan's modern wars have dealt primarily with the victims of the Imperial Army—enslaved women and girls, forced laborers, survivors of the Nanking massacre, and the formerly colonized in general (Fuhrt 1996; Schmidt 1997; Fogel 2000; and Tanaka N. 2002). Interestingly, the military and soldiers generally have been excluded from the analysis of most of these historiographical representations of war, violence, and defeat.

12. The Imperial Rescript was a long, 2,700-character document distinguished by such obscure Chinese characters that it was difficult even for a college graduate to read. The entire text was read to the troops on special occasions, such as the National Foundation Day (February 11) or Army Day (March 10). Recruits also had to memorize and recite on command a shorter version of the rescript, *Five Principles of the Soldier* (Kurushima 1899: inside front cover; see also Drea 1998:81–82).

13. Widely reappropriated as a postwar symbol of Japanese culture, Mount Fuji was militarized as a symbol of the Japanese empire. Mount Fuji also frequently appears in poem collections and textbooks. The cover of the Atarashii Kyōkasho Tsukurukai's textbook, *Kokumin no dōtoku*, published by the *Sankei Shinbun* in 2000 for the third and fourth year of elementary school, also features a representation of Mount Fuji (Tan'o 2004:113), as did the first defense white paper (Bōeichō 2004a:348).

14. Modern Japanese military history is a huge and densely researched field. Investigations of the relations between military and society, as well as the social and cultural aspects of the Imperial Army and Navy, however, have only just begun. The studies of the following authors cover new ground: Hirota Teruyuki 1998; Drea 1998; Lone 1994, 2000, 2007; Katō Yōko 1996; Arakawa 2001; Harada 2001; and T. Fujitani 2000.

15. The cover illustration includes drawings of six castles and the Imperial Army and Navy flags. The issue was reprinted by Kokusho Kankōkai on August 10, 1973.

16. Tsutsui Ryōzō (1987) has found that the magazine *Boys' Club (Shōnen Kurabu)* is especially militaristic. According to Yamasaki Hiroshi's (2001) and my own analysis (Frühstück 2003:14–54), however, mass culture for children

and youth generally became more and more blatantly militaristic after the Sino-Japanese War and especially after the Russo-Japanese War.

17. "Three stars" most probably refers to the highest rank in the Imperial Army, a general *(taishō)*. However, the rank name is not entirely clear because several different ranks' insignia had three stars—including those of superior privates *(jōtōhei)*, sergeant major *(sōchō)*, captain *(taii)*, and colonel *(taisa)*—whereas the color and stripes of the insignia changed (see http://patriot.net/~jstevens/Isiu-Island/ranks.html).

18. The MSDF Sasebo Shiryōkan, which was established in 1997, and the ASDF Hamamatsu Kōhōkan, which opened in 1999, are similar public relations centers for the other two service branches. I received the information about the painter's identity from the GSDF Public Relations Center in an email on July 15, 2003. The center's homepage is www.eae.jgsdf.go.jp/prcenter/info.html. Ono Hisako has also painted the portrait of Elsie Mpatlanyane, who was honored with a Global 500 Award by the United Nations in recognition of her work at Ecolink. The portrait is hanging at the U.N. Headquarters in New York (www.un.org/Pubs/chronicle/2001/issue4/0104p50.html, accessed March 1, 2006). See also the controversy over John Keane's works at http://ebc.chez.tiscali.fr/ebc126.html and www.mdr.de/artour/archiv/631883.html.

19. When first admitted to the NDA, female cadets were called "cherry blossoms," but today cherry blossoms have cultural currency to a degree that belies their militarist history. The so-called "cherry blossom viewing," for example, is a popular leisure activity and as a social phenomenon is an enormously complex process that eludes one-dimensional classification (Ohnuki-Tierney 1998:213–236). In pachinko parlors, "cherry blossoms" signify those employees who are hired to play pachinko in order to attract more customers.

20. It was used from October 26, 1951, to April 27, 1952. All of these flags are displayed on the following websites: www.fotw.us/flags/jp^icb.html and www.fotw.us/flags/jp^nsahb.html.

21. I received this response when I asked whether the bird on the emblem signified a carrier pigeon or the peace symbol dove and whether the blossoms were cherry blossoms or chrysanthemums, in an exchange with Ishiwata Aiko at the NDA on September 8, 2004.

22. This information came from my email exchange with Kikuchi Shigeru, the public relations officer of the Japanese Association for Carrier Pigeons, on September 10, 2004.

23. Between the establishment of the National Police Reserve and the formation of the Self-Defense Forces, service members who created the insignia not only drew on the worldwide established peace symbolism of the dove but also on what they thought of as other "symbols of traditional Japanese culture"—Mount Fuji, cherry blossoms, and Shinto gates. The first division, for example, features Mount Fuji in the center surrounded by a row of cherry blossoms; the Eastern Army's insignia features the Chinese character for cherry blossom; and the insignia of the first mixed group, which is located on Okinawa, features a red Shinto gate on a black background—also a symbol associated with wartime militarism at a time when Shinto was the one and only state religion. A similar level of amnesia and/or ignorance is at work in public relations material for U.S. bases

in Okinawa. There, Shinto gates are used to make Okinawa seem especially attractive and exotic as a posting location for the U.S. service members.

24. According to Kerry Smith (2002:35), more than a hundred museums and exhibition halls had been established by the late 1990s that dealt with the experience of war, defeat, and the peace movement in Japan. Important analyses of such museums, monuments, and exhibitions include those by Yoshida Reiji 1997; Figal 1997, 2001; Igarashi 2000; Nishikawa S. 1999; Hein and Selden 2000; Thomas 1998; Nelson 2002b; and Tanaka N. 2002. Gesine Foljanty-Jost (1979) has written the first critical analysis of an early textbook controversy concerning Ienaga Saburō's history textbook in the 1970s.

25. The raising of the national flag for festive occasions in schools was within the authority of schoolmasters until August 1999. Only then did Prime Minister Obuchi Keizō implement a new law by which the Hinomaru flag became the national flag and the tune Kimigayo the national anthem. The use of both became mandatory for certain holidays and other events. The Japanese left, as well as activists in Japan's former colonies, reject the flag that was used during the Asia-Pacific War together with the national anthem, and some schools have refused to use either (Aspinall and Cave 2001; Kokka o kangaeru kai 1990; Shimizu 1999). For the exact wording of the law, see Bōeichō 2004a:373).

EPILOGUE

1. The exact title of the article in the *Financial Times* (April 14, 2004) was "A Grown-up Nation? The Hostage Crises in Iraq Sharpens Debate over Japan's Proper Role on the International Stage." The montage that accompanied the article featured Japanese and U.S. military officials signing the peace treaty in 1945 and a service member of the Self-Defense Forces in a camouflage uniform and full gear in the foreground. The article in the *New York Times* was illustrated by a photograph of the entrance to the Asahikawa military base, where the troops that were sent to Iraq had been trained. The title of the article was, "Mission to Iraq Eases Japan toward a True Military."

2. All of these professional labels were conveyed to me in interviews in which service members described how they saw themselves and their roles in the Self-Defense Forces and in Japanese society at large.

3. Abe promised to make the revision of Article 9 of Japan's constitution one of his primary concerns as prime minister. See David Pilling, "The Son Also Rises: The Man Set to Become Japan's Next Prime Minister Is from a Family Line of Leaders But Will His Policies Win the Approval of His Ancestors?" *Financial Times,* September 16 and 17, 2006, W1–W2.

4. An opinion survey among 37 nations of 1989–1991 on the question, "Would you fight for your country in the event of war?" showed Japan at the bottom of the statistics of affirmative responses by percentage of respondents by country: Japan 10 percent, Italy 25 percent, Belgium and Germany about 31 percent. China, Turkey, and India have the highest percentages at around 90 percent. The United States is positioned in the middle with 70 percent, similar to Finland, Iceland, and Russia. The original survey was published by Dentsū Sōken and Yoka Kaihatsu Sentā in 1995: *37ka-koku: 'Sekai kachikan chōsa' repōto*

(Report on the "Survey on Social Values in the World" covering 37 countries). For an extensive interpretation of the survey, see Sven Saaler 2005:37–38.

5. The operation in Iraq had effectively been completed by the end of 2005. Thereafter, the troops spent their days mostly within the camp. They did so not only because their mission was completed but also because the camp came under rocket fire about ten times, which belied the notion of this mission being in a "noncombat zone," as had been proclaimed by the Japanese government (Konishi 2006:172–174).

6. Japan has also helped to reconstruct Iraq in the fields of culture and education for the explicit purpose of "diffusing Japan's image as a likeable country" (Ministry of Foreign Affairs 2005:101). The Foreign Ministry has provided various sports-related assistance through grants. In Al-Muthanna, Japan built a soccer stadium (the Olympic Stadium) and provided soccer equipment to the youth and sports department. Japan also provided equipment to the Iraqi Football Association and the Iraqi Judo Association (Ministry of Foreign Affairs 2005:101–102).

7. These issues have been debated in other countries as well. In Germany, for example, the military was shrunk and reformed in order to be able to "respond to crises." For Germany, these changes became the passport to full NATO membership, possible military activities even outside of NATO territory, and a seat on the U.N. Security Council.

8. Operation Restore Hope in Somalia was an intervention commanded and controlled by the United States that lasted from December 1992 through May 1993.

References

Note: *Japanese publications have been published in Tokyo unless otherwise noted.*

Abe Kanichi, Tsukahara Yasuko, Hosokawa Shūhei, Tōya Mamoru, and Takazawa Tomomasa. 2001. *Burasu bando no shakaishi (A social history of the brass band), Seikyūsha Raiburarî 20.* Seikyūsha.

Abe Kōbo. 1972. Te. In: *Abe Kōbo zenshū 2 (Abe Kōbo's collected works 2),* Shinchōsha.

Abenheim, Donald. 1988. *Reforging the iron cross: The search for tradition in the West German armed forces.* Princeton: Princeton University Press.

Adams, Abigail E. 1997. The "military academy": Metaphors of family for pedagogy and public life. In *Wives and warriors: Women and the military in the United States and Canada,* ed. Laurie Weinstein and Christie C. White. Westport: Bergin and Garvey, 63–77.

Addis, Elisabetta. 1994. Women and the economic consequences of being a soldier. In *Women soldiers: Images and realities,* ed. Valeria E. Russo, Lorenza Sebesta, and Elisabetta Addis. New York: St. Martin's Press.

Addis, Elisabetta, Valeria E. Russo, and Lorenza Sebesta. 1994a. Introduction. In *Women soldiers: Images and realities,* ed. Valeria E. Russo and Lorenza Sebesta Elisabetta Addis. New York: St. Martin's Press, xi–xxiv.

———, eds. 1994b. *Women soldiers: Images and realities.* New York: St. Martin's Press.

Adorno, Theodor W. 1986 (1959). What does coming to terms with the past mean? trans. Timothy Bahti and Geoffrey H. Hartman. In *Bitburg in moral and political perspective,* ed. Geoffrey H. Hartman. Bloomington: Indiana University Press, 114–129.

Akibayashi Kozue. 2003. "Anzen hosho" no saiteigio mezasu: Josei no rentai (Towards a redefinition of the Security Treaty). *Asoshie* 11:172–178.

———. 2004. Anzen hosho to jendā ni kansuru kōsatsu (A study on the Security Treaty and gender). *Jendā Kenkyū* 7:73–85.

Akiyama Ichirō. 2003. Tokushū: Kokusai Jieikan—Sekai kakkoku de katsuyaku suru kokusai Jieikan (Special: International service members who are active in countries all over the world). *Securitarian* 1:24–28.

Akiyama Masami. 1992a. *Rajio ga kataru kodomotachi no Shōwa-shi (Shōwa history of children told on the radio).* Vol. 1. Ozorosha.

———. 1992b. *Rajio ga kataru kodomotachi no Shōwa-shi (Shōwa history of children told on the radio).* Vol. 3. Ozorosha.

Alagappa, Muthiah. 2001a. Investigating and explaining change: An analytical framework. In *Coercion and governance: The declining political role of the military in Asia,* ed. Muthiah Alagappa. Stanford: Stanford University Press, 29–66.

———. 2001b. Military professionalism: A conceptual perspective. In *Military professionalism in Asia,* ed. Muthiah Alagappa. Honolulu: East-West Center, 1–18.

Allen, Judith A. 2002. Men interminably in crisis? Historians on masculinity, sexual boundaries, and manhood. *Radical History Review* 82: 191–207.

Amano Yasukazu. 1993. Japan's peace movement in the post-cold war. *AMPO Japan-Asia Quarterly Review* 24 (1):14–22.

Ames, Christopher. 2006. American village: Reversing the gaze. Unpubl. paper presented at the annual meeting of the Association for Asian Studies, San Francisco, April 19.

AMPO. 1991a. Strategies for war: Fujii Haruo and Douglas Lummis discuss the PKO Bill and the future of Japanese militarism. *AMPO Japan-Asia Quarterly Review* 23 (2): 32–35.

———. 1991b. Suing for the right to live in peace. *AMPO Japan-Asia Quarterly Review* 23 (1): 10.

———. 1992. Inside Japan: the struggle over the PKO Bill. *AMPO Japan-Asia Quarterly Review* 23 (3): 62–64.

———. 1993. Voices from the SDF. *AMPO: Japan-Asia Quarterly Review* 24 (1): 20.

———. 1995. Peace and anti-war: the postwar peace movement. *AMPO Japan-Asia Quarterly Review* 26 (2):32–37.

Angst, Linda Isako. 2003. The rape of a schoolgirl: Discourses of power and gendered national identity in Okinawa. In *Islands of discontent: Okinawan responses to Japanese and American power,* ed. Laura Hein and Mark Selden. Lanham: Rowman and Littlefield, 135–157.

Aoyama Shigeru. 1998. Jieitai no seikatsu wa ikaga deshita ka (How was your life in the SDF?). *Securitarian* 9:7–23.

Apter, David, and Nagayo Sawa. 1984. *Against the state: Politics and social protest in Japan.* Cambridge, MA: Harvard University Press.

Arai Shinichi, Katsumoto Saotome, and Hashimoto Susumu, eds. 1995. *Ano hi o kataritsugu (Passing on stories about that day).* Kusa no ne shuppankai.

Arakawa Shōji. 2001. *Nihon kindai kara no toi: Guntai to chiiki (Questions of modern Japanese history: The military and local communities)*. Vol. 6. Aoki shobō.

Araki Hajime. 1999. *Jieitai to iu gakkō (The school named SDF)*. Namiki shobō.

———. 2002. *Gakkō de oshienai Jieitai: Sono rekishi, sōbi, arasoikata (What schools do not teach about the SDF: Their history, equipment, and ways to fight)*. Namiki shobō.

———. 2004. *Gakkō de oshienai: Nihon rikugun to Jieitai (What schools do not teach: The old army and the SDF)*. Namiki shobō.

Arase, David. 1995. A militarized Japan? *Journal of Strategic Studies* 18 (3): 84–103.

Armitage, John. 2003. Militarized bodies: An introduction. *body & society* 9 (4):1–12.

Arrington, Aminta. 2002. Cautious reconciliation: The change in societal-military relations in Germany and Japan since the end of the cold war. *Armed Forces & Society* 28 (4):531–554.

Asahi Gurafu. 1941. Hitori hitori ga tsutsu toru kokoro (The spirit of each taking up a gun). *Asahi Gurafu* January 29, cover illustration.

Asahi.com. 2006. Iraku rikuji, kikokugo sannin jisatsu: Bōeichō 'genin tokutei dekinu' (Three suicides among GSDF returnees from Iraq: According to the JDA, the "cause cannot be determined." *Asahi.com* March 9. http://www.asahi.com/national/update/0310/TKY200603090525.html

Asai Haruo. 2001. Dansei keiseiron gaisetsu (Commentary on the formation theories of men). In *Nihon no otoko wa doko kara kite, doko e iku no ka? (Where did Japanese men come from? Where are they going?)*, ed. Itō Satoru, Murase Yukihiro, and Asai Haruo. Jūgatsusha, 12–30.

Asai Haruo, Itō Satoru, and Murase Yukihiro, eds. 2001. *Nihon no otoko wa doko kara kite, doko e iku no ka? (Where did Japanese men come from? Where are they going?)*. Jūgatsusha.

Asato Eiko. 2003. Okinawan identity and resistance to militarization and maldevelopment. In *Islands of discontent: Okinawan responses to Japanese and American power,* ed. Laura Hein and Mark Selden. Lanham: Rowman and Littlefield, 228–242.

Asayama Masami. 1998. *Sensō manga no sekai (The world of war comics)*. Natsume shobō.

Aspinall, Robert, and Peter Cave. 2001. Lowering the flag: Democracy, authority and rights at Tokorozawa High School. *Social Science Journal Japan* 4 (1): 77–93.

Assmann, Aleida. 1999. *Erinnerungsräume. Formen und Wandlungen des Kulturellen Gedächtnisses (Spaces of memory: Forms and transformations of cultural memory)*. Munich: C. H. Beck.

Atkins, E. Taylor. 1998. The war on jazz, or jazz goes to war: Toward a new cultural order in wartime Japan. *positions: east asia cultures critique* 6 (2): 345–392.

Auslitz-Blesch, Kyra. 1989. *Akademikerinnen in Japan: Familie, Beruf und Frauengruppen.* Munich: Deutscher Studien-Verlag.

Azaryahu, Maoz. 1999. The independance day parade: a political history of a patriotic ritual. In *The military and militarism in Israeli society,* ed. Edna

Lomsky-Feder and Eyal Ben-Ari. Albany: State University of New York Press, 89–116.

Baba Kimihiko. 2001. Japan and East Asia: Shifting images on an imagined map. *Japanese Studies* 21 (3):237–260.

Bacevich, Andrew J. 2005. *The new American militarism: How Americans are seduced by war*. Oxford: Oxford University Press.

Bald, Detlef. 2000. Kriegskult und Friedensmentalität der militärischen Elite in den neunziger Jahren (The military elite's cult of war and peace mentality during the 1990s). In *Von der Kriegskultur zur Friedenskultur? Zum Mentalitätswandel in Deutschland seit 1945 (From a culture of war to a culture of peace? On the transformation of German mentality since 1945)*, ed. Thomas Kühne. Münster: LIT Verlag, 110–127.

Ball, Nicole. 1984. Measuring third world security expenditure: a research note. *World Development* February:157–164.

Bamba Nobuya. 1982. Peace movement at a standstill. *Bulletin of Peace Proposals* 13 (1):39–41.

Bandō Tomiko. 1990. Joshi jieitaiin tte donna seikatsu? (What kind of life do female soldiers live?). *Fujin Kōron* 5:284–289.

Barker, E. J. 1979. *Japanese army handbook*. London: Ian Allan Ltd.

Barthes, Roland. 1982(1970). *Empire of signs*, trans. Richard Howard. New York: Hill and Wang.

Bartjes, Heinz. 2000. Der Zivildienst als die modernere 'Schule der Nation'? (Civil service as the more modern "school of the nation?") In *Von der Kriegskultur zur Friedenskultur? Zum Mentalitätswandel in Deutschland seit 1945 (From a culture of war to a culture of peace? On the transformation of German mentality since 1945)*, ed. Thomas Kühne. Münster: LIT Verlag, 128–143.

Bederman, Gail. 1995. *Manliness and civilization: A cultural history of gender and race in the United States, 1880–1917*. Chicago: University of Chicago Press.

Befu, Harumi. 1990. *Ideorogī toshite no Nihon bunkaron (Theories on Japanese culture as ideology)*. Shisō no kagakukai.

Belkin, Aaron, and Melissa Sheridan Embser-Herbert. 2002. A modest proposal: Privacy as a flawed rationale for the exclusion of gays and lesbians from the U.S. military. *International Security* 27 (2):178–197.

Belkin, Aaron, and Melissa Levitt. 2001. Homosexuality and the Israel Defense Forces: Did lifting the gay ban undermine military performance? *Armed Forces & Society* 27 (4):541–565.

Ben-Ari, Eyal. 2001. *Mastering soldiers: conflict, emotions and the enemy in an Israeli military unit*. Oxford: Berghahn Books.

———. 2003. Sake and "space time": Culture, organization and drinking in Japanese firms. *Senri Ethnological Studies* 64: 89–101.

———. 2004. Review essay: The military and militarization in the United States. *American Ethnologist* 31 (3):340–348.

Ben-Ari, Eyal, and Sabine Frühstück. 2003. The celebration of violence: A live-fire demonstration carried out by Japan's contemporary military. *American Ethnologist* 30 (4):538–553.

Bender, Shawn. 2005. Of roots and race: Discourses of body and place in Japanese *taiko* drumming. *Social Science Japan Journal* 8: 197–212.

Benjamin, Walter. 1969 (1963). *Das Kunstwerk im Zeitalter seiner technischen Reproduzierbarkeit (The work of art in the age of mechanical reproduction)*. Frankfurt am Main: Suhrkamp Verlag.

Berger, Thomas. 1993. From sword to chrysanthemum: Japan's culture of antimilitarism. *International Security* 17 (4):119–150.

Berger, Thomas U. 1996. Norms, identity, and national security in Germany and Japan. In *The culture of national security: Norms and identity in world politics*, ed. Peter J. Katzenstein. New York: Columbia University Press.

———. 1998. *Cultures of antimilitarism: National security in Germany and Japan*. Baltimore: John Hopkins University Press.

Berghahn, Volker R. 1984. *Militarism: a history of an international debate, 1861–1979*. Cambridge: Cambridge University Press.

Bernauer, Thomas. 1996. Wird Japan zur Nuklearmacht? (Is Japan becoming a nuclear power?) *NZZ*, December 16.

Bessatsu Takarajima. 1991. *Nippon to sensō. Wareware no wangan sensō o dō katatta no ka? (Japan and war. How was our gulf war reported on?)*.

———. 1993 (1991). *Hadaka no Jieitai! Okashikute iyagararete kanashiki, sekai daisani no guntai no jittai (Naked SDF! Strange, hated, sad, the real condition of the world's third-ranking military.*

———. 1999. *Ima koso shiritai! Jieitai no jitsuryoku (I want to know it particularly now! The real power of the SDF)*.

———. 2004. *Hadaka no jieitai Iraku hakenban: Shinbun, terebi ja zettai ni mirarenai (Naked SDF! Iraq deployment number: What you definitely won't see in the papers or on TV)*.

Bix, Herbert P. 1992. The Showa emperor's "monologue" and the problem of war responsibility. *Journal of Japanese Studies* 18 (2):295–363.

Block, Ralph. 1948/49. Propaganda and the free society. *Public Opinion Quarterly* 1948/49:677–686.

Bobrow, Davis B. 1991. Non-military determinants of military budgets: The Japanese case. *International Studies Quarterly* 35:39–61.

Bōei Kenkyūkai, ed. 1996. *Jieitai no kyōiku to kunren (Education and training of the SDF)*. Kaya shobō.

Bōei Kyōryokukai. 1999. *Jieitai seito (SDF students)*. Seizandō.

Bōei Nippōsha, ed. 1997. *Jieitai genkyō (The present condition of the Self-Defense Forces)*. Boei Nippōsha.

Bōeichō. 1997. *Jieitai, bōei mondaitō ni kan suru kokumin ishiki no chōsa (Public opinion survey on questions about the SDF and defense)*. Bōeichō chōkan kanbō kōhōka.

———. 1998a. *Fuji sōgō karyoku enshū. Fire power '98 (Fuji general live-firing exercise. Fire power '98)*. Bōeichō.

———. 1998b. *Jieitai ongaku matsuri (SDF music festival). Marching festival '98 in Budokan*. Adachi video seisakushitsu.

———, ed. 1999a. *Heisei 10-nenban bō ei hakusho (1998 defense white paper)*. Bōeichō.

———. 1999b. *We are Rikujō Jieitai. Catch your dream (We are the Ground Self-Defense Force. Catch your dream).* Bōeichō.

———. 1999c. *'Bōeichō shokuin sekushuaru harasumento, ankēto chōsa' kekka no gaiyō (Outline of results of the "Survey on sexual harassment among personnel of the National Defense Agency").* Unpublished survey (January 14).

———, ed. 2000a. *Heisei 11-nenban bō ei hakusho (1999 defense white paper).* Bōeichō.

———. 2000b. *Heisei 12-nendo Bōei Ika Daigakkō dai27-ki gakusei boshū annai (Heisei 12 [2000] Medical Defense Academy 27th student recruitment information).* Bōeichō.

———. 2001a. *Defense of Japan: Toward a more vigorous and professional SDF in the 21st century.* Urban Connections.

———. 2001b. *Heisei 13-nenban bōei hakusho (2001 defense white paper).* Bōeichō.

———, ed. 2002. *Heisei 14-nenban bōei hakusho (2002 defense white paper).* Bōeichō.

———, ed. 2003. *PKO to the next stage: Heiwa to tomo ni, tsugi no 10-nen e (PKO to the next stage: With peace into the next 10 years).* Bōeichō.

———, ed. 2004a. *Heisei 16-nenban bōei hakusho (2004 defense white paper).* Bōeichō.

———, ed. 2004b. *Defense of Japan 2004.* Bōeichō.

———, ed. 2005. *Heisei 17-nenban bōei hakusho (2005 defense white paper).* Bōeichō.

Bōeichō Kōhōka, ed. 2003. *All for peace: Bōeichō, Jieitai—defense.* Bōeichō.

Boyer, Peter J. 2002. A different war: Is the army becoming irrelevant? *New Yorker,* July 1, 54–66.

Brandt, Susanne. 1999. The memory makers: Museums and exhibitions of the First World War. *History & Memory* 11 (1):95–122.

Braudy, Leo. 2003. *From chivalry to terrorism: War and the changing nature of masculinity.* New York: Alfred A. Knopf.

Bresche. 1994. Blauhelmdiskussion in Japan: Interview mit Tatsuya Yoshioka (Blue helmet debate in Japan: Interview with Tatsuya Yoshioka). *Bresche* May:49–50.

Bröckling, Ulrich. 1997. *'Disziplin'. Soziologie und Geschichte militärischer Gehorsamsproduktion (Discipline: Sociology and history of the production of military obedience).* Munich: Wilhelm Fink Verlag.

Brook, Timothy. 2001. The Tokyo judgment and the rape of Nanking. *Journal of Asian Studies* 60 (3):673–700.

Buchholz, Petra. 2003. *Schreiben und Erinnern: Über Selbstzeugnisse japanischer Kriegsteilnehmer (Writing and remembering: About personal memories of Japanes war participants).* Munich: Iudicium Verlag.

Buck, James H. 1975. *The modern Japanese military system.* Beverly Hills: Sage.

Bunch, Ralph. 1998. *Reshaping the US-Japan alliance: from containment to regional stability.* Institute on the United Nations of the City University of New York.

Burk, James. 1998a. Introduction: Ten years of new times. In *The adaptive mil-*

itary: armed forces in a turbulent world, ed. James Burk. New Brunswick, London: Transaction Publishers, 1–23.

———. 1998b. Thinking through the end of the cold war. In *The adaptive military: armed forces in a turbulent world,* ed. James Burk. New Brunswick, London: Transaction Publishers, 25–48.

———. 2002. Theories of democratic civil-military relations. *Armed Forces & Society* 29 (1):7–29.

Buruma, Ian. 1994. *Wages of guilt.* London: Vintage.

Butler, Judith. 1995. Melancholy, gender/refused indentification. In *Constructing masculinity,* ed. Brian Wallis, Simon Watson, and Maurice Berger. New York and London: Routledge.

———. 2004. *Precarious life: The powers of mourning and violence.* New York: Verso.

Calder, Kent. 1996. *Pacific defense: Arms, energy, and America's future in Asia.* New York: Morrow.

Campbell, D'Ann. 1999. Lessons on gender integration from the military academies. With Francine D'Amico. In *Gender camouflage: Women and the U.S. military,* ed. Francine D'Amico and Laurie Weinstein. New York: New York University Press, 67–79.

Carnes, Mark C., and Clyde Griffen, eds. 1990. *Meanings for manhood: Constructions of masculinity in Victorian America.* Chicago: University of Chicago Press.

Cavanaugh, Carol. 2001. A working ideology for Hiroshima: Imamura Shōhei's Black Rain. In *Word and image in Japanese cinema,* ed. Dennis Washburn and Carole Cavanaugh. Cambridge: Cambridge University Press.

Chamban, R. K. 1997. Japan and its armed forces. *Asian Defense Journal:*6–13.

Chaney, David C. 2000. Contemporary socioscapes: Books on visual culture. *Theory, Culture & Society* 17 (6):111–124.

Chang, Iris. 1997. *The rape of Nanking: The forgotten Holocaust of World War II.* New York: Basic Books.

Chiba Hitoshi. 2005. "Peace and peacekeeping. *Japan Journal* 2 (2):6–11.

Chinworth, Michael W. 1992. *Inside Japan's defense.* Washington: Brassey's Inc.

Chūma Kiyofuku. 1987. What price the defense of Japan? *Japan Quarterly* 34 (3): 251–258.

———. 1990. An end to the cold war? *Japan Quarterly* 37 (3):270–275.

Chung Chin Sung. 1997. The origins and development of the military sexual slavery problem in imperial Japan. *positions: east asia cultures critique* 5 (1):219–243.

Cohn, Carol. 1987. Sex and death in the rational world of defense intellectuals. *Signs* 12 (4):687–728.

Confino, Alon. 1997. Collective memory and cultural history: Problems of method. *American Historical Review* 102 (5):1386–1403.

Connell, R. W. 1995. *Masculinities.* Berkeley: University of California Press.

Conrad, Sebastian. 2001. Thema: Geschichtspolitik in Japan (Topic: History politics in Japan). In *Periplus: Jahrbuch für aussereuropäische Geschichte*

(Periplus: Yearbook for non-European history), ed. Dietmar Rotermund. Münster: LIT Verlag.

Cook, Haruko Taya, and Theodore F. Cook. 1992. *Japan at war: an oral history.* New York: The New Press.

Cook, Theodore F. 2005. Making "soldiers": The Imperial Army and the Japanese man in Meiji society and state." In *Gendering modern Japanese history,* ed. Barbara Molony and Kathleen Uno. Cambridge, MA: Harvard University Asia Center, 259–294.

Coox, Alvin D. 1975. The Japanese army experience. In *New dimensions in military history: an anthology,* ed. Russel F. Weigley. San Rafael: Resido Press.

Cortazzi, Hugh. 1986. A former British ambassador speaks out. *Japan Quarterly* 33 (2):196–201.

Cossa, Ralpha A. 1992. Avoiding new myths: US-Japan security relations. *Security Dialogue* 28 (2):219–230.

Crane, Susan A. 1997. Writing the individual back into collective memory. *American Historical Review* 102 (5):1372–1385.

Crespi, Leo P., and and Edmund A. Stanley Jr. 1948/49. Youth looks at the Kinsey Report. *Public Opinion Quarterly* 1948/49:687–696.

Creswell, H. T., J. Hiraoka, and R. Namba. 1946 (1942). *A dictionary of military terms: English-Japanese, Japanese-English.* Chicago: University of Chicago Press.

Croissant, Aurel. 2004. Riding the tiger: Civilian control and the military in democratizing Korea. *Armed Forces & Society* 30 (3):357–408.

Cronin, Patrick M. 1996. The U.S.-Japan alliance redefined. *Strategic Forum* 75: 1–4.

Cronin, Richard P. 1992. *Japan, the United States, and prospects for the Asia-Pacific century: three scenarios for the future.* Singapore: Institute of Southeast Asian Studies.

Crowley, James B. 1976. Imperial Japan and its modern discontents: The state and the military in pre-war Japan. In *Military and state in modern Asia,* ed. Harold Z. Schiffrin. Jerusalem: Academic Press, 31–59.

Cumings, Bruce. 1993. Japan's position in the world system. In *Postwar Japan as history,* ed. Andrew Gordon. Berkeley: University of California Press, 34–63.

———. 1998. On the strategy and morality of American nuclear policy in Korea, 1950, to the present. *Social Science Japan Journal* 1 (1): 57–70.

Cwiertka, Katarzyna. 1998. Spirit versus matter: Nutritional policies in wartime Japan. Unpubl. paper presented at the International Convention of Asian Scholars. Leiden (The Netherlands, June 25–28).

———. 2002. Popularizing a military diet in wartime and postwar Japan. *Asian Anthropology* 1 (1):1–30.

Dakāpo. 2001. Nihon ga shin ni risupekuto sareru tame ni wa? (What does Japan need to do to become truly respected?). *Dakāpo,* December 5, 8–33.

———. 2003. Jinbun ga senshi suru ka mo tte kangaeta koto arimasu ka? (Have you ever thought that you might die in a war?). *Dakāpo,* June 4, 30–31.

Dai Nippon obenkai Kōdansha. 1933. Shōnen Kurabu dainijū-kan daijūichi-gō furoku: Teikoku Rikugun dai shashin ten (Boys' club volume 20, number 11 supplement: Photo album of the Imperial Army). *Dai Nippon obenkai Kō-dansha.*

Dallaire, Roméo. 2003. *Shake hands with the devil: The failure of humanity in Rwanda.* New York: Caroll and Graf Publishers.

Da Matta, Roberto. 1984. Carnival in multiple planes. In *Rite, drama, festival, spectacle: Rehearsals toward a theory of cultural performance,* ed. John J. MacAloon. Philadelphia: Institute for the Study of Human Issues, 208–240.

D'Amico, Francine, and Laurie Weinstein, eds. 1999. *Gender camouflage: Women and the U.S. military.* New York: New York University Press.

Dandeker, Christopher, and James Gow. 1997. The future of peace support operations: Strategic peacekeeping and success. *Armed Forces & Society* 23 (3):327–348.

Dandeker, Christopher, and Mady Wechsler Segal. 1996. Gender integration in armed forces: Recent policy developments in the United Kingdom. *Armed Forces & Society* 23 (1):29–47.

Darrow, Margaret H. 1996. French volunteer nursing and the myth of war experience in World War I. *American Historical Review* 101 (1):80–106.

Dasgupta, Romit. 2003. Creating corporate warriors: The "salaryman" and masculinity in Japan. In *Asian masculinities: The meaning and practice of manhood in China and Japan,* ed. Kam Louie and Morris Low. London: RoutledgeCurzon, 118–134.

Davenport, Brian A. 1995. Civil-military relations in the post-Soviet state: 'Loose coupling' uncoupled? *Armed Forces & Society* 21 (2):175–191.

Davis, Darrell, and Noël Burch. 1997. Orientarizumu to jidaigeki (Orientalism and period films). In *Jidaigeki eiga to wa nani ka (What are period films?),* ed. Kyōto Eigasai Jikkō Iin-kai. Jinbun shoin, 213–228.

Davis, Darrell William. 1996. *Picturing Japaneseness: Monumental style, national identity, Japanese film.* New York: Columbia University Press.

Denim. 1993. Jieikan, fujin keikan, gādoman: genshoku seifuku bijo zukan (SDF, police women, guards: picture book of beautiful women in their working uniforms). *Denim* 6:83–96.

Dime. 1998. Shōchō posutā kyara no wake ari kiyō jijō (Reasons for the use of ministerial poster characters). *Dime,* August 20, 88–89.

Dobson, Hugo. 2002. Japanese postage stamps: propaganda and decision making. *Japan Forum* 14 (1):21–39.

———. 2003. *Japan and United Nations peacekeeping: new pressures, new responses.* London: RoutledgeCurzon.

Doi Haruo. 1968. Kōbe kaigun sōrenjō shikō (Study on the training institute for the navy in Kōbe). *Gunji Shigaku* 13:67–84.

Dore, Ronald. 1997. *Japan, internationalism and the UN.* London: Routledge.

Douglas, Mary. 1986. *How institutions think.* Syracuse, NY: Syracuse University Press.

Dower, John W. 1993. *Japan in war and peace: Selected essays.* New York: The New Press.

Drea, Edward. 1998. *In the service of the emperor: Essays on the Imperial Japanese Army.* Lincoln: University of Nebraska Press.

Drifte, Reinhart. 1986. *Arms production in Japan. The military applications of civilian technology*. Boulder and London: Westview Press.

Duus, Peter. 2001. Presidential address: Weapons of the weak, weapons of the strong—The development of the Japanese political cartoon. *Journal of Asian Studies* 60 (4):965–997.

Ebata Kensuke. 1999. *Kō mo tsukaeru Jieitai no sōbi (The equipment of the SDF is usable in these ways too)*. Namiki shobō.

Eccleston, Bernard. 1989. *State and society in post-war Japan*. London: Polity Press.

Economist. 1995a. Japan's nice new nationalism. January 14.

———. 1995b. Japan's defense industry: slow seppuku. August 12.

———. 1995c. The Japan that cannot say sorry. August 12.

Edwards, Marie E. 2003. The "ladies league": Gender politics, national identity, and professional sports in Japan. PhD diss., University of Michigan.

Ehrenreich, Barbara. 1983. *The hearts of men: American dreams and the flight from commitment*. New York: Anchor Press/Doubleday.

Eifler, Christine. 2001. Bewaffnet und geschminkt: Zur sozialen und kulturellen Konstruktion der Soldatin in Russland und den USA (In arms and makeup: On the social and cultural construction of the female soldier in Russia and the U.S.). *L'Homme: Zeitschrift für Geschichtswissenschaft (L'Homme: Journal of Historiography)* 12 (1):73–97.

Eifler, Christine, and Ruth Seifert, eds. 1999. *Soziale Konstruktionen—Militär und Geschlechterverhältnis (Social constructions: Military and gender relations)*. Münster: Westfälisches Dampfboot.

———, 2003. Zur Einführung: Gender und Militär (Introduction: Gender and the military). In *Gender und Militär: Internationale Erfahrungen mit Frauen und Männern in Streitkräften (Gender and the military: International experiences of men and women in the armed forces)*, ed. Christine Eifler and Ruth Seifert. Königstein: Ulrike Helmer Verlag and Heinrich Böll Stiftung, 10–22.

Eirei ni Kotaeru Kai. 2001. *Tōkyō saiban no maindo kontorōru (The mind control of the Tokyo Trial)*. Nihon Izokukai.

Eisenhart, R. Wayne. 1975. You can't hack it little girl: A discussion of the covert psychological agenda of modern combat training. *Journal of Social Issues* 31 (4):13–23.

Endō Hiroko. 2004. *"Shōjo no tomo" to sono jidai ("Girl's Companion" and its time)*. Hon no izumi-sha.

Endō Mayumi. 2002. Shinshin o supōtsu de kitae mokuhyō ni mukau, kenkōteki na waraigao no rikujō jieikan (Toward the drilling of mind and body through sports, a member of the SDF with a healthy smile). *Securitarian* 9:44–45.

Endō Yōichi. 1993. Jieitai de seikatsu suru to iu koto (What it means to live in the SDF). *Gunshuku Mondai Shiryō* 9 (154):32–35.

Endō Yoshinobu. 1974. Rikugun shōkō ni yoru kyōikugaku kenkyūjo (The Center of Pedagogical Studies according to an army officer). *Gunji Shigaku* 36:17–25.

Enloe, Cynthia H. 1990. *Bananas, beaches and bases: Making feminist sense of international politics*. Berkeley: University of California Press.

———. 1993. *Sexual politics at the end of the cold war: The morning after*. Berkeley and Los Angeles: University of California Press.

———. 1994. The politics of constructing the American woman soldier. In *Women soldiers: Images and realities*, ed. Valeria E. Russo, Lorenza Sebesta, and Elisabetta Addis. New York: St. Martin's Press, 81–110.

———. 2000. *Maneuvers: The international politics of militarizing women's lives*. Berkeley: University of California Press.

Eschebach, Insa. 1993. 'Das Opfer deutscher Männer' Zur Funktion des Opferbegriffs in der Rezeptionsgeschichte der Schlacht um Stalingrad ("The sacrifice of German men" on the function of "sacrifice in the history of the reception of the battle of Stalingrad). *Sozialwissenschaftliche Informationen (Social Science Information)* 22 (1):37–41.

Etō Jun. 1995. A nation in search of reality. *Japan Echo* 22:63–71.

Farr, Robert M. 1998. From collective to social representations: Aller et retour. *Culture and Psychology* 4 (3):275–296.

Farris, William Wayne. 1995. *Heavenly warriors: The evolution of Japan's military, 500–1300*. Cambridge, MA: Harvard University Press.

Featherstone, Mike. 1992. "The heroic life and everyday life." *Theory, Culture and Society* 9: 159–182.

Feldmann, Doris. 1997. Literaturwissenschaft, New Men's Studies und das Drama der englischen Renaissance (Literary studies, new men's studies and the drama of the English renaissance). In *Wann ist der Mann ein Mann? Zur Geschichte der Männlichkeit (When is a man a man? On the history of masculinity)*, ed. Walter Erhart and Britta Herrmann. Stuttgart: J. B. Metzler, 134–148.

Ferguson, Kathy E., and Phyllis Turnbull. 1999. *Oh, say, can you see?* Minneapolis: University of Minnesota Press.

Fernandez, James. 1986. *Persuasions and performances: The play of tropes in culture*. Indiana: Indiana University Press.

Figal, Gerald. 1997. Historical sense and commemorative sensibility at Okinawa's cornerstone of peace." *positions: east asia cultures critique* 5 (3):745–778.

———. 2001. Waging peace on Okinawa. *Critical Asian Studies* 33 (1):37–69.

Finer, Samuel. 1962. *The men on horseback*. London: Pall Mall Press.

Firestone, Juanita M., and Richard J. Harris. 1994. Sexual harassment in the U.S. military: Individualized and environmental contexts. *Armed Forces & Society* 21 (1):25–43.

Flash. 2003a. 'Sora no hiroin ni aitai' ("I want to meet the heroines of the sky"). *Flash*, May 13, no pp. given.

———. 2003b. 'Toppu gan'—Nihon hatsu josei kyōkan wa konna ni bijin ("Top gun"—This is how beautiful Japan's first female instructor is). *Flash*, June 10, 40–41.

Fleckenstein, Bernhard. 1993. *Homosexuality and military service in Germany*. Munich: Sozialwissenschaftliches Institut der Bundeswehr.

Focus. 1985. Saishō de saigo no "hare sugata" (For the first time in the last "best clothes"). *Focus*, December 13, 46–47.

———. 1994. "Jieitai hatsu no josei pairotto" tanjō (The birth of the "first female SDF pilot"). *Focus*, February 2, 44–45.

———. 1995. Hatsu no "josei shotaichō" wa 27 sai, dokushin (The first "woman platoon leader" is 27 years old and single). *Focus*, September 20, 44–45.

———. 1996. Jieitai hatsu no josei kichō tanjō (The birth of the first female plane leader in the SDF). *Focus,* April 3, 20–21.

———. 2001. Washinton 'bōei chūzaikan' buka o kette kōtetsu (The "defense attaché" to Washington caused a shake-up by kicking a subordinate). *Focus,* June 13, 64–65.

Foljanty-Jost, Gesine. 1979. *Schulbuchgestaltung als Systemstabilisierung in Japan: Berliner Beiträge zur sozial- und wirtschaftswissenschaftlichen Japan-Forschung 1 (The creation of textbooks as system stabilization in Japan: Berlin contributions to the social scientific and economic research on Japan I).* Bochum: Brockmeyer.

Foucault, Michel. 1967 (1998). On the ways of writing history. In *Aesthetics, method, and epistemology: Essential works of Foucault 1954–1984,* ed. Robert Hurley. London: Penguin Press, 15–21.

———. 1972 (1998). Return to history. In *Aesthetics, method, and epistemology: Essential works of Foucault 1954–1984,* ed. Robert Hurley. London: Penguin Press, 419–432.

———. 1995 (1975). *Discipline and punish: The birth of the prison.* New York: Vintage Books.

Fravel, M. Taylor. 2002. Towards civilian supremacy: Civil-military relations in Taiwan's democratization. *Armed Forces & Society* 29 (1):57–84.

Frevert, Ute. 1995. *'Mann und Weib, und Weib und Mann:' Geschlechterdifferenzen in der Moderne ("Man and woman, and woman and man": Gender differences in modernity).* Munich: Verlag C. H. Beck.

———. 1996. Soldaten, Staatsbürger: Überlegungen zur historischen Konstruktion von Männlichkeit (Soldiers, citizens: Thoughts on the historical construction of masculinity). In *Männergeschichte—Geschlechtergeschichte (Men's history—gender history),* ed. Thomas Kühne. Frankfurt am Main: Campus Verlag.

———. 2001. *Die kasernierte Nation: Militärdienst und Zivilgesellschaft in Deutschland (A nation in barracks: Modern Germany, military conscription and civil society).* Munich: Verlag C. H. Beck.

Frewer, Douglas. 2002. Japanese postage stamps as social agents: some anthropological perspectives. *Japan Forum* 14 (1):1–19.

Friday. 1996. Tafu de yasashiku nakereba onna ja nai!? Rikuji sensha taiin & daigaku yakyū buin no otome pawā (If you are not tough and kind you are not a woman!? The girl power of the members of an army tank unit and a university baseball team). October 4, 14–15.

Frühstück, Sabine. 1999a. Immer noch auf dem Weg zur Chancengleichheit? Zur Situation der Frau in Japan (Still on the way to equality? On the situation of women in Japan). *Zeitschrift für angewandte Sozialforschung* 21 (1/2):23–44.

———. 1999b. Jieitainai no danjo (Men and women in the SDF). Unpubl. paper presented in Ueno Chizuko's Gender Colloquium, Tokyo University (January 28):11.

———. 2000. A passion for power: Geography and the culture of empire building in Japan. Unpubl. paper presented at the Annual Meeting of the Association for Asian Studies, San Diego, March 9–12.

———. 2002. Rhetorics of reform: On the institutionalization and deinstitutionalization of old age. In *Aging and social policy: A German-Japanese comparison*, ed. Harald Conrad and Ralph Lützeler. Munich: Iudicium.

———. 2003. *Colonizing sex: Sexology and social control in modern Japan.* Berkeley: University of California Press.

———. 2004a. 'Nur nicht kampflos aufgeben!' Die Geschlechter der japanischen Armee ("Don't give up without a fight!" The genders of the Japanese army). In *Gender und Militär (Gender and the military)*, ed. Christine Eifler and Ruth Seifert. Berlin: Ulrike Helmer Verlag (Heinrich Böll Stiftung).

———. 2004b. Manufacturing militarism: Japan's armed forces and opinion polls. Unpubl. paper presented at the Annual Meeting of the Association for Asian Studies, San Diego, March 4–7.

———. 2005a. Awangyarudo toshite no Jieitai: Shōrai no guntai ni okeru gunjika sareta otokorashisa" (The SDF as avant-garde: Militarized masculinity in the army of the future). *Jinbun Gakuhō* 89 (1).

———. 2005b. Male anxieties: Nerve force, nation, and the power of sexual knowledge in modern Japan. *Journal of the Royal Asiatic Society* 15 (1):71–88.

———. 2005c. Von Männern, Tauben und Kirschblüten: Kollektives Gedenken in Militärmuseen (On men, doves, and cherry blossoms: Collective memory in military museums). In *Über Japan denken, Japan überdenken. Festschrift für Sepp Linhart zum 60. Geburtstag (Thinking about Japan, rethinking Japan: Festschrift for Sepp Linhart for his 60th birthday)*, ed. Roland Domenig, Susanne Formanek and Wolfram Manzenreiter. Münster: LIT-Verlag.

———. 2007a. De la militarisation de la culture impériale du Japan (Militarizing visual culture in imperial Japan). In *Société et militarisme au Japan,* ed. Jean-Jacques Tschudin and Claude Hammon. Arles: Editions Picquier.

———. 2007b. J-Militarisierung: 'Go, Go, Peace.' In *J-Nationalismus*, ed. Jaqueline Berndt and Steffi Richter. Berlin: Konkursbuchverlag Claudia Gehrke.

———. 2007c. The spirit to take up a gun: Militarizing gender in the Imperial Army. In *Gender, nation and state in modern Japan,* ed. Andrea Germer, Ulrike Wöhr and Vera Mackie. London: RoutledgeCurzon.

Frühstück, Sabine, and Eyal Ben-Ari. 2002. "Now we show it all!" Normalization and the management of violence in Japan's armed forces. *Journal of Japanese Studies* 28 (1):1–39.

Fuhrt, Volker. 1996. Von der Bundesrepublik lernen? Der Vergleich mit Deutschland in der japanischen Diskussion über Kriegsschuld und Vergangenheitsbewältigung (Learning from Western Germany? The comparison with Germany in the Japanese discussion about war responsibility and overcoming the past). *Japanstudien* 8:337–353.

Fujii Haruo. 1995. Jieitai no hensen to bōei taikō (The transformation of the SDF and the fundamental rules of defense). *Gunshuku Mondai Shiryō* 11 (180):24–29.

Fujin Kōron. 2002. PKO haken kara 4-kagetsu, higashi Chimōru no fujin Jieikantachi (Four months since the peace-keeping dispatch: The female members of the SDF in East Timor). *Fujin Kōron*:142–145.

Fujitani, T. 2000. The masculinist bonds of nation and empire: The discourse on

Korean "Japanese" soldiers in the Asia Pacific war. In *Japanese civilization in the modern world: Nation-state and empire (Senri Ethnological Studies)*, ed. Takashi Fujitani, Tadao Umesao, and Eisei Kurimoto. Suita: National Museum of Ethnology, 133–161.

Fujitani, Takashi, Geoffrey M. White, and Lisa Yoneyama, eds. 2001. *Perilous memories: The Asia-Pacific war(s)*. Durham: Duke University Press.

Fukuda Kazuya. 2001. Obahan de mo wakaru 'Nihon kokukenpō' ("Japan's constitution" for idiots). *Shinchō 45*, December, 76–85.

Fukuda Tsuneari. 1995. Some questions for the peaceniks. *Japan Echo* 22:32–37.

Fukukawa Keiko. 1995. *Rikujō jieitai kanbu kōhosei gakkō (Cadet school of the GSDF)*. Funabashi.

Fukushima Shingo. 1954. Sengo Nihon no keisatsu to chian (Police and internal security in postwar Japan. *Shakai Kagaku Kenkyū* 5 (1):17–81.

Fukuyoshi Shoji. 1995. Higashi Ajia shokoku no gunjiryoku kindaika to Ajia no anzen hosho (Military modernization of East Asian countries and Asian security). *Asian Forum* 11:38–67.

Fussell, Paul. 1975 (2000). *The Great War and modern memory*. New York: Oxford University Press.

———. 2002. *Uniforms and why we are what we wear*. Boston: Houghton Mifflin.

Fūzoku Gahō. 1894. Nihon teikoku rikugun tokubetsu daienshū kiji oyobi fukusei zue (Reports and uniform illustrations of the great special maneuver of the Japanese Imperial Army). *Fūzoku Gahō* 54.

Garon, Sheldon. 1997. *Molding Japanese minds: The state in everyday life*. Princeton, N.J.: Princeton University Press.

Gendai. 2001. Asada Jirō Ichigaya e kaeru (Asada Jirō returns to Ichigaya). *Gendai* 6:60–66.

Gendai Shisō. 1997. Kyōkasho mondai (The textbook problem). *Gendai Shisō* 25 (10):36–287.

Gerow, Aaron. 2000. Consuming Asia, consuming Japan: The new neonationalist revisionism in Japan. In *Censoring history: Citizenship and memory in Japan, Germany, and the United States*, ed. Laura Hein and Mark Selden. Armonk, NY: M. E. Sharpe, 74–95.

———. 2006. Fantasies of war and nation in recent Japanese cinema. *Japan Focus* at http://japanfocus.org.

Gibney, Frank, ed. 1995. *Senso: The Japanese remember the Pacific War: Letters to the editor of Asahi shinbun*. trans. Beth Cary. Armonk, NY: M. E. Sharpe.

Giddens, Anthony. 1985. *The nation-state and violence*. Cambridge: Polity Press.

Gill, Tom. 2002. When pillars evaporate: Structuring masculinity on the Japanese margins. In *Men and masculinities in contemporary Japan: Dislocating the salaryman doxa*, ed. James E. Roberson and Suzuki Nobue. London: Routledge, 144–161.

Gilmore, David D. 1990. *Manhood in the making: Cultural concepts of masculinity*. New Haven: Yale University Press.

Giuffre, Patti A., and Christine L. Williams. 1994. Boundary lines: Labeling sexual harrassment in restaurants. *Gender & Society* 8 (3):378–401.

Gluck, Carol. 1993. The past in the present. In *Postwar Japan as history*, ed. Andrew Gordon. Berkeley: University of California Press, 64–98.

Goldstein, Joshua S. 2001. *War and gender*. Cambridge: Cambridge University Press.

Gotō Masako. 1981. 'Yasukuni no tsuma' o kobamu (Rejecting the "wife of Yasukuni"). *Sekai*, September, 122–126.

Green, Michael. 1995. *Arming Japan: defense production, alliance politics, and the postwar search for autonomy*. New York: Columbia University Press.

Griffiths, Owen. 2002. Japanese children and the culture of death, January–August 1945. In *Children and war*, ed. James Marten. New York: New York University Press, 160–171.

Gunji Mondai Kenkyū. 1968. Tokushū: Keisatsu, kidōtai no genkyō (Special: The current situation of the police and the mobile troops). *Gunji Mondai Kenkyū* 6 (7):34–49.

Gunji Nenkan. 1943a. *Baji (Concerning horses)*. Kokusai gunji kenkyūkai.

———. 1943b. Kodomo no hoken: Fukoku chōhei (Children's insurance: Rich country, conscription). *Gunji Nenkan*:advertisement section at the end.

Gurney, Joan Neff. 1985. Not one of the guys: the female researcher in a male-dominated setting. *Qualitative Sociology* 8 (1):42–62.

Gusterson, Hugh. 1999. Feminist militarism. *PoLAR* 22 (2):17–26.

Hacking, Ian. 1995. *Rewriting the soul: Multiple personality and the sciences of memory*. Princeton: Princeton University Press.

Hakoda Keizō. 2001. Shimai toshi teikei jigyō ni sanka (Participation in the cooperation business of sister cities). *Sōyū: So You* 145 (4):84.

Halberstam, Judith. 1998. *Female masculinity*. Durham and London: Duke University Press.

Hall, Peter. 1993. Policy paradigms, social learning, and the state: the case of economic policymaking in Britain. *Comparative Politics* 25 (3):275–296.

Halloran, Richard. 1994. Is Japan a military threat to Asia? *Arms Control Today* 24:12–17.

Hamada Koichi. 1996. The pacifist constitution in post-war Japan—economic dividends or political burdens? *Disarmament* 19 (3):46–62.

Handelman, Don. 1997. Rituals/spectacles. *International Social Science Journal* 153:387–399.

———. 1998. *Models and mirrors: Towards an anthropology of public events*. Oxford: Berghahn Books.

Hara Kazuo. 1987. Yukiyukite shingun: The emperor's naked army marches on, ed. Kazuo Hara. Shisso production.

Harada, Keiichi. 2001. *Kokumingun no shinwa: Heishi ni naru to iu koto (The myth of the people's army: What it meant to become a soldier)*. Yoshikawa Kyōbunkan.

Hardacre, Helen. 1989. *Shintō and the state, 1868–1988*. Princeton: Princeton University Press.

Harootunian, H. D. 1988. Foucault, genealogy, history: The pursuit of otherness. In *After Foucault: Humanistic knowledge, postmodern challenges*, ed. Jonathan Arac. New Brunswick: Rutgers University Press.

———. 2004. *The empire's new clothes: Paradigm lost, and regained*. Chicago: Prickly Paradigm Press.

Harootunian, H. D., and Masao Miyoshi. 2002. Introduction: The "afterlife" of area studies. In *The afterlife of area studies*, ed. Masao Miyoshi and H. D. Harootunian. Durham: Duke University Press, 1–18.

Harrison, Selig S., and Masashi Nishihara. 1995. *UN peacekeeping: Japanese and American perspectives*. Washington, D.C.: Carnegie Endowment for International Peace.

Harwit, Martin. 1996. *An exhibit denied: Lobbying the history of Enola Gay*. New York: Copernicus.

Hayakawa Satio, and Morris F. Low. 1991. Science policy and politics in postwar Japan: The establishment of the KEK high energy physics laboratory. *Annals of Science* 48:207–229.

Hayashi Yōko. 1994. Meiji Jingu Seitoku Kinen Egakan ni tsuite (About the Meiji Shrine Memorial Gallery). *Meiji Seitoku Kinen Gakkai Kiyō* 11:82–109.

Heginbotham, Eric, and Richard J. Samuels. 2002. Japan's dual hedge. *Foreign Affairs* 81 (5):110–121.

Hein, Laura, and Mark Selden. 2000. *Censoring history: Citizenship and memory in Japan, Germany, and the United States*. Armonk, NY: M. E. Sharpe.

———. 2003. Culture, power, and identity in contemporary Okinawa. In *Islands of discontent: Okinawan responses to Japanese and American power*, ed. Laura Hein and Mark Selden. Lanham: Rowman and Littlefield, 1–35.

Heinrich, William L. Yoshihide Soeya, and Akiho Shibata. 1999. *United Nations peace-keeping operations: A guide to Japanese policies*. Tokyo: United Nations University Press.

Henisch, Walter. 2003. *Brutale Neugier (Brutal curiosity)*. Vienna: Verlag Christian Brandstätter.

Hicks, George L. 1997. *Japan's war memories: Amnesia or concealment*. Aldershot, United Kingdom: Ashgate Publishing.

Higa Kōjin. 2001. Daigakusei Jieitai taiken nyūtai tsuā-ki (Notes on an experience the SDF tour of university students). *Securitarian* 11:38–42.

High, Peter B. 2003(1995). *The imperial screen: Japanese film culture in the Fifteen Years' War, 1931–1945*. Madison: University of Wisconsin Press.

Higuchi Ryōko. 2002. Sasebo shiryōkan 'sēru tawā' de kashiwade no eraseru gaido o mezasu kaijō Jieikan (A member of the ASDF who pursues the laudable position of a guide of the "sales tower" at the Sasebo library). *Securitarian* 11:44–45.

Hikosaka Tai. 1991. *Dansei shinwa (Myths of men)*. Komichi shobō.

Hirakawa T. 1946. *Kamu kamu ebburibodi: Illustrated text, English conversation (Come come everybody: Illustrated text, English conversation)*. Daiichi Gekkansha.

Hirata Toshiharu. 1977. Meiji guntai ni okeru 'chūkun aikoku' no seishin no seiritsu (The foundation of "loyalty and patriotism" in the Meiji era's armed forces). *Gunji Shigaku* 50:2–20.

Hirota Tadashi. 1998. Jieitai no kōhō no monomōsu (What the public relations office of the Self-Defense Forces wants to say). *Securitarian* 4:13–15.

Hirota Teruyuki. 1998. *Rikugun shōkō no kyōiku shakaishi. Risshin shusse to tennōsei (Social history of the education at the army academy. Careerism and the Tennō ideology)*. Yokohama.

Hisauchi Michio. 1993. Japan's junglest day. In *Monkey brain sushi: New tastes in Japanese fiction*, ed. and trans. Alfred Birnbaum. Kodansha International.

Hixson, Walter L. 2000. *Historical memory and representation of the Vietnam War*. New York: Garland Publishers.

Hoe Isamu. 1993. Kanbojia to Jieitai (Cambodia and the SDF). *Gunshuku Mondai Shiryō* 9 (154):30–31.

Holmes, Robert L. 1998. The challenge of nonviolence in the new world order. In *The adaptive military: armed forces in a turbulent world*, ed. James Burk. New Brunswick, London: Transaction Publishers.

Honda Noriko. 2001. Kichi o kage de sasaeru seieitachi (The powerful who support the base behind the scenes). *Securitarian* 10:30–35.

Honda Shōichi. 1990. Hinkon naru seishin: Jieitai wa beigun no banken ka? (Impoverished soul: Are the SDF the watchdog of the U.S. armed forces?). *Asahi Jānaru*, October 26, 94–95.

Hook, Glenn D. 1982. Education as business: whither peace education? *Bulletin of Peace Proposals* 13 (1):15–23.

———. 1996. *Militarization and demilitarization in contemporary Japan*. London: Routledge.

———. 1998. Japan and the ASEAN regional forum: bilateralism, multilateralism or supplementalism. *Japanstudien: Jahrbuch des Deutschen Instituts für Japanstudien der Philipp Franz von Siebold Stiftung* 10:159–188.

Hook, Glenn D., and Gavan McCormack. 2001. *Japan's contested constitution: Documents and analysis*. London: Routledge.

Horner, Charles. 1996/97. The third side of the triangle: the China-Japan dimension. *The National Interest* 10 (46):23–31.

Hoshi Tōru. 2001. Shinryaku no nagare ni hankōshikirenakatta watashi (I could not resist the pressure of aggression). *Shūkan Kinyōbi* 371:54–57.

Hosokawa Shūhei. 2002. Experiencing blackness from afar. In *Popular music studies*, ed. Keith Negus and David Hesmondalgh. London: Blackwell.

Hoston, Germain A. 1996. *The state, identity, and the national question in China and Japan*. Princeton: Princeton University Press.

Howe, Leo. 2000. Risk, ritual and performance. *Journal of the Royal Anthropological Institute* 6:63–79.

Hoyt, Edwin P. 1985. *The militarists: the rise of Japanese militarism since WW II*. New York: Donald I. Fine.

Hummel, Hartwig. 1996. Das Ende der Aufrüstung in Japan: Chancen für eine Friedensdividende? (The end of Japanese rearmament: Chances for a peace dividend?) Bonn: Bonn International Center for Conversion.

Humphreys, Leonard A. 1995. *The way of the heavenly sword: the Japanese army in the 1920's*. Stanford: Stanford University Press.

Hunt, David. 2000. War crimes and the Vietnamese people: American representations and silences. In *Censoring history: Citizenship and memory in Japan*,

Germany, and the United States, ed. Laura Hein and Mark Selden. Armonk, NY: M. E. Sharpe.

Hunt, Leslie. 1961. Air force mascots. *Royal Air Forces Quarterly* 1 (1):36–39.

lbraith, Stuart, and IV. 1994. *Japanese science fiction, fantasy and horror films: A critical analysis of 103 features released in the United States, 1950–1992.* Jefferson, NC: McFarland.

Ichikawa Homi. 2001. Kuriādo fō teiku ofu (Cleared for take off). *Sōyū: So You* 145 (4):81.

Igarashi Takeshi, and Akio Watanabe. 1997. Die Verteidigungsrichtlinien im übergeordneten Zusammenhang (The Security Guidelines in the larger context of security concerns). *Japan Echo* 3:83–87.

Igarashi Yoshikuni. 2000. *Bodies of memory: Narratives of war in postwar Japanese culture, 1945–1970.* Princeton: Princeton University Press.

Ignatieff, Michael, ed. 2005. *American exceptionalism and human rights.* Princeton: Princeton University Press.

Ikeda Itsunori. 1994. Giving the SDF new fangs. *AMPO Japan-Asia Quarterly Review* 25 (2):7–9.

Ikegami Eiko. 1995. *The taming of the samurai.* Cambridge, MA: Harvard University Press.

Ikemoto Kaoru. 2001. Nijū isseiki o ninau rikusō (Soldiers carrying the 21st century). *Sōyū: So You* 145 (4):93.

Imada Erika. 2003. Jendā-ka sareru 'kodomo' (Gendered "children"). *Soshioroji* 48 (1):57–74.

Inaba Masaki. 1998. Some comments on the legal position in Japan by Occur program director. The International Lesbian and Gay Association, (accessed June 12). Available at http://www.aglbic.org.

Inoguchi Takashi. 1991. Japan's response to the gulf crisis: an analytic overview. *Journal of Japanese Studies* 17 (2):257–273.

———. 1992. Japan's role in international affairs. *Survival* 34 (2):71–87.

"Inokura" Kichi Bukai, eds. 1998. *Kichi no yomikata arukikata (How to read and walk a base).* Meiseki shoten.

Inoue Kazuhiko. 2001. Sekai no naka no Nippon (Japan in the world). *Sōyū: So You* 145 (4):44–45.

Inoue Kazuhiko, Masaaki Minegishi, and Shinji Hasuo. 2001. Jieitai 'senjo e!' (The SDF to the front!). *Sapio,* November 14, 7–9.

Inoue Kyoko. 1991. *MacArthur's Japanese constitution.* Chicago: University of Chicago Press.

Inoue Teruko, Ueno Chizuko, and Ehara Yumiko, eds. 1995. *Danseigaku (Men's studies).* Iwanami shoten.

International Peace Academy. 1992. *The United Nations peace-keeping operations: recent experiences and future prospects.* Report of the Tokyo symposium, September 3–4, 1991. Tokyo: United Nations University, International Peace Academy.

Ioka Kumi. 2002a. Tokushū: Josei Jieikan o yomu—Josei Jieikan no ishiki (Special: Reading female Jieikan—The consciousness of female Jieikan). *Securitarian* 2:16–19.

———. 2002b. Josei Jieikan no ayumi (The progress of female Jieikan). *Securitarian* 2:20–22.

Ishibashi Masashi. 1984. The road to unarmed neutrality. *Japan Quarterly* 31 (2): 142–143.

Ishihara Shintaro. 1989. *The Japan that can say no.* New York: Simon and Schuster.

Ishii-Kuntz, Masako. 2002. Balancing fatherhood and work: Emergence of diverse masculinities in contemporary Japan. In *Men and masculinities in contemporary Japan: Dislocating the salaryman doxa,* ed. James E. Roberson and Suzuki Nobue. London: Routledge, 198–216.

Ishikawa Mao. 1995a. Okinawa no Jieitai to watashi (The SDF in Okinawa and I). *Gunshuku Mondai Shiryō* 11 (180):30–33.

———. 1995b. *Okinawa to Jieitai (Okinawa and the SDF).* Kōbunken.

Ishizuki Shizue, and Yabuta Yutaka. 1999. *Joseishi o manabu hito no tame ni (For people who study women's history).* Seikai shisōsha.

Ito Kenichi. 1991. The Japanese state of mind: deliberations on the gulf crisis. *Journal of Japanese Studies* 17 (2):275–290.

Itō Kimio. 1996. *Danseigaku nyūmon (Introduction to men's studies).* Sakuhinsha

Itō Narihiko. 1995. Guntai de kuni ga mamoreru ka (Can one protect a country with the military?). *Gunshuku Mondai Shiryō* 11 (180):4–9.

Itō Nobuyuki. 2001. Bōeichō kara no senshi: Manshū bōjū daijiken (History from the Defense Agency: That Manchurian incident). *Securitarian* 9:56–57.

Itō Toshiya. 1999. *Puraido: unmei no shunkan (Pride: A moment of fate).* Toei video.

Itoh, Mayumi. 1995. Expanding Japan's role in the United Nations. *Pacific Review* 8 (2): 283–302.

Iwabashi Ikurō. 1988. *"Shōnen Kurabu" to dokushatachi ("Youth Club" and its readers).* Zōonsha.

Izawa Motohiko. 2003. Tokushū: Zakkubaran ni Jieitai—Dokusha no koe de kiku "koko ga shiritai Jieitai" (Special: Outspoken SDF—What readers want to know about the SDF). *Securitarian* 3:19–22.

Jager, Sheila Miyoshi. 1997. Manhood, the state and the Yongsan war memorial, South Korea. *Museum Anthropology* 21 (3):33–39.

Jahoda, G. 1988. Critical notes and reflections on "social representations." *European Journal of Social Psychology* 18:195–209.

James, Daniel. 1997. Meatpackers, Peronists, and collective memory: A view from the South." *American Historical Review* 102 (5):1404–1412.

Japan Defense Agency. 1999. *Bōeichō chōkan Norota Hōsei (The director of the Defense Agency Norota Hōsei).* http:www.kantei.go.jp/jp/9901kakuryo/16norotahousei.html:July 6.

———. 2005. *Defense of Japan.* Tokyo: Japan Defense Agency.

Japan Defense Agency Public Information Division, ed. 2003. *All for peace: JDA, Japan SDF—defense.* Tokyo: Japan Defense Agency.

Japan Echo. 2004. Japan dispatches the SDF to Iraq. *Japan Echo* 2:6–12.

Japan VAWW-NET, ed. 2001. *Koko made hidoi! 'Tsukuru kai' rekishi kōmin kyōkasho (This is terrible! History and civics textbooks by the "Tsukuru kai").* Akashi shoten.

Jay, Martin. 2003. *Refractions of violence.* London: Routledge.

Jidō Hyakka Daijiten Kankōkai. 1937. *Jidō hyakka daijiten (Encyclopedia for children).* Jidō hyakka daijiten kankōkai.

Jodelet, D. 1984. The representation of the body and its transformations. In *Social representations,* ed. R. M. Farr and Serge Moskovici. Cambridge: Cambridge University Press.

Johnson, Chalmers. 1996a. American military bases in San Diego and Okinawa. *JPRI Critique* 3 (6): http://www.jpri.org.

———. 1996b. Go-banken-sama, go home! *The Bulletin of the Atomic Scientists* July/August:22–29.

———. 2003. *Three rapes: The Status of Forces Agreement and Okinawa.* http://www.japanfocus.org (accessed November 29).

Jones, Peter D. 1991. The Asian arms market. *AMPO Japan-Asia Quarterly Review* 23 (2):14–17.

Josei Jishin. 2001. Chichi ni akogarete: Watashi mo 'jieitai pairotto' (Adoring my father: I also became an "SDF pilot"). *Josei Jishin,* March 6, 131–132.

———. 2001. Jieikan tsumatachi no 'chinmoku no sakebi'! (The "silent shouts" of the wives of members of the Self-Defense Forces!). *Josei Jishin,* December 4, 191–192.

Jun Jinsok. 2001. South Korea: Consolidating democratic civilian control. In *Coercion and governance: The declining political role of the military in Asia,* ed. Muthiah Alagappa. Stanford: Stanford University Press, 121–142.

Kaizuma Keiko. 2004. *Kindai Nihon no fuseiron to jendā poritikku (Theories on modern Japanese fatherhood and gender politics).* Sakuhinsha.

Kakehashi Kumiko. 2002a. Tokushū: Josei Jieikan o yomu—Bōeichō ga susumeru danjo kyōdō sanka e no torikumi (Special: Reading female Jieikan—the Defense Agency's position on matters of the integration of women). *Securitarian* 2:23–24.

———. 2002b. Tokushū: Josei Jieikan o yomu—Kore kara no josei Jieikan to Jieitai (Special: Reading female service members—the future of female service members and the SDF). *Securitarian* 2:25–28.

———. 2002c. Tokushū: Kanbu kyōiku no arikata (Special: Officers training). *Securitarian* 10:12–28.

Kakiya Isao. 2001. Meiyo naki Jieikan no 'hahei': Jieikan wa 'banken' de wa nai (The gloryless "dispatch" of the members of the Self-Defense Forces: They are not watchdogs). *Seiron,* December, 130–141.

Kamata Takeshi. 2002. Guntai no rekishi to kōhō (The history and aftermath of the military). *Securitarian* 9:20–23.

Kameyama Michiko. 1997(1984). *Kindai Nihon kangoshi II: Sensō to kango (History of nursing in modern Japan II: War and nursing).* Domesu shuppan.

Kaneko Hiromasa, Sasaki Kiyomitsu, Chiba Tokuji, and Konishi Masayasu. 1992. *Nihon-shi no naka no dōbutsu-shi (Animal history within the history of Japan).* Tōkyōdō shuppan.

Kaneko, Martin. 1998. Daigaku no sensō—sengo sekinin to 'Taiheiyō sensōka no seishun'-ten ni tsuite (The war of universities—postwar responsibilities and the exhibition "Youth during the Pacific War"). *Nihon Joshi Daigaku Ningen Shakaigakubu Kiyō* 8:101–126.

Kaneko, Mātin. 2001. Nihonkoku no sengo shori to Nihonjin no sensōkan (Postwar reparations by the Japanese state and the view of the war by the Japanese people). *Buraku Kaihō Hiroshima* 54 (9):59–83.

Kaneko Ryūichi. 2003a. The origin and development of Japanese art photography. In *The history of Japanese photography*, ed. Dana Friis–Hansen, Anne Wilkes Tucker, Kaneko Ryūichi, and Takeba Joe. New Haven: Yale University Press, 100–141.

———. 2003b. Realism and propaganda: The photographer's eye trained on society. In *The history of Japanese photography*, ed. Dana Friis-Hansen, Anne Wilkes Tucker, Kaneko Ryūichi, and Takeba Joe. New Haven: Yale University Press, 184–207.

Kanō Mikiyo. 1995. *Onnatachi no 'jūgo' (Women's "home front")*. Inpakuto shuppankai.

———. 2002. *Tennōsei to jendā (The emperor system and gender)*. Inpakuto shuppankai.

Kansteiner, Wulf. 2002. Finding meaning in memory: A methodological critique of collective memory studies. *History and Theory* 41 (May):179–197.

Karlin, Jason G. 2002. The gender of nationalism: Competing masculinities in Meiji Japan. *Journal of Japanese Studies* 28 (1):41–77.

Kasson, John F. 2001. *Houdini, Tarzan, and the perfect man: The white male body and the challenge of modernity in America*. New York: Hill and Wang.

Katahara Eiichi. 2001. Japan: From containment to normalization. In *Coercion and governance: The declining political role of the military in Asia*, ed. Muthiah Alagappa. Stanford: Stanford University Press, 69–91.

Katō Mikirō. 1997. Maegaki: Jidaigeki no inwentorī (Preface: The inventory of period films). In *Jidaigeki eiga to wa nani ka (What are period films?)*, ed. Kyōto Eigasai Jikkō Iin-kai. Jinbun shoin, 7–10.

Katō Yōko. 1996. *Chōheisei to kindai Nihon, 1868–1945 (The conscription system and modern Japan, 1868–1945)*. Yoshikawa kobunkan.

Katō Yōzō. 1979. *Shiroku: Jieitaishi (Personal record: History of the Self-Defense Forces)*. Gekkan seisaku seiji geppōsha.

Katsumoto Saotome. 1998. *Sensō o kataritsugu (Passing down a story of war)*. Iwanami shoten.

Katsuno Katsumi. 1927. Shinkei suijaku to sono ryōhō (Neurasthenia and its cures). *Senyū* 203:28–34.

Katzenstein, Mary Fainsod. 1998. *Faithful and fearless. Moving feminist protest inside the church and military*. Princeton: Princeton University Press.

Katzenstein, Peter J. 1996a. *Cultural norms and national security: Police and military in postwar Japan*. Ithaca: Cornell University Press.

———. 1996b. Introduction: Alternative perspectives on national security. In *The culture of national security: Norms and identity in world politics*, ed. Peter J. Katzenstein. New York: Columbia University Press, 1–32.

Kawamura Sumihiko. 1999. The SLOC protection and Korea-Japan cooperation. Paper presented at the "Conference on future strategic cooperation among the United States, Japan, and Korea for securing peace in the Korean peninsula," Seoul, Korea, April 22–23.

Kayajima Hitoshi. 2001. Waga kokoro no furusato Jieitai (Home of our hearts: The SDF). *Sōyū: So You* 145 (4):50–51.

Keller, Jörg. 2003. Küss' die Hand gnäd'ge Frau . . . —oder: Ist die Soldatin möglich? (Respectfully madam or is the female soldier possible?) In *Gender und Militär: Internationale Erfahrungen mit Frauen und Männern in Streitkräften*, ed. Christine Eifler and Ruth Seifert. Königstein: Ulrike Helmer Verlag (Heinrich Böll Stiftung), 248–266.

Kelsky, Karen. 2001. *Women on the verge: Japanese women, Western dreams.* Durham: Duke University Press.

Kennedy, M. D. 1973[1924]. *The military side of Japanese life.* Westport: Greenwood Press.

Kenyon, Elizabeth, and Sheila Hawker. 1999. "Once would be enough": some reflections on the issue of safety for lone researchers. *International Journal of Social Research Methodology* 45 (2):313–327.

Kikuchi Katsuo. 1997. 'Senyū' Mishima Yukio-san kara no tegami (Letters from "comrade" Mr. Mishima Yukio). *Bungei Shunjū*, December, 166–176.

Kikuchi Masayuki. 2000. *Ganbare josei jieikan (Good luck women soldiers).* Ikarosu shuppan.

Kikuchi Tetsuo. 1991. Kyōkasho ni nai Nihonshi (Japanese history that is not in the textbooks). *Rekishi Hyōron* 493:1–8.

Kim Hakjoon. 1988. The American military government in South Korea, 1945–1948: Its formation, policies, and legacies. *Asian Perspective* (Spring–Summer): 51–83.

Kim Kyun Hyun. 2004. *The remasculinization of Korean cinema.* Durham: Duke University Press.

Kim Tai Sung. 1974. Japan's security policy: A study of the relationships among the decision makers' perceptions, the press, and public opinion during 1952–1971. PhD diss., Michigan State University.

Kimijima Kazuhiko. 2000. The continuing legacy of Japanese colonialism: The Japan-South Korea Joint Study Group on History Textbooks. In *Censoring history: Citizenship and memory in Japan, Germany, and the United States*, ed. Laura Hein and Mark Selden. Armonk, NY: M. E. Sharpe, 203–225.

Kimoto Shigeo. 1993. Following the troops into Cambodia. *AMPO Japan-Asia Quarterly Review* 24 (1):29–33.

Kinmonth, Earl H. 1981. *The self-made man in Meiji Japanese thought: From samurai to salary man.* Berkeley: University of California Press.

Kinoshita Hideaki. 1998. Jaianto na Jieitai no taiiku (Sports of the giant SDF). *Securitarian* 5:6–25.

Kinoshita Naoyuki. 2000. From weapon to work of art: "sword hunts" in modern Japan. *Senri Ethnological Studies* 54:119–136.

———. 2003. The early years of Japanese photography. In *The history of Japanese photography*, ed. Dana Friis-Hansen, Anne Wilkes Tucker, Kaneko Ryūichi, and Takeba Joe. New Haven: Yale University Press with Museum of Fine Arts, Houston, 14–99.

Kinsella, Sharon. 1995. Cuties in Japan. In *Women, media and consumption in*

Japan, ed. Lise Skov and Brian Moeran. Richmond, Surrey, England: Curzon Press, 220–254.

———. 2000. *Adult manga: Culture and power in contemporary Japanese society.* Honolulu: University of Hawaii Press.

Kitami Kenichi. 2002. Hotto suru warai ni kodawari tsuzuketai (I always want to show comedy that makes people feel relieved) *Securitarian* 1:62–64.

Kitaoka Shinichi. 1995. Die Torheit der Resolution zum fünfzigsten Jahrestag des Kriegsendes. *Japan Echo* 3:71–78.

———. 1996. Plädoyer für den Ausbau des Sicherheitsvertrags. *Japan Echo* 3:73–81.

Kitazawa Masakuni. 1975. Militarism and the cloak of management society. *Japan Interpreter* 9 (3):324–330.

Kiyotani Shinichi. 2002. *Konna Jieitai ni dare ga shita! (Who has made the SDF like this!).* Kosaidō shuppan.

Klein, Kerwin Lee. 2000. On the emergence of memory in historical discourse. *Representations, Special issue: Grounds for remembering* 69:127–150.

Klein, Paul. 1997. *Vers des armées post-nationales? Das Ende der Nationalarmee?* Strausberg: Sozialwissenschaftliches Institut der Bundeswehr.

Klompmakers, Inge. 2003. *Of brigands and bravery.* Amsterdam: Hotei Publishing.

Ko, Kilhee. 1995. Gakkō kyōiku ni okeru Nikkan sōgō ninshiki no mondai (The problem of mutual understanding of Japan and Korea in school education). *Tōkyō Daigaku Daigakuin Kyōikugaku Kenkyūka Kiyō* 35:12–19.

Kobayashi Hiroaki. 1991. Sollen die Japaner Blauhelme tragen? Verfassungsrechtliche Perspektiven. (Shall the Japanese wear blue helmets? Constitutional perspectives). *Comparative Law (Nihon University)* 8:63–73.

———. 1995. Der Verfassungswandel und die Verfassungsauslegung in der japanischen Verfassung: in Memoriam Friedrich August Freiherr von der Heydte (Changes and interpretations of the Japanese constitution: In memory of Friedrich August Freiherr von der Heydte). *Comparative Law (Nihon University)* 12:39–66.

———. 1998. Die Richtlinien (Guidelines) zur japanisch-amerikanischen Zusammenarbeit für die Verteidigung aus der Sicht der japanischen Verfassung (The guidelines for Japanese-American cooperation for defense from the perspective of the Japan constitution). *Comparative Law (Nihon University)* 15:27–72.

Kobayashi Naogeki. 1999. Haisen kinenbi tokushū: 55 nenme no 'itsuka kita michi' (Anniversary of defeat special: 55th year of "the path we took that day"). *Shūkan Kinyōbi,* 6 August.

Kobayashi Yoshinori. 1998. *Shin gōmanizumu senden (New arrogance manifesto).* Shōgakkan.

Kōda Tsūji. 2001. Kūkō Jieitai Hamamatsu kichi o kenshū (Research visit to the ASDF Hamamatsu camp). *Sōyū: So You* 145 (4):84.

Kōdansha no Ehon. 1940. *Kōdansha no ehon: Nippon no rikugun (Kōdansha picture book: Japan's army).* Kōdansha.

———. 1952. *Kōdansha no ehon: Orinpikku (Kōdansha picture book: Olympics).* Dai Nippon Benikai Kōdansha.

Kohler, Chris. 2004. *Power up: How Japanese video games gave the world extra life*. Brady Games.

Koike Eiko. 2001. Gurabia no shigoto o tsūjite mananda koto ga aru (What I have learned from photogravure). *Securitarian* 10:62–63.

Koike Seishun. 1993. Bōeichō 'Jieikan boshū CM' meguru kōbō (Attacking and defending the "Self-defense personnel recruitment CM" of the Defense Agency). *Sō* 10:116–123.

Kōjima Michiko. 1985. *Sensō o ikita onnatachi—shōgen, Kokubō Fujinkai (Women who lived the war—testimony, the Women's Association for National Defense)*. Mineruba shobō.

Kokka o Kangaeru Kai. 1990. *Nan no hata, nan no uta: Hi no maru, kimi ga yo (Flag of what? Song of what? The national flag and anthem)*. Kokka o kangaeru kai.

Kokubu Ichitarō. 1940. *Senchi no kodomo (Children on the battlefield)*. Chūō kōronsha.

Kokumin Bunka Kaigi, eds. 1996. *Shiru ya shirazu ya (The ones who know, the ones who don't)*. 12 vols. Shinkyō shuppansha.

Komachi Hiiragi. 1998. Bōei daigakkō ni manabu joshi gakusei no kyanpasu raifu (Campus life of female students at the National Defense Academy). *Securitarian* 4:42–48.

Komatsu Ichinosuke. 2001b. Tsuma o shikikan ni akarui katei o (A happy family under the guidance of my wife). *Sōyū: So You* 145 (4):89.

Komatsu Zenpō. 2001a. Jinsei kōro, ōhanami kohanami o norikoete. *Sōyū: So You* 145 (4):78–79.

Kōmuin Shiken Jōhō Kenkyūkai. 2002. *Daigaku sotsugyō teido [ippan kanbu kōhosei] Jieitai enyō shiken (University graduate level [officer cadet] SDF exam)*. Hitotsubashi shoten.

Kondo, Dorinne. 1990. *Crafting selves: Power, gender, and discourses of identity in a Japanese workplace*. Chicago: University of Chicago Press.

Kondō Shinji. 1982. Gunji shigaku no magarikado (Turning point in military history). *Gunji Shigaku* 72:2–8.

Konishi Makoto. 2002. *Jieitai no tai tero sakusen (The SDF strategy against terrorism)*. Shakai hihyōsha.

———. 2006. *Jieitai: Sono transfōmēshon: taitero, gerira, komandō sakusen e no saihen (The transformation fo the Self-Defense Forces: Reorganization for anti-terror and guerrilla commando strategies)*. Shakai hihyōsha.

Konishi Makoto, Watanabe Nobutaka, and Yabuki Takashi. 2004. *Jieitai no Iraku hahei (The Iraq deployment of the Self-Defense Forces)*. Shakai hihyōsha.

Konoe Fumimaro. 1995. Against a pacifism centered on England and America. *Japan Echo* 22:12–14.

Koven, Seth. 1994. Remembering and dismemberment: Crippled children, wounded soldiers, and the Great War in Great Britain. *American Historical Review* 99 (4):1167–1202.

Krämer, Hans Martin. 2005. Just who reversed the course? The red purge in higher education during the occupation of Japan. *Social Science Japan Journal* 8 (1):1–18.

Krebs, Gerhard. 1993. Das Ende des Shōwa-Tennō oder Der Shōwa-Tennō und kein Ende: Die Diskussion in Politik und Literatur. *Japanstudien* 5: 35–88.

Krüger, Arnd. 1999. Breeding, bearing and preparing the Aryan body: Creating supermen the Nazi way. In *Shaping the superman: Fascist body as political icon—Aryan fascism*, ed. J. A. Mangan. London: Frank Cass.

Kühne, Thomas, ed. 1996. . . . . aus diesem Krieg werden nicht nur harte Männer heimkehren': Kriegskameradschaft und Männlichkeit im 20. Jahrhundert (". . . not only tough men will return from this war": War comrades and manliness in the 20th century). In *Männergeschichte—Geschlechtergeschichte: Männlichkeit im Wandel der Moderne*, ed. Thomas Kühne. Frankfurt and New York: Campus, 174–192.

———. 2000. 'Friedenskultur', Zeitgeschichte, historische Friedensforschung ("Culture of peace": Contemporary history, peace research). In *Von der Kriegskultur zur Friedenskultur? Zum Mentalitätswandel in Deutschland seit 1945*, ed. Thomas Kühne. Münster: LIT Verlag, 13–33.

Kümmel, Gerhard. 2002. Complete access: Women in the Bundeswehr. *Armed Forces & Society* 28 (4):555–574.

Kümmel, Gerhard, and Stefan Spangenberg. 1998. *Gewalt, Gesellschaft und Bundeswehr: Zur Wahrnehmung der Entwicklung eines gesellschaftlichen Phänomens (Violence, society, and the German military: Perceptions of the development of a social phenomenon) (Sowi Arbeitspapier 111)*. Strausberg: Sozialwissenschaftliches Institut der Bundeswehr.

Kurita Sukenari. 2001. Renjā tamashî o hakki shite iku zo! (Demonstrate the ranger spirit!). *Sōyū: So You* 145 (4):86.

Kuroda Toshio. 1996. The world of spirit pacification: issues of state and religion. *Japanese Journal of Religious Studies* 23 (3–4):321–351.

Kurosumi Nobuaki. 1967. Bōei Daigakkō yūkai gunjishi kenkyūbu Shōwa 41 nendo no jōkyō (The army history research club at the NDA, the situation in 1966). *Gunji Shigaku* 8:118–119.

Kurushima Takehiko. 1899. Nichiyō hyakka zensho dai yonjūhen: Kokumin hikkei rikugun ippan (Everyday use encycloedia 40: Indispensable army handbook for the people). Hyakubunkan.

Kushner, Barak. 2006. *The thought war: Japanese imperial propaganda*. Honolulu: University of Hawai'i Press.

Kuwahata Hiroshi (scenario) and Tomonaga Taro (illustration). 1995. *Pikurusu ōji no Jieitai nikki (Prince Pickles' SDF diary)*. Bōeichō.

Kuwazawa Kei. 1998. Jieitai no toshihajime gyōji (Activities of the SDF at the beginning of the year). *Securitarian*, 26–32.

Kyōto Eigasai Jikkō Iin-kai/Tsutsui Kiyotada and Katō Mikirō, eds. 1997. *Jidaigeki eiga to wa nani ka (What are period films?)*. Jinbun shoin.

Laqueur, Thomas W. 2000. Introduction. *Representations, Special issue: Grounds for remembering* 69:1–8.

Leal, David L. 2005. American public opinion toward the military. *Armed Forces & Society* 32 (1):123–138.

LeGoff, Jacques. 1992(1977). *History and memory, trans. Steven Rendall and Elisabeth Claman*. New York: University of Columbia Press.

Lenzen, Dieter. 1997. Kulturgeschichte der Vaterschaft (A cultural history of fatherhood). In *Wann ist der Mann ein Mann? Zur Geschichte der
Männlichkeit*, ed. Walter Erhart and Britta Herrmann. Stuttgart: J. B. Metzler, 87–113.

Levy, Edna. 2003. Die paradoxe Geschlechterpolitik der israelischen Armee (The
paradoxical gender politics of the Israeli army). In *Gender und Militär: Internationale Erfahrungen mit Frauen und Männern in Streitkräften*, ed. Christine Eifler and Ruth Seifert. Königstein: Ulrike Helmer Verlag (Heinrich Böll
Stiftung), 52–73.

Lindee, M. Susan. 1998. The repatriation of atomic bomb victim body parts to
Japan: Natural objects and diplomacy. *Osiris* 13:376–409.

Lo, Chih-cheng. 2001. Taiwan: The remaining challenges. In *Coercion and governance: The declining political role of the military in Asia*, ed. Muthiah Alagappa. Stanford: Stanford University Press.

Loewen, James W. 2000. The Vietnam war in high school American history. In
*Censoring history: Citizenship and memory in Japan, Germany, and the
United States*, ed. Laura Hein and Mark Selden. Armonk, NY: M. E. Sharpe,
150–172.

Lone, Stewart. 1994. *Japan's first modern war: Army and society in the conflict
with China, 1894–95.* New York: St. Martin's Press.

———. 2000. *Army, empire, and politics in Meiji Japan: The three careers of
General Katsura Tarō.* New York: St. Martin's Press.

———, ed. 2007. *Daily lives of civilians in wartime Asia: From the Taiping Re-
bellion to the Vietnam War.* Westport: Greenwood Press.

Lorentzen, Lois Ann, and Jennifer Turpin, eds. 1998. *The woman and war
reader.* New York: New York University Press.

Lory, Hillis. 1943. *Japan's military masters: The Army in Japanese life.* Westport:
Greenwood Press.

Low, Morris. 2003. The emperor's sons go to war: Competing masculinities in
modern Japan. In *Asian masculinities: The meaning and practice of manhood
in China and Japan,* ed. Kam Louie and Morris Low. London: Routledge-
Curzon, 81–99.

Lummis, C. Douglas. 1982. Japanese pacifism under the U.S. war machine: the
latent force. *Bulletin of Peace Proposals* 13 (1):43–48.

Lutz, Catherine. 2001. *Homefront: The military city and the American twentieth century.* Boston: Beacon Press.

Maase, Kaspar. 2000. 'Give peace a chance'—Massenkultur und Mentalitätswandel: Eine Problemskizze ("Give peace a chance": Mass culture and
the transformation of metality—An overview of the problem). In *Von der
Kriegskultur zur Friedenskultur? Zum Mentalitätswandel in Deutschland seit
1945,* ed. Thomas Kühne. Münster: Lit Verlag, 262–279.

MacAloon, John J. 1984. Olympic games and the theory of spectacle in modern
societies. In *Rite, drama, festival, spectacle: Rehearsals toward a theory of
cultural performance,* ed. John J. MacAloon. Philadelphia: Institute for the
Study of Human Issues, 241–280.

Maeda Ai, and Shimizu Isao, eds. 1986. *Taishō-kōki no manga: Kindai manga*

6 *(Comics in the latter half of the Taishō era: Modern comics 6)*. Chikuma shobō.

Maeda Tetsuo. 1990 (1988). *Bokutachi no guntai (Our military)*. Iwanami shoten (Iwanami junia shinsho 150).

———. 1992. *Jieitai o dō suru ka (What shall we do about the SDF?)*. Iwanami shoten.

———. 1993. *Kanbojia PKO jūgunki*. Mainichi shinbunsha.

———. 1994. Kanbojia PKO o sōkatsu suru (Summarizing the peace-keeping mission to Cambodia). *Gunshuku Mondai Shiryō* 9 (166):28–33.

Maekawa Mitsuo. 2004. Samawa shimin o shitsubō saseru Nihon no fukkyō shien (Japan's reconstruction aid that leaves the citizens of Samawa disappointed). *Shūkan Kinyōbi*:22–23.

Mann, Michael. 1987. War and social theory: Into battle with classes, nations and states. In *The sociology of war and peace*, ed. Colin Creighton and Martin Shaw. Bowling Green: Bowling Green University Popular Press, 3–32.

Marten, James. 2002. Introduction. In *Children and war: A historical anthology*, ed. James Marten. New York: New York University Press, 1–10.

Martinez, Maria Lourdes. 2001. Zwangsprostitution und Entschädigung: Zur Diskussion über die 'Trostfrauen' in Japan (Forced prostitution and compensation: On the debate about "comfort women" in Japan). In *Periplus: Jahrbuch für aussereuropäische Geschichte*, ed. Dietmar Rotermund. Münster: LIT Verlag, 26–42.

Masaki, Hisane. 2000. Foreign Ministry vs. Defense Agency. *Japan Times*, December 17.

Masuda Megumi. 2003. 'Kōdo seichōki' ni okeru joshi 'rōdōsha' no sanshutsu katei (Curriculum practices in commercial high schools: The production process of female "workers" during the "high growth period" in Japan). *Soshioroji* 48 (1):75–92.

Mathews, Gordon. 2002. Can "a real man" live for his family? Ikigai and masculinity in today's Japan. In *Men and masculinities in contemporary Japan: Dislocating the salaryman doxa*, ed. James E. Roberson and Suzuki Nobue. London: Routledge, 109–125.

Matsui Minoru. 2001. *Riben guizi (Devils of the past/Japanese devils)*. New York: Riben Guizi Production Committee.

Matsui Shinji. 1935. Sensō to jūgo no josei (The war and women on the home front). *Rikugun Gahō* 3 (3):33–40.

Matsumoto Reiji. 1998. Manga to Jieitai (Comics and the SDF). *Securitarian* 2:11–16.

Matsumoto Toshiaki. 1998. Hana no fujin Jieikan 1-man'in dansei shūdan no naka no funtō (The struggle of a female SDF member flower in a 10,000-men male group). *Shūkan Taishū*, 17 August, 51–53.

Matsushima Eiichi. 1993. Nihon no kyōiku to 'gakuto shutsujin' (Japanese education and "students" departure for the front). *Rekishi Chiri Kyōiku* 508: 8–13.

Matsuzawa Shintarō. 2001. Ashita ni kagayake, renjā kisho (Let the ranger badge sparkle for tomorrow). *Sōyū: So You* 145 (4):87.

McCormack, Gavan. 2000a. Flight from the violent 20th century. *Japanese Studies* 20 (1):5–14.

———. 2000b. The Japanese movement to "correct" history. In *Censoring history: Citizenship and memory in Japan, Germany, and the United States,* ed. Laura Hein and Mark Selden. Armonk, NY: M. E. Sharpe, 53–73.

———. 2005. Okinawa and the revamped U.S.-Japan alliance. *Japan Focus:* http://www.japanfocus.org/products/details/2088.

McLaren, Angus. 1997. *The trials of masculinity: Policing sexual boundaries 1870–1930.* Chicago: University of Chicago Press.

McLean, Alasdair, and Michael Sheehan. 1992. Making space for Japan. *Pacific Review* 5 (1):68–77.

McVeigh, Brian J. 2000a. *Wearing ideology: State, schooling and self-presentation in Japan.* Oxford: Berg.

———. 2000b. Hello Kitty commodifies the cute, cool and camp: "Consumutopia" versus "control" in Japan. *Journal of Material Culture* 5 (2):225–245.

———. 2000c. Postwar nationalism of Japan: The management and mysticism of identity. *New Zealand Journal of Asian Studies* 2 (1):24–39.

Melman, Billie. 1993. Gender, history and memory: The invention of women's past in the nineteenth and early twentieth centuries. *History & Memory* 5 (1):5–41.

Mertens, Wolfgang. 1997. Männlichkeit aus psychoanalytischer Sicht (Masculinity from a psychoanalytical perspective). In *Wann ist der Mann ein Mann? Zur Geschichte der Männlichkeit,* ed. Walter Erhart and Britta Herrmann. Stuttgart: J. B. Metzler, 35–57.

Messaris, Paul. 1997. *Visual persuasion: The role of images in advertising.* London: Sage.

Meyer, John W., John Boli, George M. Thomas, and Francisco O. Ramirez. 1997. World society and the nation-state. *American Journal of Sociology* 103 (1): 144–181.

Mihara Haruki. 2001. Etegami ni miserarete (Charmed by illustrated letters). *Sōyū: So You* 145 (4):79.

Miller, Laura. 2000. Media typifications and hip bijin. *U.S.–Japan Women's Journal (English supplement 19)*:176–205.

———. 2003. "Male beauty work in Japan." In *Men and masculinities in contemporary Japan: Dislocating the salaryman doxa,* ed. James E. Roberson and Nobue Suzuki. London: Routledge, 37–57.

Miller, Laura L. 1997. Do soldiers hate peacekeeping? The case of preventive diplomacy operations in Macedonia. *Armed Forces & Society* 23 (3): 415–450.

———. 1998. Feminism and the exclusion of Army women from combat. *Gender Issues* 16 (3–36).

Miller, Laura L., and Charles Moskos. 1995. Humanitarians or warriors? Race, gender, and combat status in Operation Restore Hope. *Armed Forces & Society* 21 (4):615–637.

Minami Hiroshi. 1971(1953). *Psychology of the Japanese people.* Tokyo: University of Tokyo Press.

Mineo Hisao. 1998. *Jieikan wa kataru, sono hōfu to kunō (SDF personnel tell, their ambitions and distress)*. Bunkyō shuppan.

Ministry of Foreign Affairs. 1997. *UN peace-keeping operations: Japanese policy and practice*. Ministry of Foreign Affairs.

———. 1999. *PKO seminar—the changing face of peacekeeping*. http://www.mofa.go.jp/policy/un/pko/.

———. 2005. *Diplomatic blue book 2005: Japanese diplomacy and global affairs in 2004*. Ministry of Foreign Affairs.

Mishima Yukio. 1977. *Yukio Mishima on hagakure*, trans. Kathryn Sparling. New York: Basic Books.

Miura Keiko. 2003. Tokushū: Zakkubaran ni Jieitai—Gairo de wakamono ni kiku 'Jieitai' kankaku ankēto (Special: Outspoken SDF—A survey of young people's sense of the SDF on the street). *Securitarian* 3:12–15.

Miura Sumie. 2001. Barē o ai suru kakkoii papa (Cool dad who loves volleyball). *Sōyū: So You* 145 (4):103.

Miyagi Harumi. 2003. Josei ni taisuru bōryoku, kichimura josei no jiritsu (Violence against women, the independence of women in base villages). *Asoshie* 11:186–187.

Miyagi Kikuko. 1995 (2002). *Himeyuri no shojo (The maiden lily student nurse corps)*. Kōbunken.

Miyanishi Kaori. 2003. Beigun dansei to kekkon shita Nihonjin tsumatachi no 9-gatsu 11-nichi—Yokosuka beikaigun kichi no jirei kara (September 11 for the Japanese wives of American soldiers: Examples from the American navy base in Yokosuka). PhD diss., Kyoto University.

Miyata Mitsuo. 1982. The politico-religion of Japan: the revival of militarist mentality. *Bulletin of Peace Proposals* 13 (1):25–30.

Miyazaki Katsuji. 1990. Time to reevaluate the security treaty. *Japan Quarterly* 37 (4):416–423.

Mizuno Hitoshi. 1997. *Kaigai hihahei no ronri (The logic of non-dispatch to foreign countries)*. Shinhyōron.

Mizushima Asaho. 1994. Heiwa kenpō to Jieitai no shōrai (The peace constitution and the future of the SDF). *Gunshuku Mondai Shiryō* 9 (166):16–21.

Mochizuki, Mike M. 1996. Toward a new Japan-U.S. alliance. *Japan Quarterly* 43 (3):4–12.

Moeller, Robert G. 1996. War stories: The search for a usable past in the Federal Republic of Germany. *American Historical Review* 101 (4):1008–1048.

Moeran, Brian. 1986. One over the seven: Sake drinking in a Japanese pottery community. In *Interpreting Japanese society*, ed. Joy Hendry and Joy Webber. Oxford: JASO Occasional Papers 5, 226–242.

Mojtaba, Sadria. 1993. The peace culture of the Japanese people and the "new world order." *AMPO Japan-Asia Quarterly Review* 24 (1):34–38.

Momoi Makoto. 2001nen—*Nihon no gunjiryoku (Japan's military strength in 2001)*. Shōdensha.

Monbushō Shakai Kyōikukyoku. 1967. *Seishōnen no ishiki: Kachikan, aikokushin-tō ni tsuite (The consciousness of youth: On values and patriotism)*. Naikaku Sōri Daijin Kanbō Kōhō-shitsu.

Moon, Seungsook. 2005. Trouble with conscription, entertaining soldiers: Popular culture and the politics of militarized masculinity in South Korea. *Men and Masculinities* 8 (1):64–92.

Morelli, Anne. 2004(2001). *Die Prinzipien der Kriegspropaganda*, trans. Marianne Schönbach. Hannover: Klampen Verlag.

Morgan, David H. J. 1994. Theater of war: Combat, the military and masculinities. In *Theorizing masculinities,* ed. Harry Brod and Michael Kaufmann. Thousand Oaks, California: Sage Publications, 165–182.

Morimatsu Matsuo. 1978. Gunkankei no kikan oyobi kenkyūsha (Military agencies and researchers). *Gunji Shigaku* 54–55:58–75.

Morrison, Alex, and James Kiras. 1996. *UN peace operations and the role of Japan.* Clementsport, Canada: Lester B. Pearson Canadian International Peacekeeping Training Center.

Morris-Suzuki, Tessa. 1994. *The technological transformation of Japan: from the seventeenth to the twenty-first century.* Cambridge: Cambridge University Press.

Morris-Suzuki, Tessa, and Takuro Seiyama, eds. *Japanese capitalism since 1945.* Armonk, NY: M. E. Sharpe.

Moskos, Charles C., John A. Williams, and David Segal, eds. 2000. *The postmodern military: Armed forces after the cold war.* New York: Oxford University Press.

Mosse, George L. 1996. *The image of man: The creation of modern masculinity.* Oxford: Oxford University Press.

Motoyama Kenichi. 2001. Kazoku no tame ni ganbaritai (I want to do my best for my family). *Sōyū: So You* 145 (4):89.

Mouer, Ross, and Sugimoto Yoshio. 1995. *Nihonjinron at the end of the twentieth century: A multicultural perspective.* Melbourne: La Trobe University Asian Studies Paper, no. 4.

Murakami Kenji. 2001. Kaiin no tame kyōryoku na rīdāshippu o motte (Cooperative strong leadership for members). *Sōyū: So You* 145 (4):1.

Murakami Takashi. 2005. Superflat trilogy: Greetings, you are alive. In *Ritoru bōi: Little boy: The arts of Japan's exploding subculture,* ed. Murakami Takashi. New York: Japan Society, and New Haven: Yale University Press, 151–163.

Murata, Koji. 1995. View from Japan. The U.S.-Japan alliance and the U.S.-South Korea alliance: Their origins, dilemas, and structures. *Comparative Strategy* 14:185–194.

Muromoto Hiromichi. 2002. Atarashii kōhō no katachi (The new form of aftermath). *Securitarian* 9:24–28.

Mushaben, Joyce Marie. 1999. Collective memory divided and reunited. *History & Memory* 11 (1):7–40.

Mushakōji, Kinhide. 1985. In search of formulas for regional peace. *Japan Quarterly* 32 (3):234–239.

Naikaku Sōri Daijin Kanbō Kōhō-shitsu. 2001. *Yoron chōsa nenkan* (Annual compilation of opinion surveys). Naikaku Sōri Daijin Kanbō Kōhō-shitsu.

Naikakufu. 2002. *Seishōnen hakusho (Youth white paper)*. Zaimushō insatsukyoku.

Naikakufu Daijin Kanbō Seifu Kōhōshitsu. 2000. Jieitai bōei mondai (The issue of SDF and defense). *Gekkan Yoron Chōsa* 32 (9):1–106.

———. 2003. Jieitai bōei mondai (The issue of the SDF and defense). *Gekkan Yoron Chōsa* 35 (6):1–100.

Nakada Toshitsune. 1979. *Bōei daigakkō (The NDA)*. Kyōikusha.

Nakamaki Hirochika. 1997. Yoshō: Keiei jinruigaku ni mukete kaisha no 'minzokushi' to sarariiman no 'shomin kenkyū' (Introduction: Toward an anthropology of management: "Ethnographies" of companies and studies of employees as "ordinary people." In *Keiei jinruigaku kotohajime: Kaisha to sarariiman (The beginning of an anthropology of management: Company and salary man)*, ed. Nakamaki Hirochika and Hioki Koichirō. Ōsaka: Tōhō shuppan, 13–29.

Nakamura Hisashi, and Malcolm Dando. 1993. Japan's military research and development: a high technology deterrent. *Pacific Review* 6 (2):177–188.

Nakamura Ken'ichi. 1982. Militarization of postwar Japan. *Bulletin of Peace Proposals* 13 (1):31–37.

Nakamura Masao. 2001. *Rikujō Jieitai pāfekuto gaido (GSDF perfect guide)*. Gakken.

Nakamura Satoshi. 1993. Tennō heika wa Jieikan no seifuku ga kirai no konkyo (The reasons the emperor dislikes SDF uniforms). *Shūkan Asahi*, October 15, 26–29.

Nakano, Koichi. 1998. Becoming a "policy" ministry: the organization and amakudari of the Ministry of Posts and Telecommunications. *Journal of Japanese Studies* 24 (1):95–117.

Nakano Tetsuya. 2001. Kenkyūshin to doryoku de: ichininmae no shomu rikusō ni (Through interest in research and hard work: becoming a skilled general affairs army soldier). *Sōyū: So You* 145 (4):88–89.

Nakano-ku Chiiki Sentā-bu Josei Seishōnen-ka. 1991. *Dansei no seikatsu to ishiki ni kan suru chōsa (Survey on men's lives and consciousness)*. Shadan Hōjin Jōhō Sentā.

Nakar, Eldad. 2003. Memories of pilots and planes: World War II in Japanese manga, 1957–1967. *Social Science Journal Japan* 6 (1):57–76.

Nakasone Yasuhiro. 1997. The security environment of the Asia-Pacific age. *Asia-Pacific Review* 4 (1):3–16.

Nakatani Ayami. 2000(1999). 'Kosodate suru otoko' toshite no chichioya (Fathers as "men who bring up children"). In *Danseiron (On men)*, ed. Yūko Nishikawa and Ogino Miho. Jinbun shoin, 46–73.

Nakayama Michiko. 1998. Ronten toshite no 'josei to guntai' ("Women and military" as point of discussion). In *Sei, bōryoku, nēshon*, ed. Ehara Yumiko. Keiso shobō, 31–60.

Nambara, Wataru. 1993. The SDF as an instrument of political expression. *AMPO Japan-Asia Quarterly Review* 24 (1):2–6.

Napier, Susan. 1998. Vampires, psychic girls, flying women and sailor scouts:

Four faces of the young female in Japanese popular culture. In *The worlds of Japanese popular culture: Gender, shifting boundaries and global cultures,* ed. D. P. Martinez. Cambridge: Cambridge University Press, 91–109.

———. 2001. *Anime: from Akira to Princess Mononoke.* New York: Palgrave, 175–192.

———. 2005. World War II as trauma, memory and fantasy in Japanese animation. *Japan Focus,* http://japanfocus.org/, posted May 31.

Nathan, John. 1974 (2000). *Mishima: A biography.* Cambridge, Mass.: Da Capo Press.

National Institute for Defense Studies. 1998. *East Asian strategic review 1997–1998.* Tokyo: The National Institute for Defense Studies.

———. 1999. *East Asian strategic review 1998–1999.* Tokyo: The National Institute for Defense Studies.

Natsume Fusanosuke. 1997. *Manga to 'sensō' (Comics and "war").* Kōdansha.

Nelson, John. 2002a. From battlefield to atomic bomb to the pure land of paradise: Employing the Bodhisattva of compassion to calm Japan's spirits of the dead. *Journal of Contemporary Religion* 17 (2):149–164.

———. 2002b. Tempest in a textbook: A report on the new middle-school history textbook in Japan. *Critical Asian Studies* 34 (1):129–148.

Newton, Judith L. 1997. Geschichtswissenschaft und Männlichkeit: The Edinburgh Review (Historiography and masculinity: The Edinburgh Review). In *Wann ist der Mann ein Mann? Zur Geschichte der Männlichkeit,* ed. Walter Erhart and Britta Herrmann. Stuttgart: J. B. Metzler, 149–169.

Nezu Shinji. 1995. *Nigetai yametai Jieitai: Genshoku Jieikan no bikkuri taikenki (The Jieitai that I want to escape and quit: The surprising experience of a current member of the Self-Defense Forces).* Gendai shokan.

Niedhart, Gottfried. 2000. Frieden als Norm und Erfahrung in der Aussenpolitik der Bundesrepublik Deutschland. In *Von der Kriegskultur zur Friedenskultur? Zum Mentalitätswandel in Deutschland seit 1945,* ed. Thomas Kühne. Münster: LIT Verlag, 182–201.

Nihon Kirisuto Kyōdan Yasukuni Jinja Mondai Tokubetsu Iinkai. 1979. 'Yasukuni jinja kōshiki sanpai wa kenpō ihan de aru': Hisan na rekishi o kurikaesanai tame ni ("Official visits to the Yasukuni Shrine are a violation of the constitution": In order to not repeat a wretched history). Nihon Kurisutokyōdan Jimukyoku.

Nihon Kyōshokuin Sōgō. 1969. *Atarashii senbotsusha o tsukuru na (Let's not create new war dead).* Nihon Kyōshokuin Sōgō (in collaboration with the Nihon Bunka Kaigi).

Nihon Senbotsu Gakusei Kinen-Kai (Japan Memorial Society for the Students Killed in the War—Wadatsumi Society). 2000 (1949). *Listen to the voices from the sea (Kike wadatsumi no koe),* trans. Midori Yamanouchi and Joseph L. Quinn. Scranton: University of Scranton Press.

Nishihara Masashi. 2004. The peril of a US-North Korea nonaggression pact. *Japan Echo* 2:13–16.

Nishii Kazuo. 1998–1999. *Fukyoka shashin: Mainichi shinbun hizō (Censured photographs: Treasures of the Mainichi Newspaper).* Mainichi shinbunsha.

Nishikawa Shigenori. 1999. 'Shōwakan' to watashitachi no kadai ('Shōwa Hall' and our tasks). *Kikan: Sensō Sekinin Kenkyū* 25:58–61.

Nishikawa Yūko. 2000 (1999). Otoko no kaishōsei toshite no ietsukuri (House-building as men's ability). In *Danseiron (On men)*, ed. Nishikawa Yūko and Ogino Miho. Jinbun shoin.

Nishimoto Tetsuya. 2002. Jieitai ni kanren suru saikin no hosei (The recent changes of the legal system concerning the SDF). *Securitarian* 8:7–16.

Nishinarita Yutaka. 1999. 'Sensōron—shin gōmanizumu senden' hihan (On war: A critique of the "New arrogance manifesto"). *Kikan: Sensō Sekinin Kenkyū* 26:40–43.

Nishio Kanji. 2001. *Atarashii rekishi kyōkasho (New history textbook)*. Fusōsha.

Noda Masaaki. 1998. *Sensō to zaiseki (War and liability)*. Iwanami shoten.

Nogan Yasuhiro. 2002a. Jibun no michi wa, jibun de hiraku (Opening my own path myself). *Securitarian* 2:37–39.

———. 2002b. Nihon no PKO ashiato to sono shōrai (Past and future of Japan's PKO). *Securitarian* 10 (529):37–40.

———. 2003. Tokushū: Zakkubaran ni Jieitai—Dokusha no koe de kiku 'koko ga shiritai Jieitai' (Special: Outspoken SDF—What readers want to know about the SDF). *Securitarian* 3:23–27.

Nojima Tsuyoshi. 2004. Jūgun taiken o furikaette (Looking back on the experience of the Imperial Army). In *Jūgun no poritekusu (The Politics of the Imperial Army)*, ed. Katō Tetsurō et. al. Seikyūsha, 247–268.

Nora, Pierre. 1989. Between memory and history. Les lieux de mèmoire. *Representations* 36:7–25.

Nornes, Abe Mark. 2003. *Japanese documentary film: The Meiji era through Hiroshima*. Minneapolis: University of Minnesota Press.

NRKSG and KBK (Nihon Rōdō Kumiai Sōhyō Gikai and Kokumin Bunka Kaigi), eds. 1969. *Manga anpō (The U.S.-Japan Security Treaty in cartoon format)*. Rōdō junpō-sha.

O'Brien, Tim. 1999 [1990]. *The things they carried*. New York: Broadway.

O'Connor, Peter, and Aaron M. Cohen. 2001. Thoughts on the precipice: Japanese postcards, c. 1903–39. *Japan Forum* 13 (1):55–62.

Odawara Atsushi. 1985. No tampering with the brakes on military expansion. *Japan Quarterly* 32 (3):248–254.

Ogawa Kazuhisa. 1999. Substantive debate needed. *Japan Quarterly* 46 (3):17–23.

Ōgoshi Aiko. 2004. Jūgun to josei (The Imperial Army and women). In *Jūgun no poritekusu (The Politics of the Imperial Army)*, ed. Katō Tetsurō et.al. Seikyūsha, 169–190.

Oguma Eiji. 2003 (2002). *"Minshū" to "aikoku": Sengo Nihon no nashonarizumu to kōkyōsei ("People" and "patriotism": Japan's postwar nationalism and communality)*. Shinyōsha.

Ogura Osamu, and Ken Hamada. 2002. *'Jipangu' kenkyū yosetsu (Research outline of "Zipangu")*. āto bukku hon no mori.

Ogura Yuji. 1996. Makkāsā to 47-nen keisatsu kaikaku (MacArthur and the police reform of 1947). *Kantō Gakuin Daigaku Keizaikei* 188: 174–180.

Ohashi Seiko. 1985. No to U.S.-Japan military intervention in the Philippines. *AMPO Japan-Asia Quarterly Review* 17 (3):38–41.

Ohnuki-Tierney, Emiko. 1998. Cherry blossoms and their viewing: A window onto Japanese culture. In *The culture of Japan as seen through its leisure,* ed. Sepp Linhart and Sabine Frühstück. Albany: State University of New York Press, 213–236.

————. 2002. *Kamikaze, cherry blossoms, and nationalisms: The militarization of aesthetics in Japanese history.* Chicago: University of Chicago Press.

Oka Yoshie (illustrations) and Koga Tadamichi (commentary). 1950. *Kōdansha no ehon 7: Dōbutsu gashū kedamonozukushi (Kodansha's picture book series 7: Animal pictures- full of beasts).* Dai Nippon Yūbenkai Kōdansha.

Okada Akio. 1979. *Nihon-shi shōhyakka: Dōbutsu (Small encyclopedia of Japanese history: Animals).* Kondo shuppansha.

Okada Toshitsune. 1979. *Bōei Daigakkō (NDA), Jiji Mondai Kaisetsu 215.* Kyōikusha.

Oku Takenoru. 2000. *Taishū shinbun to kokumin kokka (Mass newspapers and the nation state).* Heibonsha.

Ōmiya Hiroshi. 2001. *Soko ga hen da yo Jieitai! (The weird world of the SDF!).* Tokyo.

Ōmori Kazuki. 1998. Eizō to Jieitai (Images and the SDF). *Securitarian* 2:17–21.

Omuka Toshiharu and Misuzawa Tsutomu. 2003. *Modanizumu/nashonarizumu (Modernism/nationalism).* Serika shobō.

Orikasa Ai. 1998. Anime hiroin to Jieitai (Anime heroine and the SDF). *Securitarian* 2: 22–26.

Orr, James J. 2001. *The victim as hero.* Honolulu: University of Hawai'i Press.

Osa Shizue. 2000(1999). Tenshi no jendā (The gender of the successor to the throne). In *Danseiron (On men),* ed. Nishikawa Yūko and Ogino Miho. Jinbun shoin, 275–296.

Osawa Mari. 1996. Bye-bye corporate warriors: The formation of a corporate-centered society and gender-biased social policies in Japan. *Annals of the Institute of Social Science*:157–194.

Ōta Yoshinobu. 2001. Kanbu kōhosei shiken o oete: ōku no hito ni sasaerare ganbareta (Completing the officers candidate examination: I worked hard and was supported by many people). *Sōyū: So You* 145 (4):88.

Ota Yuri. 2001. Risu no anzen mo kichin to mamoru kuni!? (Is this a country that protects the safety of squirrels too!?). *Securitarian* 12:54–55.

————. 2002a. Bōdaisei ga yatte kita (The NDA students came). *Securitarian* 4:41–43.

————. 2002b. Iyo iyo kikoku, dokusha no minasama, arigatō (Return at last, thank you, readers). *Securitarian* 2:40–43.

————. 2002c. Oya toshite kangaesaserareru dekigoto (A matter to think about as a parent). *Securitarian* 10:37–39.

Ōtsuka Shinichi, ed. 2001 (1993). *Iwanami kōza Nihon to shokuminchi 7: Bunka no naka no shokuminchi (Iwanami course Japan and the colonies 7: The colonies within culture).* Iwanami shoten.

Overby, Charles. 1994. A quest for peace with article 9. *AMPO Japan-Asia Quarterly Review* 25 (2):39–46.

Ōya Sōichi. 1981. Sararîman no seikatsu to shisō (Salary men's lives and thoughts). In *Oya Sōichi zenshū—dainikan (Collected works of Oya Sōichi—volume 2)*, ed. Ōya Sōichi. Chikuma shobō.

Ōzawa Gentarō. 2001. *Otona no sankōsho: 'Jieitai' ga wakaru! (A reference book for adults: Understanding the "SDF"!)*. Seishun shuppansha.

Ozawa, Ichiro. 1994. *Blueprint for a new Japan: The rethinking of a nation*, trans. Louisa Rubinfien. Tokyo: Kodansha International.

Peach, Lucinda Joy. 1997. Behind the front lines: Feminist battles over women in combat. In *Wives and warriors: Women and the military in the United States and Canada*, ed. Laurie Weinstein and Christie C. White. Westport: Bergin and Garvey, 99–135.

Pearton, Maurice. 1982. *The knowledgable state*. London: Burnett Books.

Peattie, Mark R. 1995. *A historian looks at the Pacific War*. Stanford: Stanford University, Hoover Institution.

Pempel, T. J. 2001. International economics and security in the study of U.S.-Japan relations. In *Japanese Studies in the United States: Survey of U.S.-Japan security studies and international economics*, ed. The National Bureau of Asian Research. Seattle: The National Bureau of Asian Research and The Japan Foundation Center for Global Partnership, 51–55.

Perault, Matthew. 2005. Moving beyond Kosovo: Envisioning a coherent theory of humanitarian intervention. *Journal of Public and International Affairs* 16: 1–25.

Petersen, Susanne. 2001. Die Schulbuchprozesse: Geschichtspolitik in japanischen Schulbüchern (The textbook lawsuits: History politics in Japanese textbooks). In *Periplus: Jahrbuch für aussereuropäische Geschichte*, ed. Dietmar Rotermund. Münster: LIT Verlag, 59–82.

Pilling, David. 2004a. A grown-up nation? The hostage crisis in Iraq sharpens debate over Japan's proper role on the international stage. *Financial Times*, April 14, 15.

———. 2004b. Tokyo's defense review names China and North Korea as security threats. *Financial Times*, December, 3.

———. 2004c. Japan restocks armoury of words as pacifist constitution takes the strain. *Financial Times*, December 13, 3.

———. 2006. Past lives, current issue: How Japan's top daily is forcing a war reappraisal. *Financial Times*, December 28, 7.

Ping-Ying Hsieh. 1939. *Onna heishi no jiden (Autobiography of a female soldier)*, trans. Morohoshi Akiko. Seinen shobō.

Postone, Moishe. 1990. After the Holocaust: History and identity in West Germany. In *Coping with the past: Germany and Austria after 1945*, ed. Lutz R. Reuter, Volker Dürr, and Kathy Harms. Madison: University of Wisconsin Press.

Puja, Kim. 2001. Global civil society remakes history: The Women's International War Crimes Tribunal 2000. *positions: east asia cultures critique* 9 (3):611–620.

Rabinbach, Anson. 1990. Beyond Bitburg: The place of the "Jewish question" in German history after 1945. In *Coping with the past: Germany and Austria after 1945*, ed. Lutz R. Reuter, Volker Dürr, and Kathy Harms. Madison: University of Wisconsin Press, 187–218.

Raine, Michael. 2001. Ishihara Yūjirō: Youth, celebrity, and the male body in late-1950s Japan. In *Word and image in Japanese cinema*, ed. Dennis Washburn and Carole Cavanaugh. Cambridge: University of Cambridge Press, 202–225.

Reid, Maree. 1998. *The shape of things to come: The US-Japan security relationship in the new era, Canberra Papers on Strategy and Defense 128*. Canberra: Strategic and Defence Studies Centre, Research School of Pacific and Asian Studies, The Australian National University.

Rekishi Kyōikusha Kyōgikai, ed. 1995. *Heiwa hakubutsukan, sensō shiryōkan gaido bukku (Guidebook for peace and war museums)*. Aoki shoten.

Research Institute for Peace and Security. 1994. *A regional approach to confidence and security building in the Far East*. Tokyo: Research Institute for Peace and Security.

Riessland, Andreas. 1997. Sweet spots: The use of cuteness in Japanese advertising. *Japanstudien: Jahrbuch des Deutschen Instituts für Japanstudien der Philipp Franz von Siebold Stiftung* 9:129–154.

Riggs, Matt L., and Patrick A. Knight. 1994. The impact of perceived group success-failure on motivational beliefs and attitudes: a causal model. *Journal of Applied Psychology* 79 (5):755–766.

Rikugun Bijutsu Kyōkai. 1939. *Seisen bijutsu (Art of the holy war)*. Rikugun Bijutsu Kyōkai.

Rikugun Gahō. 1935. Jūgo no josei: Jūgun fujin katsuyaku (Women on the home front: The activities of war women/women during the war). *Rikugun Gahō* 3 (3): 33–40.

————. 1943. Daitōa sensō shin buki o kataru zadankai (A discussion on the new weapons of the Greater East Asia war). *Rikugun Gahō* 11 (1):14–26.

Rikugun Shikan Gakkō Ikan, eds. 1898. *Rikugun shikan gakkō jōrei, Rikugun shikan gakkō kyōiku kōryō, Rikugun shikan gakkō kyōsoku (The Military Academy's rules, education outlines, and rules for teaching)*. Rikugun shikan gakkō.

Rikugunshō Henshūbu. 1934. *Heishi to haha (Soldiers and mothers)*. Tsuwamono hakkōsho, Rikugunshō.

Rikugunshō jōhō-bu and Kaigunshō jōhō-bu. 1939 [1922]. Kōgun banzai suguroku (Suguroku hailing the Imperial Army). *Shojo Kurabu (Girls' Club)* 18 (1) supplement.

Rikujō Bakuryō Kanbu Kōhōshitsu. 2006. *We are Rikujō Jieitai (We are the GSDF)*. Bōeichō.

Rikujō Jieitai, eds. 1998a. *We are Rikujō Jieitai: catch your dream*. Rikujō bakuryō kanbu kōhōshitsu.

————, eds. 1998b. *Dokyumento Jieitai: Rikujō Jieitai (Document SDF: The GSDF), Bunshun nonfiction video*. Bungei shunju.

Roberson, James E. 2002. Japanese working-class masculinities: Marginalized complicity. In *Men and masculinities in contemporary Japan: Dislocating the salaryman doxa*, ed. James E. Roberson and Suzuki Nobue. London: Routledge, 126–143.

———. 2005. Fight!! *Ippatsu*!!: "Genki" Energy drinks and the marketing of masculine ideology in Japan. *Men and Masculinities* 7 (4):365–384.

Roberson, James E., and Suzuki Nobue. 2002. Introduction. In *Men and masculinities in contemporary Japan: Dislocating the salaryman doxa*, ed. James E. Roberson and Suzuki Nobue. London: Routledge, 1–19.

Robertson, Jennifer. 1998. *Takarazuka: Sexual politics and popular culture in modern Japan*. Berkeley: University of California Press.

Rohlen, Thomas, and Gerald LeTendre, eds. 1996. *Teaching and learning in Japan*. Cambridge: Cambridge University.

Rohlen, Thomas P. 1973. "Spiritual education" in a Japanese bank. *American Anthropologist* 75 (5):1542–1562.

Roland, Alex. 1985. Technology and war: A bibliographical essay. In *Military enterprise and technological change: Perspectives on the American experience*, ed. Merritt Roe Smith. Cambridge, MA: MIT Press, 347–379.

Rosen, David M. 2005. *Armies of the young: Child soldiers in war and terrorism*. New Brunswick: Rutgers University Press.

Rosenfeld, Alvin H. 1986. Another revisionism: Popular culture and the changing image of the Holocaust. In *Bitburg in moral and political perspective*, ed. Geoffrey H. Hartman. Bloomington: Indiana University Press, 90–102.

Russo, Valeria E. 1994. The constitution of a gendered enemy. In *Women soldiers: Images and realities*, ed. Valeria E. Russo, Lorenza Sebesta, and Elisabetta Addis. New York: St. Martin's Press, 49–158.

Saaler, Sven. 2005. *Politics, memory and public opinion*. Munich: Iudicium.

Saitō Gorō. 1976. Kantō daishinsai ni okeru guntai no kōdō (Military activities during the Kantō earthquake). *Gunji Shigaku* 47:64–73.

Saitō Minako. 2003 (2001). *Kōittenron (On being the only girl in a group of men)*. Chikuma bunkō.

Saito Naoki. 1992. Financing of U.N. peacekeeping operations: U.S. and Japanese responses, Policy Paper 84E. Tokyo: International Institute for Global Peace.

Sakai Takeshi. 1988. A matter of faith. *Japan Quarterly* 35 (4):357–364.

Sakamoto Yoshikazu. 1982. Introduction: Japan in global perspective. *Bulletin of Peace Proposals* 13 (1):1–6.

Sakata Kiyo. 2002 (1942). *Onna no mita senjo (The battle field viewed by a woman)*. Nagoya: Arumu.

Sakurai Hitoshi. 1940. *Jūgo yori shussei heishi e imonbun no kakikata (How to write comfort letters to soldiers at the front)*. Daidō shuppansha.

Sakurai Tadayoshi. 1911a. Enshū (Maneuver). *Senyū* 14:33–38.

———. 1911b. Senyū toshite no dōbutsu (Animals as comrades). *Senyū* 13:28–34.

Sakurai Yoshiko. 1999. Anadarake no Jieitai 'Nihon bōei'(The holy SDF "Japan's defense"). *Shūkan Shinchō*, July 22, 134–138.

Samuels, Richard J. 1994. *"Rich nation, strong army": National security and the technological transformation of Japan*. Ithaca: Cornell University Press.

Sandler, Mark H. 2001. A painter of the "holy war": Fujita Tsuguji and the Japanese military. With Eleanor Kerkham. In *War, occupation and creativity: Japan and East Asia 1920–1960*, ed. Marlene J. Mayo and J. Thomas Rimer. Honolulu: University of Hawai'i Press, 188–211.

Sangi'in Naikaku Iinkai Chōsashitsu. 1997. *Nichibei bōei kyōryoku no tame no shikei (gaidorain) kankei shiryōshū (Collection of material on the guidelines of Japan–U.S. defense cooperation).* Sangi'in Naikaku Iinkai Chōsashitsu.

Saoyama Sachie. 2001. Benkyō o ganbaru! (I study hard!). *Sōyū: So You* 145 (4): 102.

Sapio. 1996a. Bijin Jieikan 9-nin no arasoi to heiwa: watashi no baai (War and peace for nine beautiful female service members: My case). *Sapio*: 128–131.

———. 1996b. Nihon wa ika ni kekkaku kokka ni natta ka? (How did Japan become a defective state?). *Sapio*:12–13.

Sasa Atsuyuki. 1994. *Poritiko-miritarī no susume (Suggestions for the politico-military complex).* Toshi shuppan.

Sasaki Yōko. 2001. *Sōryokusen to josei heishi (Total war and female soldiers).* Seikyūsha raiburarî 19. Seikyūsha.

Sase Minoru. 1980. *Jieitai no 30-nen sensō (The 30-year war of the SDF).* Kōdansha.

Sasson-Levy, Orna. 2003. Frauen als Grenzgängerinnen im israelischen Militär: Identitätsstrategien und –praktiken weiblicher Soldaten in "männlichen" Rollen (Women as border crossers in the Israeli military: Strategies and practices of identity among female soldiers in "male" roles). In *Gender und Militär: Internationale Erfahrungen mit Frauen und Männern in Streitkräften*, ed. Christine Eifler and Ruth Seifert. Königstein: Ulrike Helmer Verlag (Heinrich Böll Stiftung), 74–100.

Satō Fumika. 1999. Nichibei no josei heishi o meguru jendā ideorogī no hensen (The transition of gender ideologies concerning female Japanese Self Defense Forces officials and female American soldiers). *Joseigaku* 7:132–152.

———. 2000a. 'Guntai to/no josei' ron no tame ni (For a theory of military and women/military women). *Joseigaku Nenpō* 21:133–150.

———. 2000b. Jieitai ni okeru jendā—'Bōei hakusho' to Jieikan boshū posutā no hyōshō bunseki kara (Gender in the SDF: An analysis of the images in the "Defense white paper" and service member recruitment posters). *Sociology Today* 10:60–71.

———. 2002. Jendāka sareta gunjika (Gendered militarization). *Joseigaku* 9: 47–65.

———. 2004. *Gunji soshiki to jendā: Jieitai no joseitachi (A military organization and gender: The women of the Self-Defense Forces).* Keiō gijuku daigakkō shuppankai.

Satō Kōichi. 1918. Gendai seinen no shinri (The psychology of present-day youth). *Shinri Kenkyū* 14 (1):1–26.

Satō Minae et. al. 2002. Kokumin to Jieitai no setten o hirogeru tame ni (In order to broaden the connections between the populace and the SDF). *Securitarian* 1:41–44.

Satō Takumi. 2002. *'Kingu' no jidai (The era of "King").* Iwanami shoten.

Satō Toshiki. 2000. Sore demo susumu 'fubyōdō shakai-ka' ("Unequal society" still expands). *Chūō Kōron* 11:92–100.

Satoh, Yukio. 1995. Emerging trends in Asia-Pacific security: the role of Japan. *Pacific Review* 8 (2):267–281.

Sauter, Johanna. 1994. *Sozio-politische Orientierungsmuster von männlichen und weiblichen Jugendlichen in Ost- und Westdeutschland und deren Einstellungen zur Bundeswehr (Sociopolitical models of male and female youth in East and West Germany and their attitudes toward the German military) (Sowi Arbeitspapier 86)*. Munich: Sozialwissenschaftliches Institut der Bundeswehr.

Schaffer, Hanne Isabell. 1994. *Konkurrenz unter Frauen: Arbeitsbeziehungen von weiblichen Beschäftigten bei der Bundeswehr (Competition among women: Work relations among female members of the German military) (Sowi-Arbeitspapier 91)*. Munich: Sozialwissenschaftliches Institut der Bundeswehr.

Schattschneider, Ellen. 2005. The bloodstained doll: Violence and the gift in wartime Japan. *Journal of Japanese Studies* 31 (2):329–356.

Scherer, Klaus. 2001. *Kamikaze: Todesbefehl für Japans Jugend (Kamikaze: Order to die for Japan's youth)*. Munich: Iudicium.

Schmidt, Petra. 1997. Wiedergutmachung in Japan (Compensation in Japan). *Nachrichten der Gesellschaft für Natur- und Völkerkunde Ostasiens* 161–162:135–168.

Schodt, Frederik L. 2004 (1996). *Dreamland Japan: Writing on modern manga*. Berkeley: Stone Bridge Press.

Scholar. 2002. Nyōbō ni suru nara 'tetsuwan bijo'! (For a wife take a "canon ball beauty"!). November:40–50.

Schwind, Martin. 1940. Japanische Raumnot und Kolonisation (Japan's lack of space and colonization). *"Mitteilungen" der Deutschen Gesellschaft für Natur- und Völkerkunde Ostasiens* 32 (C):1–23.

Sebesta, Lorenza. 1994. Women and the legitimation of the use of force: The case of female military service. In *Women soldiers: Images and realities,* ed. Valeria E. Russo and Lorenza Sebesta, and Elisabetta Addis. New York: St. Martin's Press, 28–47.

Securitarian. 1997. Daigakusei Jieitai seikatsu taiken tsuā (University students' SDF experience tour). *Securitarian* 10:52–53.

———. 1998a. Tokushū: Bōeichō, Jieitai Q&A (Special: Questions and answers about the JDA and the SDF). *Securitarian,* 10–25.

———. 1998b. "Kigyō no kōhō" to "Jieitai no kōhō" ("Company PR" and "SDF PR"). *Securitarian,* 7–24.

———. 1998c. Jieitai no kōhō katsudō, zurari shōkai (An introductory line-up of the SDF PR activities). *Securitarian* 4:16–20.

———. 1998d. Jieitai no minsei kyōryoku (The SDF cooperation with civilians). *Securitarian* 5:29–33.

———. 1998e. Jieitai no sōbi-ing (The SDF equipment). *Securitarian* 7:7–24.

———. 1998f. Taiken nyūtai no haru (The spring of trial enlistment in the SDF). *Securitarian* 6:62–63.

———. 1999. Tokushū 4: Bōeichō Naikyoku shokuin kara no imēji (Special 4: Image by officers at the Defense Agency). *Securitarian* 11:24–28.

———. 2000a. Tokushū 3: Jieikan no puro ishiki ni fureta 'Josei goikenban' (A "female critic" who talked about professional consciousness of service members). *Securitarian* 1:22–23.

———. 2000b. Ikushima Noriko: Kotoba wa iranai (Ikushima Noriko: Words are unnecessary). *Securitarian* 2:2–3.

———. 2000c. Tokushū 1: Bōei daigakkō (Special 1: The NDA). *Securitarian* 3:6–19.

———. 2000d. Tokushū 2: Bōei daigakkō Q & A (Special 2: NDA Q & A). *Securitarian* 3:20–23.

———. 2000e. Tokushū 3: Bōdaisei tte, donna gakusei? (Special 3: What kind of students are the NDA cadets?). *Securitarian* 3:24–28.

———. 2000f. Tokushū 1: Jieitai no gochisō (Special 1: Food in the SDF). *Securitarian* 5:6–18.

———. 2000g. Daigakusei: Jieitai seikatsu taiken tsuā (University students: A trial tour of life in the SDF). *Securitarian* 6:36.

———. 2000h. Tokushū 1: Kokumin no bōei ishiki (Special 1: The defense knowledge of the population). *Securitarian* 8:6–18.

———. 2000i. Watanabe Emiko: Misu heripōto (Watanabe Emiko: Miss Heliport). *Securitarian* 12:2–3.

———. 2001a. Tokushū: Gaikokujin kara mita Nihon (Special: Japan as seen by foreigners). *Securitarian* 1:9.

———. 2001b. Zadankai: Jieitai ni okeru mentaru herusu (Round-table discussion: Mental health in the SDF). *Securitarian* 2:40–45.

———. 2001c. Hanseiki no kontentsu: Shōwa 50-nen (1975 nen) (The contents of half a century: 1975). *Securitarian* 4:40–42.

———. 2001d. Tokushū 3: Otona ni natta seitotachi (Special 3: The students who have become adults). *Securitarian* 6:23–28.

———. 2001e. SDF ibento jōhō (SDF event information). *Securitarian* 11:58.

———. 2001f. PKO de katsuyaku suru josei (The women who are active in PKO). *Securitarian* 9:41–45.

———. 2001g. Human sketch: Tanaka Miho. *Securitarian* 9:2–3.

———. 2001h. Rikujō Jieitai Kenkyū Honbu Settei (The establishment of a Ground SDF Research Headquarters). *Securitarian* 9:37–39.

———. 2001i. Human sketch: Fukuyama Sayumi. *Securitarian* 10:2–3.

———. 2001j. Human sketch: Kuroiwa Toshihiko. *Securitarian* 11:2–3.

———. 2001k. Human sketch: Ishihara Shinya. *Securitarian* 12:2–3.

———. 2001l. Sōgō no genzai to mirai (The present and future of synergy). *Securitarian* 12:2–3.

———. 2002a. Dēta de miru Ichigayadai tsuā (An Ichigaya camp tour in data). *Securitarian* 7:40–41.

———. 2002b. SDF ibento jōhō (SDF event information). *Securitarian* 7:57–58.

———. 2002c. 'Rikujō Jieitai Kōhō Sentā' ga opun (The opening of the "GSDF Public Relations Center"). *Securitarian* 5:37–39.

———. 2002d. Wakai josei no tame no Jieitai taiken: Paseri-chan tsuā (SDF experience for young women: The Parsley tour. *Securitarian* 4:57.

———. 2002e. Human sketch: Ikeuchi Keiji. *Securitarian* 2:2–3.

———. 2002f. Human sketch: Sanagashi Masanori. *Securitarian* 3:2–3.

———. 2002g. Human sketch: Watanabe Hidetsugu. *Securitarian* 4:2–3.

———. 2002h. Human sketch: Yokota Yoshinori. *Securitarian* 5:2–3.

———. 2002i. Human sketch: Kuboyama Yasushi. *Securitarian* 6:2–3.

———. 2002j. Human sketch: Suzuki Makoto. *Securitarian* 7:2–3.

———. 2002k. Human sketch: Murai Hirofumi. *Securitarian* 8:2–3.

———. 2002l. Jieikan no ichinichi (One day in the life of a SDF service member). *Securitarian* 5:6–16.

———. 2002m. Jieitai no 'tenkin' ("Job transfer" in the SDF). *Securitarian* 3:6–18.

———. 2002n. Jieitai o meguru hōsei (Toward a legal system for the SDF). *Securitarian* 8:6–16.

———. 2002o. Human sketch: Yamaguchi Shinji. *Securitarian* 2:2–3.

———. 2002p. Human sketch: Mukasa Noriko. *Securitarian* 10:2–3.

———. 2002q. Human sketch: Osumi Yasuhiko. *Securitarian* 11:2–3.

———. 2002r. Human sketch: Murano Shinji. *Securitarian* 10:2–3.

———. 2002s. 'Atarashii Jieitai no sugata' o hakken dekiru eiga ga kansei (Fim completed that allows the discovery of the "new appearance of the SDF"). *Securitarian* 11:42–43.

———. 2002t. Tokushū: Josei Jieikan o yomu—Watashitachi ga mamorimasu (Special: Reading female Jieikan—We protect). *Securitarian* 2:6–15.

———. 2002u. Tobe, Jieitai nāsu (Fly, nurse of the SDF). *Securitarian* 9:40–43.

———. 2003a. Human sketch: Kaneta Daisuke. *Securitarian* 1:2–3.

———. 2003b. Tokushū: Kokusai Jieikan—Kokusai Jieikan no hyōka (Special: International Jieikan—Their reputation). *Securitarian* 1:19–23.

———. 2003c. Human sketch: Gawa Hitoshi. *Securitarian* 3:2–3.

———. 2003d. Human sketch: Murata Hideyuki. *Securitarian* 4:32–33.

Sedgwick, Eve Kosofsky. 1995. Gosh, Boy George, you must be awfully secure in your masculinity! In *Constructing masculinity*, ed. Brian Wallis and Simon Watson Maurice Berger. New York: Routledge, 11–20.

Seifert, Ruth. 2003. Diskurse und Konjunkturen im Verhältnis von Militär und Geschlecht in Deutschland und USA (Discourses and cycles concerning the issue of gender in the military in Germany and the U.S.). In *Gender und Militär: Internationale Erfahrungen mit Frauen und Männern in Streitkräften*, ed. Christine Eifler and Ruth Seifert. Königstein: Ulrike Helmer Verlag (Heinrich Böll Stiftung), 23–51.

Sekiguchi Hisashi. 2001. Taiiku, supōtsu ni miru 'otokorashisa' baiyō no rekishi (The history of the cultivation of "masculinity" in gymnastics and sports). In *Nihon no otoko wa doko kara kite, doko e iku no ka? (Where did Japanese men come from? Where are they going?)*, ed. Itō Satoru and Murase Yukihiro Asai Haruo. Jūgatsusha, 72–96.

Sekizaki Yōko. 1995. Onna datera no Bōdai ikkisei shimatsuki (Reflective writing by female students of the first year class at the NDA). *Shinchō* 45:172–184.

Selden, Kyoko, and Mark Selden. 1989. *The atomic bomb: Voices from Hiroshima and Nagasaki*. Armonk, NY: M. E. Sharpe.

Sengoku Tamotsu. 1982. *Nihon no sarariiman (The Japanese salary man)*. Nippon hōsō shuppan kyōkai.

Senjo Shikan. 1905. Senjo shikan no tsuma (The wives of front officers). *Senjo Shikan (Front Officer)* 1:5.

Senshi-gakari. 1967. Rikujō Jieitai Fuji Gakkō no senshi (War history at the Fuji School of the Ground SDF). *Gunji Shigaku* 9 (3/1):111–112.

Senyū. 1899. Kokumin no heiji shisō (Thoughts about the military in the population). *Senyū* 1:19–21.

———. 1911. Chōhei tekireisha kokoroe (Information for people of conscription age). *Senyū* 2:1–4.

———. 1912a. Chihōjin no heiei sanka (Participation of local people in military matters). *Senyū* 21:87–88.

———. 1912b. Fukusō kaisei (Uniform reform). *Senyū* 18:87–88.

Seo Tetsushi. 2001. Masumedia ni miru danseizō (Representations of men in mass media). In *Nihon no otoko wa doko kara kite, doko e iku no ka? (Where did Japanese men come from? Where are they going?)*, ed. Itō Satoru, Murase Yukihiro, and Asai Haruo. Jūgatsusha, 150–169.

Seraphim, Franziska. 2001. Im Dialog mit den Kriegstoten: Erinnerungspolitik zwischen Nationalismus und Pazifismus (In dialogue with the war dead: Memory politics between nationalism and pacifism). In *Periplus: Jahrbuch für aussereuropäische Geschichte*, ed. Dietmar Rotermund. Münster: LIT Verlag, 12–25.

Serlin, David. 2003. Crippling masculinity: Queerness and disability in U.S. military culture. *GLQ* 9 (1/2):149–179.

Shambaugh, David. 2002. *Modernizing China's military: Progress, problems, and prospects*. Berkeley: University of California Press.

Sheehan, James. 2003. What it means to be a state: States and violence in twentieth-century Europe. *Journal of Modern European History* 1 (1):11–23.

Shidehara Hiroshi. 1912. Ai subeki shinryōmin (The new colonized who must be loved). *Senyū* 24:28–31.

Shigeri Katsuhiko. 1999. 'Pojitibu' ga ima ureru ("Positive" sells now). *Aera*, (February 8):34–37.

Shikata Toshiyuki. 1995. Security for the 21st century: Lessons from the 20th century. *Journal of Japanese Trade and Industry* 14 (4):20–23.

———. 1998. Otsukaresama dēsu! Jieitai to sekuhara mondai (Good job! The SDF and the problem of sexual harrassment). *Securitarian* 8:36–37.

Shils, Edward A., and Morris Janowitz. 1948. Cohesion and disintegration in the Wehrmacht in World War II. *Public Opinion Quarterly* (September): 280–315.

Shimada Kei. 1994. Nuclear curse: a report from Rokkasho-Mura. *AMPO Japan-Asia Quarterly Review* 25 (2):33–36.

Shimada Yoshiko. 2002. *Escape from oneself: Jieitai no onna (Escape from oneself: The women of the SDF)*. Ota Fine Arts.

Shimaha Setsuko. 1935. Hijōji ni okeru Nippon joshi no katsudō (The activities of Japanese women during times of emergency). *Rikugun Gahō* 3 (3):61–62.

Shimanuki Takeji, and Ueda Shūichi. 1973. Bōdaisei to senshi kenkyū (NDA cadets and research in war history). *Gunji Shigaku* 7 (3):108–118.

Shimizu Isao. 1990. *Bigō Nihon sobyōshū (Bigot's rough sketches of Japan)*. Iwanami shoten.

———. 2001. *Nihon kindai manga no tanjō (The birth of comics in modern Japan), Nihonshi riburetto 55*. Yamakawa shuppansha.

Shimizu Tateo. 1999. Japan, the ambiguous, and its flag and anthem. *Japan Quarterly* 46 (4):3–9.

Shimizu-Niquet, Valérie. 1994. Japan's new strategy: a new menace? *Pacific Review* 7 (2):163–170.

Shimokawa Kōshi. 1995. *Nihon ero shashin-shi (A history of erotic photographs in Japan)*. Seikyōsha.

Shinchō 45. 2002. Chōjō taidan: Jieitai tōgō bakuryō kaigi gichō Takegōchi Shōji vs. Bîto Takeshi (Summit discussion: The director of the SDF general headquarter's meeting Takegōchi Shōji vs. Bîto Takeshi). *Shinchō 45*:98–110.

Shinn, James. 1997. Testing the United States-Japan security alliance. *Current History* (December):425–430.

Shirai Hisaya. 1989. Edajima sengo umare no 'kaigun heigakkō' sei (Edojima's navy academy students born after the war). *Chō* 4:272–285.

Shokun! 2001. Hidō tero ni 'Jieitai haken'—doko ga warui!! (What is wrong with "dispatching" the SDF against incredible terrorism!!). *Shokun* 11:42–55.

Shōnosuke Susumu. 1919. Sensō to shinkeibyō (War and mental illness). *Shinri Kenkyū* 15 (6):104–108.

Shufu no Tomo. 1941. Kessen katei keizai (The decisive war of household economics). *Shufu no Tomo* 27 (4):cover illustration.

———. 1943. Kokushi bōei (Defense of the homeland). *Shufu no Tomo* 27 (12): cover illustration.

Shūkan Asahi. 1970. Sekai no yangu 6000 nin no ishiki chōsa: sekkusu, sensō, aikokushin etc (Worldwide survey of 6,000 young people's attitudes: Sex, war, patriotism etc.). *Shūkan Asahi*, 22–26.

———. 2001. Watashiteki ni Jieitai (The SDF my way). *Shūkan Asahi*, (June 22):9–14.

Shūkan Bunshun. 1993. Tennō kōgo ryōheika wa 'Jieikan no seifuku' ga okirai (His and her majesty the emperor and the empress dislike "SDF uniforms"). *Shūkan Bunshun*, (September 30):36–39.

Shūkan Gendai. 1990. Jieitai josei taiin hachi-nin (Eight female service members of the SDF). *Shūkan Gendai*, (November 24):221–228.

———. 1992. Kaijō jieitai jiken (The Maritime SDF incident). *Shūkan Gendai*, (July 18):28–32.

———. 1999. Moto fujin Jieikan ga hea nūdo de kataru: Jieitai no sei (A former female SDF member tells it through nudes: Sex in the SDF). *Shūkan Gendai*, (September 11):238–241.

Shūkan Hōseki. 1995. '95-nen kakukai chūmoku no josei: Jitsuryoku no bijo, Kawaue Hitomi ('95 women to pay attention to: The beauty with real strength, Kawaue Hitomi). *Shūkan Takaraseki*, (February 23):223–225.

Shūkan Josei. 2001a. Otto wa sensō suru tame ni Jieitai ni haitta wake ja nai!! (My husband did not join the SDF to go to war!!). *Shūkan Josei*, (October 23):208–209.

————. 2001b. Risō no kare to ichinen inai ni shiawase kekkon keikaku 2001: Vol. 15 Rikujō Jieitai daisotsu kanbu to kekkon suru no kan—jō (Plan 2001 for a happy marriage with the ideal man/boyfriend within a year: Vol. 15 Part on marriage with a university graduate GSDF officer—A). *Shūkan Josei,* (April 17):176–177.

————. 2001c. Risō no kare to ichinen inai ni shiawase kekkon keikaku 2001: Vol. 16 Rikujō Jieitai daisotsu kanbu to kekkon suru no kan—ge (Plan 2001 for a happy marriage with the ideal man/boyfriend within a year: Vol. 16 Part on marriage with a university graduate GSDF officer—B). *Shūkan Josei,* (April 24):132–133.

Shūkan Kinyōbi. 2001. Mondai wa kokkai giin dake de wa nai! Seifuku sugata no Jieikan tsunezune Yasukuni sanpai (The problem is not only diet members! Members of the SDF commonly visit Yasukuni Shrine in their uniforms). *Shūkan Kinyōbi,* (September 7):24–27.

Shūkan Shinchō. 1977. Otoko ni takkuru suru onna futari (Two women who tackle men). *Shūkan Shinchō,* (February 10): no page numbers.

————. 1995. Shufu shashin-ka ga totta josei Jieikan no seitai (The lives of female service members taken by a housewife photographer). *Shūkan Shinchō,* (June 3):189–191.

————. 1997. Fūzokukai o kaeta Tōdaisotsu nyū hāfu to moto jieikan sutorippā (A new half graduate from the University of Tokyo who has changed the entertainment world and a former service member stripper). *Shūkan Shinchō,* (July 3):64–65.

————. 1999. Tsumako sute Kanbojia josei to kekkon 'PKO taiin' no muzan (The cruelty of a "PKO participant" to have abandoned his wife and child and married a Cambodian woman). *Shūkan Shinchō*:139.

————. 2002. Futatsu no kao (Two faces). *Shūkan Shinchō,* (August 29):18–19.

Shūkan Taishū. 1989. Kore ga Heisei no Jieitai da!! (This is the Heisei era Self-Defense Force!!). *Shūkan Taishū,* (July 10):182–185.

Shūkan Yomiuri. 1999a. Minisuka 'Jieikan' (A "member of the Self-Defense Force" in a mini skirt). *Shūkan Yomiuri,* (July 11):3–6.

————. 1999b. 'Watashi wa yurusanai' (I won't allow it). *Shūkan Yomiuri,* (November 28):30–33.

Silver, Alain. 2005. *The samurai film.* Woodstock: Overlook Press.

Singer, P. W. 2005. *Children at war.* New York: Pantheon Books.

Skabelund, Aaron. 2006. To become a "beloved Self-Defense Force": The early postwar Japanese miltary's efforts to woo wider society. Unpubl. paper presented at the annual meeting of the Association for Asian Studies, San Francisco, April 19.

Smith, Kerry. 2002. The Shōwa Hall: Memorializing Japan's war at home. *Public Historian* 24 (4):35–64.

Sodei, Rinjirō. 2001. *Dear General MacArthur: Letters from the Japanese during the American occupation.* Lanham, Maryland: Rowman and Littlefield.

Somit, Albert. 1948. The military hero as presidential candidate. *Public Opinion Quarterly* (Summer 1948):192–200.

Sontag, Susan. 1990 (1973). *On photography.* New York: Farrar, Straus and Giroux.

————. 2003. *Regarding the pain of others.* New York: Farrar, Straus and Giroux.

Sōrifu. 1995. Kongo no Jieitai no yakuwari ni kan suru yoron chōsa (Opinion poll on the role of the SDF in the future).

Soysal, Yasemin Nuhoglu. 2000. Indentity and transnationalization in German school textbooks. In *Censoring history: Citizenship and memory in Japan, Germany, and the United States,* ed. Laura Hein and Mark Selden. Armonk, NY: M. E. Sharpe, 127–149.

Sōyū: So You. 2001a. Umi katsudō memoriaru foto (Memorial photographs of federation activities). *Sōyū: So You* 145 (4):32–33.

————. 2001b. Beikoku de no jissenteki shageki kunren ni sanka (Participation in real shooting exercises in the United States). *Sōyū: So You* 145 (4):74–77.

Spakowski, Nicola. 2003. Die Konstruktion der Soldatin in der Volksrepublik China: Das sozialistische Gleichheitspostulat und seine Untergrabung (The construction of the female soldier in the People's Republic of China: The socialist postulate of equality and its destruction). In *Gender und Militär: Internationale Erfahrungen mit Frauen und Männern in Streitkräften,* ed. Christine Eifler and Ruth Seifert. Königstein: Ulrike Helmer Verlag and Heinrich Böll Stiftung, 188–220.

Spangenberg, Stefan. 1998. *Bundeswehr und öffentliche Meinung: Betrachtungen zum aktuellen Verhältnis zwischen Gesellschaft und Streitkräften (The German military and public opinion: Observations concerning the current relations between society and armed forces) (= Sowi Arbeitspapier 114).* Strausberg: Sozialwissenschaftliches Institut der Bundeswehr.

Späth, Thomas. 1997. Männerfreundschaften—politische Freundschaften? Männerbeziehungen in der römischen Aristokratie (Friendships among men—political friendships? Relationships between men in the Roman aristocracy). In *Wann ist der Mann ein Mann? Zur Geschichte der Männlichkeit,* ed. Walter Erhart and Britta Herrmann. Stuttgart: J. B. Metzler, 192–211.

Spencer, Sarah W. 2005. Making peace: Preventing and responding to sexual exploitation by United Nation peacekeepers. *Journal of Public and International Affairs* 16:167–181.

Standish, Isolde. 2000. *Myth and masculinity in the Japanese cinema: towards a political reading of the "tragic hero."* Richmond: Curzon.

Stearns, Peter N., and Timothy Haggerty. 1991. The role of fear: Transitions in American emotional standards for children, 1850–1950. *American Historical Review* 96 (1):63–94.

Steger, Brigitte. 2002. Schlafen als Forschungsgegenstand der sozialwissenschaftlich orientierten Japanologie (Sleep as a research topic in Japanese Studies). In *Japanforschung-Mitteilungen der Gesellschaft für Japanforschung* 2: 6–20.

————. 2004. *(Keine) Zeit zum Schlafen? Kulturhistorische und sozialanthropologische Erkundungen japanischer Schlafgewohnheiten (No time for sleep? Cultural-historical and socioanthropological investigations into Japanese customs of sleep).* Münster: LIT Verlag.

Steinbruner, John, and Jeffrey Lewis. 2002. The unsettled legacy of the Cold War. *Daedalus* (Fall):5–10.

Steinhoff, Patricia. 1989. Hijackers, bombers, and bank robbers: Managerial style in the Japanese Red Army. *Journal of Asian Studies* 48 (4):724–740.

Stevens, Carolyn S. 1999. Rocking the bomb: A case study in the politicization of popular culture. *Japanese Studies* 19 (1):49–67.

Stiehm, Judith Hicks. 1989. *Arms and the enlisted woman*. Philadelphia: Temple University Press.

Sugihara Yūsuke, and Sugihara Gōsuke. 1997. *Mishima Yukio to Jieitai (Mishima Yukio and the SDF)*. Naragi shobō.

Sugimoto, Yoshio. 1981. *Popular disturbances in postwar Japan*. Hong Kong: Asian Research Service.

Sugiyama Takao. 1998a. *Heishi ni kike (Listen to the soldiers)*. Shinchō Bunkō.

———. 1998b. *Heishi o miyo (Look at the soldiers)*. Shinchō Bunkō.

Suleiman, Susan Rubin. 2002. History, memory, and moral judgment in documentary film: On Marcel Ophul's Hotel Terminus: The life and times of Klaus Barbie. *Critical Inquiry* 28:509–541.

Sung Kim Tai. 1974. Japan's security policy: A study of the relationships among the decision makers' perceptions, the press, and public opinion during 1952–1971. PhD diss., Michigan State University.

Suzuki Masahiro. 2001. Sensō ni okeru dansei sekushuariti (Male sexuality at war). In *Nihon no otoko wa doko kara kite, doko e iku no ka? (Where did Japanese men come from? Where are they going?)*, ed. Itō Satoru, Murase Yukihiro, and Asai Haruo. Jūgatsusha, 98–119.

Szpilman, Christopher W. 1993. The politics of cultural conservatism: the national foundation society in the struggle against foreign ideas in prewar Japan, 1918–1936. PhD diss., Yale University.

Tachibana Koichirō. 1912. Yasukuni Jinja ni tsuite (About Yasukuni Shrine). *Senyū* 21:18–20.

Takagi Hiroshi. 1999. Sakura to nashonarizumu: Nisshin sensō ikō no someiyoshino no shokuju (Cherry blossoms and nationalism: The planting of Someiyoshino after the Sino-Japanese war). In *Seiki tenkanki no kokusai chitsujo to kokumin bunka no keisei (World order and the formation of a popular culture around the turn of the century)*, ed. Nishikawa Nagao and Watanabe Kōzo. Kashiwa shobō, 147–170.

Takahashi Kenji. 1999. Datsu gōmanizumu saiban. (Out of the arrogance manifesto trial) *Kikan: Sensō Sekinin Kenkyū* 26:36–39.

Takahashi Mika. 2001. Taimu to katei o ryōritsu sase (Coexistence of unit duties and family). *Sōyū: So You* 145 (4):82–83.

Takahashi Tetsuya, and Takao Saitō. 2004. *Heiwa to byōdō o akiramenai (We cannot give up peace and equality)*. Shobunsha.

Takase Shōji. 1985. What "star wars" means to Japan. *Japan Quarterly* 32 (3):240–247.

Takayama Tatsuki. 1997. Shokuba kekkon: Omuko-san sagashinagara Jieitai ni dōzo (Workplace marriage: While looking for a groom, welcome to the SDF). *Securitarian* 12:64.

Takazato Suzuyo. 1996. *Okinawa no onnatachi: Josei no jinken to kichi, guntai*

(The women of Okinawa: The human rights of women, the bases, and the military). Akashi shoten.

———. 2003. Okinawa no kichi: Guntai no genjō to undō (Okinawa bases: The condition of the military and the movement). *Asoshie* 11:179–185.

Takazawa Tomomasa, Abe Kanichi, and Tōya Mamoru. 2001. Bandoman Takazawa Tomomasa no raifu hisutorii (The life history of the band man Takazawa Tomomasa). In *Burasu bando no shakaishi, Seikyūsha raiburarî 20 (A social history of the brass band)*, ed. Hosokawa Shūhei, Abe Kanichi, Tsukahara Yasuko, Tōya Mamoru, and Takazawa Tomomasa. Seikyūsha, 151–238.

Takeba, Joe. 2003. The age of modernism: From visualization to socialization. In *The history of Japanese photography*, ed. Dana Friis-Hansen, Anne Wilkes Tucker, Kaneko Ryūichi, and Takeba Joe. New Haven: Yale University Press, 142–183.

Takeishi Chikako. 1996. Japanese national identity in transition: Who wants to send the military abroad? *International Sociology* 11 (2):239–268.

Takemori Kazuo. 1978. *Heishi no gendaishi (A soldier's contemporary history)*. Jiji tsūshinsha.

Takeuchi Yō. 1997. Sarariiman-kei ningen-zō no tanjō to shūen (The birth and death of the salary man type figure). In *Keiei jinruigaku kotohajime: Kaisha to sarariiman (The beginning of an anthropology of management: Company and salary man)*, ed. Nakamaki Hirochika and Hioki Koichirō. Osaka: Tōhō shuppanl, 223–235.

Takeuchi Yoshimi. 1995. Peace with China: the road not taken. *Japan Echo* 22:56–62.

Takeyama Akiko. 2002. *Rajio no jidai (The radio era)*. Sekai shisōsha.

Takino Takahiro. 2002. *Jieitai shikikan (SDF officers)*. Kōdansha.

Tanabashi Masahiro, ed. 1989. *Nihon shoshigaku taikei 48 (I) (Compendium for Japanese bibliography 48 (I))*. Seishōdō.

Tanaka Akihiko. 2003. Atarashii sensō to yokushiryoku no igi (A new war and the significance of a checkmate). *Securitarian* 4:20–25.

Tanaka Giichi. 1911. Guntai to chihō to no kankei (The relations between the military and the regions). *Senyū* 7 :9–14.

———. 1912. Kokumin no kyōryoku o nozomu (Requesting the cooperation of the people). *Senyū* 21:11–13.

Tanaka Hiromi. 1977. Atarashii gunji shigaku no kōsō ni tsuite (On new concepts of military history in Japan). *Gunji Shigaku* 49:2–11.

Tanaka Hisao. 1985. *Nihon no sensōga: Sono keifu to tokushitsu (Japanese war paintings: Their geneology and characteristics)*. Perikansha.

Tanaka Masahiro, and Masuda Kōhei. 1998. Tokushū: Kōhō saizensen 'Kigyō no kōhō' to 'Jieitai no kōhō' (Special: Public relations: The public relations forefront "Industry PR" and "SDF PR"). *Securitarian* 4 :7–12.

Tanaka Masakazu. 1998. *Bōryoku no bunka jinruigaku (The Cultural Anthropology of Violence)*. Kyōto: Kyōto Daigaku gakujutsu shuppankai.

———. 2005a. Yoron (Outline). *Jinbun Gakuhō 90. Tokushū Ajia no guntai no rekishi, jinruigakuteki kenkyū: Bunmyaku ni okeru guntai (Jinbun Gakuhō*

90. Special issue. *Historical and anthropological research on Asian militaries: Military organizations in their sociocultural contexts).*

Tanaka Masasumi. 1997. Jidaigeki eiga shiron no tame no yobiteki shokōsatsu (Preliminary remarks for a historiography of period films). In *Jidaigeki eiga to wa nani ka (What are period films?)*, ed. Kyōto Eigasai Jikkō Iin-kai. Jinbun shoin, 17–44.

Tanaka Nobumasa. 2002. *Yasukuni no sengoshi (The postwar history of Yasukuni)*. Iwanami shoten.

Tanaka Yuki. 1994. Will Japan go nuclear? *AMPO Japan-Asia Quarterly Review* 25 (3):49–53.

———. 1996. *Hidden horrors*. Boulder: Westview Press.

———. 2002. *Japan's comfort women*. London and New York: Routledge.

Tani Tomio, ed. 2002 (1996). *Raifu hisutorī o manabu hito no tame ni (For people who study life histories)*. Sekai shisōsha.

Tanin, O. 1973 (1934). *Militarism and fascism in Japan*. Westport: Greenwood Press.

Tan'o Yasunori. 1998. Le traitement alusif de la guerre dans la peinture: un oubli (The allusive treatment of war in painting: A lapse of memory). In *Japan pluriel 2*, ed. Jean-Pierre Berthon and Josef A. Kyburz. Paris: Edition Philippe Picquier, 13–28.

———. 2001. 'Heiwa kokka' no 'meisshihōkō'. *Hikaku Bungaku Nenshi: Annales de Litterature Comparee* 37:1–21.

———. 2004. Daitōā no Fuji—toshi no seihoku yori, sanyō o nozomu (Fuji of Greater East Asia—looking at three oceans from a northwestern city). *Kokubungaku* 49 (2):108–116.

Tan'o Yasunori, and Kawada Akihisa. 1996. *Imēji no naka no sensō (The war in images)*. Iwanami shoten.

Taoka Shunji. 1991. Jieitai: futatsu no kiki ga ōu (SDF: two overlapping crises). *Aera* (November 26):31–35.

Taylor, Dena. 1988. *Red flower: rethinking menstruation*. Freedom, CA: Crossing Press.

Terada Junki. 2001. Kanū fōramu no kōza ni sanka (Participation in the Canoo Forum Course). *Sōyū: So You* 145 (4):87.

Thomas, Julia A. 1998. Photography, national identity, and the "catarct of times": Wartime images and the case of Japan. *American Historical Review* 103 (5): 1475–1501.

Thomson, Alistair. 1995. A crisis of masculinity? Australian military manhood in the Great War. In *Gender and war: Australians at war in the twentieth century*, ed. Joy Damousi and Marilyn Lake. Cambridge: Cambridge University Press, 133–147.

Tokoro Etsuo. 2001. Furūtsu no sato ni tawawa ni minoru ringo (A fruit village overbowed with ripening apples). *Sōyū: So You* 145 (4):85.

Tōkyō Joshi Daigaku Joseigaku Kenkyūjo. 1997. *Kōgakureki josei no kyaria diberoppumento ni kan suru chōsa hōkokusho II (Survey report II about the career development of women with a high level education)*. *Tōkyō Joshi Daigaku Joseigaku Kenkyūjo Kenkyū Hōkoku* 17.

Tomie Naoko. 2005. The political process of establishing the Mother-Child Protection Law in prewar Japan. *Social Science Japan Journal* 8:239–251.

Tomino Yoshiyuki, Ueno Toshiya, Ōtsuka Eiji, and Sasakibara Gō. 2002. *Sensō to heiwa (War and peace)*. Tokuma shoten.

Tomiyama Ichirō. 1995. *Senjo no kioku (War memories)*. Nihon keizai hyōronsha.

Tomonaga Taro. 1991. *Pikurusu ōji: Heiwa e no tabi (Prince Pickles: The journey to peace)*. Bōeichō.

Tonelson, Alan. 1997. Time for a new U.S.–Japan security relationship. *Comparative Strategy* 16:1–11.

Toritani Shō. 1912. Kokumin to guntai (The people and the military). *Senyū* 19: 21–28.

Toriyama Takeo. 1994. Nitchū rekishi kyōiku sinpōjiumu sankaki (Notes of the symposium on Japanese-Chinese history education). *Rekishigaku Kenkyū* 656:28–31, 64.

Tow, William T. 1987. The U.S., mainland China and Japan: military technology transfer policies and strategic collaboration. *Issues & Studies* (October):110–128.

Tsuchida Kuniyasu. 1980. Boei daigakkō kyōiku to senshi (On the significance of war history for the education at the NDA). *Gunji Shigaku* 62:14–15.

Tsuchiya Yutaka. 1997. What do you think about the war responsibility of emperor Hirohito? In *Japanese Panorama,* ed. Tsuchiya Yutaka. Tokyo, video recorded at Yasukuni Shrine, August 15; screened at YIDFF 1997, Japanese Panorama: Video Act!

Tsuda Sadako. 2002. Kōkū Jieitai seitotai de no 2 haku 3 ka (Two nights and three days in the student unit of the ASDF). *Securitarian* 11:22–26.

Tsukahara Yasuko. 2001. Gungakutai to senzen no taishū ongaku (Military music units and prewar mass music). In *Burasu bando no shakaishi, Seikyūsha raiburarî 20 (A social history of the brass band),* ed. Hosokawa Shūhei, Kanichi Abe, Tsukahara Yasuko, Tōya Mamoru, and Takazawa Tomomasa. Seikyūsha, 83–124.

Tsukakoshi Emi. 2000. *Jieitaikan-juku wakazuma nikki (The diary of a young wife in a SDF apartment)*. Wani bukkusu.

Tsukitari Hironori. 2001. Risō no niwa o mezashite (Toward an ideal garden). *Sōyū: So You* 145 (4):85.

Tsuru Bunka Daigaku Hikaku Bunka Gakka, ed. 2003. *Kioku no hikaku bunkaron (Comparative cultural studies of memory)*. Tokyo: Kashiwa shobō.

Tsurumi Kazuko. 1970. *Social change and the individual: Japan before and after the defeat in Word War II*. Princeton: Princeton University Press.

Tsurutani Taketsugu. 1981. *Japanese policy and East Asian security*. New York: Praeger.

Tsutsui, William. 2004. *Godzilla on my mind: Fifty years of the King of Monsters*. New York: Palgrave Mcmillan.

Tyson, Ann Scott. 2005. For female GI's, combat is a fact. *Washington Post,* May 13.

Ueno Chizuko. 1994. *Kindai Kazoku no seiritsu to shūen (The emergence of the modern family and its demise)*. Iwanami Shoten.

————. 1998. Josei heishi no kōchiku (The construction of female soldiers). In *Sei bōryoku nēshon (Sexuality, violence, nation)*, ed. Ehara Yumiko. Keiso shobō, 3–30.

————. 2004. *Nationalism and gender*, trans. Beverly Yamamoto. Gosford, Australia: Trans Pacific Press.

Ueno Nakae. 2001. Missile-defense proposal rocks Japan. *Mainichi Daily News*, http://www12.mainichi.co.jp.

Ueyama Kazuo. 2002. *Teito to guntai (Imperial cities and the military)*. Nihon keizai hyōronsha.

Ui Jun. 2003. "Beigun kichi to kankyō mondai" (American bases and the environment). trans. Sabine Frühstück and Yumiko Tokita-Tanabe. *Gunshuku Mondai Shiryō* 5 (271): 18–25. *Japan Focus* at http://japanfocus.org.

Umeda Toshihide. 2001. *Posutā no shakaishi—Ōhara Shaken korekushon (A social history of posters—The collection of the Ohara Research Institute for Social Problems)*. Hitsuji Shobō.

uno! 1997. Sentō shūdan 'Jieitai:' Onna ga nozomu subete ga koko ni wa aru (The battle organization SDF: Everything women desire is here). *uno!* (February 1):161–165.

Urquhart, Brian. 2004. The good general: Tom Clancy, with General Tony Zinni (Ret.) and Tony Koltz. Battle Ready. New York: Putnam. 2004. *New York Review of Books*, (September 23):28–33.

Van Creveld, Martin. 1991. *Technology and war: from 2000 B.C. to the present*. New York: The Free Press.

Van den Dungen, Peter, and Terence Duffy, eds. 1998. *Exhibiting peace: The proceedings of the third international conference of peace museums*. Kyoto and Osaka: The Organizing Committee.

Van Vranken Hickey, Dennis 1998. The revised U.S.-Japan security guidelines: implications for Beijing and Taipei. *Issues & Studies* 4:72–89.

Virilio, Paul. 2000 (1984). *War and cinema: The logistics of perception*, trans. Patrick Camiller. New York: Verso.

————. 2002 (1991). *Desert screen: War at the speed of light*. New York: Continuum.

Virilio, Paul, and Sylvère Lotringer. 1984 (1983). *Der reine Krieg*. Berlin: Merve Verlag.

Vogel, Ezra. 1963. *Japan's new middle class: The salary man and his family in a Tokyo suburb*. Berkeley: University of California Press.

Vogel, Kerstin Katharina. 1997. Von der Unmöglichkeit, Politikerin werden zu wollen und von der Möglichkeit, es zu sein. In *Getrennte Welten, gemeinsame Moderne? Geschlechterverhältnisse in Japan*, ed. Ilse Lenz and Michiko Mae. Opladen: Leske + Budrich, 247–270.

Voice. 2001. Tokushū: Kaigai hahei suru Nihon (Special: Japan dispatches [its forces] abroad). (December):54–103.

Vollmer, Klaus. 2001. Review article: The anatomy of an age: Interpretations of modern history in postwar Germany and Japan. *Monumenta Nipponica* 56 (2):239–254.

Wacquant, Loic J. D. 1995. Review article: Why men desire muscles. *body & society* 1 (1):163–179.

Wada Haruki. 2002. Sengo Nihon heiwashugi no genten (The origin of postwar Japanese pacifism). *Shisō* 944:5–26.

Wagner-Pacifici, Robin, and Barry Schwartz. 1991. The Vietnam veterans' memorial: commemorating a difficult past. *American Journal of Sociology* 97 (2):376–420.

Waldron, Arthur. 1991. The warlord: Twentieth-century Chinese understandings of violence, militarism, and imperialism. *American Historical Review* 96 (4): 1073–1100.

Wallis, Brian. 1994. Selling nations: International exhibitions and cultural diplomacy. In *Museum culture: Histories, discourses, spectacles*, ed. Daniel J. Sherman and Irit Rogoff. Minneapolis: University of Minnesota Press.

Wang Hsui-hsiung (Wang Xiuxiong). 2001. The development of official art exhibitions in Taiwan during the Japanese occupation. With H. Eleanor Kerkham. In *War, occupation and creativity: Japan and East Asia, 1920–1960*, ed. Marlene J. Mayo and J. Thomas Rimer. Honolulu: University of Hawai'i Press, 92–120.

Wang Qingxin Ken. 2000. Taiwan in Japan's relations with China and the United States after the cold war. *Pacific Affairs* 73 (3):353–373.

Warren, Carol A. B., and Jennifer Kay Hackney. 2000. *Gender issues in ethnography*, ed. Peter K. Manning, John Van Maanen, and Marc L. Miller. 2nd ed. Vol. 9, *Qualitative research methods series*. London: Sage.

Washburn, Dennis. 1995. Manly virtue and the quest for self: The Bildungsroman of Mori Ōgai. *Journal of Japanese Studies* 21 (1):1–32.

Wasmuht, Ulrike C. 1997. *Der Krieg hat auch ein weibliches Gesicht (War has a female face too) (= Sowi Arbeitspapier 100)*. Munich: Sozialwissenschaftliches Institut der Bundeswehr.

Watanabe Morio. 2001. Imagery and war in Japan: 1995. In *Perilous memories: The Asia-Pacific war(s)*, ed. Geoffrey M. White, Lisa Yoneyama, and Takashi Fujitani. Durham: Duke University Press.

Watanabe Yasushi. 2001. Rentai suiji kyōgikai yūshō (Regiment cooking competition champion). *Sōyū: So You* 145 (4):78–79.

Weinstein, Laurie, and Christie White, ed. 1997. *Wives and warriors: Women and the military in the United States and Canada*. Westport: Bergin and Garvey.

Wengeler, Martin. 2000. 'Unerträglich aber notwendig'? Öffentliche Sprachsensibilität als Indikator kulturellen Wandels in der Bundesrepublik Deutschland (Unbearable but necessary? Public language sensibility as indication of cultural change in the Federal Republic of Germany). In *Von der Kriegskultur zur Friedenskultur? Zum Mentalitätswandel in Deutschland seit 1945*, ed. Thomas Kühne. Münster: LIT Verlag, 280–293.

Wette, Wolfram. 2000. Der Beitrag des Nuklearpazifismus zur Ausbildung einer Friedenskultur (The contribution of nuclear pacifism to the emergence of a culture of peace). In *Von der Kriegskultur zur Friedenskultur? Zum Mentalitätswandel in Deutschland seit 1945*, ed. Thomas Kühne. Münster: LIT Verlag, 144–167.

White, Geoffrey M. 2001. Moving history: The Pearl Harbor film(s). In *Perilous memories: The Asia-Pacific war(s)*, ed. Geoffrey M. White, Lisa Yoneyama, and Takashi Fujitani. Durham: Duke University Press, 267–295.

White, Hayden. 1988. Historiography and historiophoty. *American Historical Review* 93 (5):1193–1199.

Whitehead, Tony Larry, and Mary Ellen Conaway, eds. 1986. *Self, sex, and gender in cross-cultural fieldwork.* Urbana: University of Illinois Press.

Widdig, Bernd. 1997. 'Ein herber Kultus des Männlichen': Männerbünde um 1900 ("The rough cult of manliness": Men's organizations around 1900). In *Wann ist der Mann ein Mann? Zur Geschichte der Männlichkeit,* ed. Walter Erhart and Britta Herrmann. Stuttgart: J. B. Metzler, 235–248.

Wildmann, Daniel. 1998. *Begehrte Körper: Konstruktion und Inszenierung des 'arischen' Männerkörpers im 'Dritten Reich' (Desired bodies: Construction and staging of the "Arian" male body during the "Third Reich").* Würzburg: Königshausen and Neumann.

Willett, Susan. 1997. East Asia's changing defense industry. *Survival: The IISS Quarterly* 39 (3):107–134.

Williams, John A. 2000. The postmodern military reconsidered. In *The postmodern military: Armed forces after the cold war,* ed. John A. Williams, David Segal, and Charles C. Moskos. New York: Oxford University Press.

Wilson, George Macklin. 1980. Time and history in Japan. *American Historical Review* 85 (3):557–571.

Wilson, Sandra. 2001. Rethinking the 1930s and the "15-year war" in Japan. *Japanese Studies* 21 (2):155–164.

Winther-Tamaki, Bert. 2003. Oil painting in postsurrender Japan: Reconstructing subjectivity through deformation of the body. *Monumenta Nipponica* 58 (3): 347–396.

Woodward, Rachel, and Patricia Winter. 2004. Discourses of gender in the contemporary British army. *Armed Forces & Society* 30 (2):279–301.

Wright, Evan. 2004. *Generation kill: Devil dogs, iceman, captain America and the new face of American war.* New York: G. P. Putnam's Sons.

XYZ. 1935. Dai Nippon Kokubō Fujinkai: Kansai honbu wa dō ni katsudō shite iru ka (Greater Japan Women's Association for National Defense: What kind of activities does the Kansai headquarters engage in?). *Rikugun Gahō* 3 (3):86–93.

Yamaguchi Jirō. 1992. The gulf war and the transformation of Japanese constitutional politics. *Journal of Japanese Studies* 18 (1):155–172.

Yamaguchi Masa. 1915. Shōnen giyūdan to jidō no shinri (Patriotic youth groups and children's psychology). *Shinri Kenkyū* 8 (3):49–54.

Yamaguchi Noboru. 2001. Japan: Completing military professionalism. In *Military professionalism in Asia,* ed. Muthiah Alagappa. Honolulu: East-West Center, 35–46.

Yamaguchi Tomomi. 2005. Feminism, timelines, and history-making. In *A companion to the anthropology of Japan,* ed. Jennifer Robertson. London: Blackwell Publishers, 51–58.

Yamamoto Mari. 2004. *Grassroots pacifism in post-war Japan.* London: RoutledgeCurzon.

Yamamura Motoki, and Kobayashi Tetsuo. 1989. Shinjinrui Jieikan 'sensō to heiwa tte nan darō' (The new type member of the SDF "what do war and peace mean?"). *Gendai* (February):358–380.

Yamamuro Ōtoji (Lieutenant colonel). 1910. Joshikan to ikuji (Female officers and child rearing). *Senjo Shikan (Front Officer)* 5:146–148.

Yamanaka Hisashi. 2001. *Shinbun wa sensō o bika seyo! (Newspapers should beautify wars!)*. Shōgakkan.

Yamanaka Tsuyu. 2002a. Kokumin to Jieitai to no setten o hirogeru tame ni (In order to broaden the interactions between the populace and the SDF). *Securitarian* 1:41–44.

———. 2002b. Moto Jieikan ga furikaetta PKO (A former SDF service member looks back upon PKO). *Securitarian* 10:26–28.

Yamanaka Tsuyu, and Fujiwara Sachiko. 2002. Kasoku suru shokyū kanbu e no yume (Accelerating toward the dream of a junior officer). *Securitarian* 11: 30–35.

Yamanaka Yukio. 2001. Konjaku monogatari (Stories from now and then). *Sōyū: So You* 145 (4):66–67.

Yamanishi Shinichi. 2001. 'Masane' to iu na no kodomo no tanjō (Birth of a child named "Masane"). *Sōyū: So You* 145 (4):82.

Yamano Shigeko. 1991. Preempting the SDF: Christian groups carry out refugee evacuation. *AMPO Japan-Asia Quarterly Review* 23 (1):8–9.

Yamasaki Hiroshi. 2001. Kindai dansei no tanjō (The birth of the modern man). In *Nihon no otoko wa doko kara kite, doko e iku no ka? (Where did Japanese men come from? Where are they going?)*, ed. Itō Satoru, Murase Yukihiro, and Asai Haruo. Jūgatsusha, 32–53.

Yamasaki Madoka. 2001. Kansha no kimochi o wasurenai fūfu (A couple that doesn't forget gratitude). *Sōyū: So You* 145 (4):102.

Yano, Christine R. 2002. The burning of men: Masculinities and the nation in Japanese popular song. In *Men and masculinities in contemporary Japan: Dislocating the salaryman doxa*, ed. James E. Roberson and Suzuki Nobue. London: Routledge.

Yashima Masami, ed. 1997. *Dansei dōseiaisha no raifu hisutorî (The life histories of male homosexuals)*. Gakubunsha.

Yasuhiko Yoshikazu. 2005. *Anime, manga, sensō: Yasuhiko Yoshikazu taidanshū (Animated films, comics, war: A collection of conversations with Yasuhiko Yoshikazu)*. Kadokawa shoten.

Yasukuni Jinja. 2003. *Yasukuni Jinja Yushukan (The Yasukuni Shrine War Memorial Hall)*. Kindai shuppansha.

Yasukuni no inori henshū iinkai. 1999. *Yasukuni Jinja no inori (The prayers of Yasukuni Shrine)*. Nihon kōgyō shinbunsha.

Yoneyama, Lisa. 1999. *Hiroshima traces: Time, space, and the dialectics of memory*. Berkeley: University of California Press.

———. 2000. Postmodernism and the symbols of history: the relationship between collection, display, and materials in the Hiroshima Peace Memorial Museum and the Muzeum of Kamigata Performing Arts. *Senri Ethnological Studies* 54:137–148.

Yoshida Reiji. 1997. Endless debate over war museums. *Japan Times Weekly International Edition*, December 22–28.

Yoshida Shigeru. 1995. The coordinates of Japan's foreign policy. *Japan Echo* 22: 51–55.

Yoshida Tetsuaki. 1926. *Sarariiman-ron (Theories on salary men)*. Ōsaka yagō shoten.

Yoshida Toshihiru. 2003. Are SDF soldiers pawns to be sacrificed? trans. Atsuko Nelson and Christopher Nelson. *Sekai* (November): http://www.japanfocus.org.

Yoshida Yutaka. 1995. *Nihonjin no sensōkan: Sengo-shi no naka no henyō (Japanese views of the war: Changes in postwar history)*. Iwanami shoten.

———. 1997. *Gendai rekishigaku to sensō sekinin (Contemporary historiography and war responsibility)*. Aoki shoten.

———. 2002. *Nihon no guntai: Heishitachi no kindaishi (The Japanese military: A modern history of soldiers)*. Iwanami shoten.

Yoshino Kosaku. 1992. *Cultural nationalism in contemporary Japan: A sociological inquiry*. London: Routledge.

Yoshioka Kyōho. 1912. Bushidō no seishin (The spirit of the way of the warrior). *Senyū* 17:13–15.

Yoshioka Shizuo. 2006. Point of view: Train safety is the responsibility of us all. *Asahi Shinbun*, June 15.

Yoshitome Roju. 1981. *Minshū no naka no bōeiron (Theories of defense among the masses)*. Gendaishi shuppankai.

Young, James E. 1986. Memory and monument. In *Bitburg in moral and political perspective*, ed. Geoffrey H. Hartman. Bloomington: Indiana University Press.

Zaidan Hōjin Bōei Kōsaikai/Securitarian. 1996. *Jieitai yūmoa jiten (SDF humor dictionary)*. Kōdansha.

———. 2004a. *Manga de yomu: Heisei 16-nenban bōei hakusho (Reading the 2004 defense white paper in comic format)*. Illus. Kiribayashi Chitose. Zaidan Hōjin Bōei Kōsaikai/Securitarian in collaboration with the Defense Agency.

———. 2004b. *Kokumin no hogo no tame no hōsei (Law for the Protection of the Populace)*. Illus. Kinashi Momoko. Zaidan Hōjin Bōei Kōsaikai/Securitarian.

Index

Text: 10/13 Sabon
Display: Sabon
Compositor: Binghamton Valley Composition
Printer and binder: Maple-Vail Book Manufacturing Group